Additional
Educational
Needs

STAND   LOAN

UNLE   R REA

371.
9
ADD

Also available:

Understanding Children's Learning: A Text for Teaching Assistants (Alfrey)
1-84312-069-0

Successful Study: Skills for Teaching Assistants (Ritchie and Thomas)
1-84312-106-0

Supporting Learning and Teaching (Bold)
1-84312-127-1

Additional Educational Needs

Inclusive Approaches to Teaching

Edited by Sue Soan

 David Fulton Publishers

David Fulton Publishers Ltd
The Chiswick Centre, 414 Chiswick High Road, London W4 5TF

www.fultonpublishers.co.uk

First published in Great Britain in 2004 by David Fulton Publishers
10 9 8 7 6 5 4 3 2

Note: The right of the author to be identified as the author of this work has been asserted by her in accordance with the Copyright, Designs and Patents Act 1988.

David Fulton Publishers is a division of Granada Learning Limited, part of ITV plc.

British Library Cataloguing in Publication Data
A catalogue record for this book is available from the British Library.

ISBN 1 84312 149 2

Typeset by RefineCatch Limited, Bungay, Suffolk
Printed and bound in Great Britain

Contents

Notes on contributors

Richard Bailey is Professor in the Centre for Educational Research at Canterbury Christ Church University College. With a degree in physical education/human movement studies, a PhD in the philosophy of education and post-doctoral study in cognitive evolution, his interests are broad and multidisciplinary, but centre on the scientific study of childhood. Before coming to Canterbury, Richard was Reader in Educational Studies at Carnegie, Leeds Metropolitan University, and before that, Head of the Centre for Physical Education and Sport Science at the University of Reading. Previously, he worked in both secondary and primary schools, in Kent and the North East. He is the author of numerous books, on different aspects of education and child development, recent examples being *Teaching Physical Education 11–18* (Continuum) and *Supporting Physical Development and Physical Education in the Early Years* (Open University Press).

Mike Blamires is a Principal Lecturer within the Centre for Enabling Learning of the Faculty of Education at Canterbury Christ Church University College. He is co-editor of *Support Services and Mainstream Schools Working Together* with John Moore, Principal Advisor for Additional Educational Needs in Kent County Council. He is a deputy director of the TTA initial teacher education professional resource network for Behaviour for Learning. His main area of research is the construction and utilisation of expertise to enable learning.

John Cornwall is a Senior Lecturer at Canterbury Christ Church University College and is currently Programme Director of the MA in 'Enabling Learning.' He is also an author, Education Consultant and Trainer. He was formerly a Head Teacher and later an independent OFSTED Inspector. He has worked in a variety of capacities since 1975 with children and young people who are vulnerable, challenging or have disabilities or disadvantages entailing additional educational needs. John has been an adviser to local and county education, community and youth organisations and has provided training support to people who work with socially excluded youngsters. He has worked with a number of LEAs since 1990 and has also been on two Government Advisory Committees. He has published four books on these subjects, contributed to a variety of professional publications over many years and is currently preparing two books on 'Therapeutic Education' and 'Inclusive Educational Practices' for publication.

Simon Ellis works jointly as a Senior Lecturer with the Centre for Enabling Learning, Faculty of Education, Canterbury Christ Church University College and as Key Stage 3 Strategy Behaviour and Attendance specialist for Kent LEA. Simon qualified as a teacher in 1988 and taught in the primary sector for eight years before joining Kent's Behaviour Support Service where he worked for over six years as a specialist teacher and a team manager.

Sue Soan trained as a teacher in Portsmouth, specialising in History and Mathematics. She has since taught in East Sussex, Shropshire and Kent, first as a class teacher and subject coordinator and then for the last decade as a SENCO in mainstream schools, a MLD Unit and a specialist EBD school. At Canterbury Christ Church University College Sue is a Senior Lecturer in Enabling Learning. She is particularly interested in the areas of social, emotional and behavioural difficulties and in children's motor control development. Sue has also recently been part of a team carrying out research into 'behaviour for learning' for the TTA.

Janet Tod is a Professor of Education at Canterbury Christ Church University College. She is a chartered educational and clinical psychologist and speech therapist. Her work involves teacher education at undergraduate and postgraduate level in the area of Special Educational Needs and Inclusion. Her publications linked to her DfES-funded research include a series of books on IEPs and articles and books on SEN policy and dyslexia.

Preface

This book aims to provide all educators, but especially those wishing to achieve the HLTA Professional Standards, with a theoretical perspective to underpin their practical understanding and knowledge of learners. It discusses areas of Additional Educational Needs (AEN) that educators have frequently 'heard about', but would welcome the opportunity to find out more about. However, with inclusive practice continuing to develop in all educational settings it is vital that all educators have a good knowledge foundation to provide insight into areas of study such as therapeutic education, AIDS and cultural issues. The book also seeks to encourage practitioners to examine and reflect on their own practice and their personal views and beliefs. In this way individuals' professional practice can constantly develop within an informed framework, thus enabling the teaching and learning experience to remain active, positive and inclusive.

The book is designed so that each chapter can 'stand alone' (perhaps with the exception of cultural issues and bilingual learners), with its own references and helpful ideas. The chapters nevertheless follow the same format with discussion points, key issues and case studies, where appropriate. The authors have also included, in the margin, a note of individual HLTA Professional Standards that they suggest will be met if the Teaching Assistant can ably demonstrate similar practice and understanding. All the Professional Standards highlighted are then presented in the conclusion of each chapter.

It is anticipated that all educators will be able to access the information. The case studies are all 'real', experienced over a 25-year period of classroom practice, but the identity of the learners and colleagues has been carefully protected, by changing names, ages and situations.

Finally, it is hoped that the information gained from reading this book will stimulate a personal interest in AEN issues and encourage further study and enquiry, developing the professional knowledge and expertise within all educational settings.

Acknowledgements

I would like first of all to thank my colleagues who have contributed to this book, particularly Janet Tod, and also many other members of the Faculty of Education at Canterbury Christ Church University College who have offered their support and encouragement throughout this venture.

I thank my family, Mark, David and Ashleigh Soan for their patience, love and encouragement. I also wish to thank Mark for so ably proofreading all the chapters and for his constant belief in me.

Illustration acknowledgements

Fig. 2.2 – Thomson Publishing/Routledge (from Riddell, S. and Tett, L. (eds) (2001) *Education, Social Justice and Interagency Working*)

Fig. 3.1 – Lawrence Erlbaum Associates Inc. (from Igoa, C. (1995) *The Inner World of the Immigrant Child*)

Fig. 4.2 – Lawrence Erlbaum Associates Inc. (from Brisk, M. (1998) *Bilingual Education*)

Fig. 4.3 – Trentham Books (from Gravelle, M. (2000) *Planning for Bilingual Learners*)

Fig. 6.2 – Continuum (from McGuiness, J. (1993) *Teachers, Pupils and Behaviour*)

Figs 6.4, 6.5 – QEd (from Haworth, E. (ed.) *Social, Emotional and Behavioral Difficulties*)

Fig. 9.1 – J. Renzulli (from 'What makes Giftedness?', *Phi Delta Kappan*, **60**, 180–4)

Fig. 11.1 – Open University Press (from Doherty, J. and Bailey, R. (2003) *Supporting Physical Development in the Early Years*)

Fig. 15.1 – Thomson Publishing (from Weare, K. (2000) *Promoting Mental and Social Health*)

List of abbreviations

AAC	augmentative and alternative communication
ADD	attention deficit disorder
ADHD	attention deficit hyperactivity disorder
AEN	additional educational needs
AIDs	acute infectious diseases
ASD	autistic spectrum disorder
BESD	behavioural, emotional and social difficulties/development
CAMHS	Child and Adolescent Mental Health Services
CAP	Communication Aids Project
CLO	Children's Liaison Officer
COP	Code of Practice for Special Educational Needs
CP	clinical psychologist
CRE	Commission for Racial Equality
DDA	Disability Discrimination Act
DfE	Department for Education
DfEE	Department for Education and Employment
DfES	Department for Education and Skills
DoH	Department of Health
EAL	English as an additional language
EBSD	emotional, behavioural and social difficulties
EiC	Excellence in cities
EP	educational psychologist
ESL	English as a second language
EWO	Education Welfare Officer
FLO	Family Liaison Officer
FSM	free school meals
HI	hearing impairment
HIV	human immunodeficiency virus
HLTA	higher level teaching assistant

HV	health visitor
IBP	individual behaviour plan
IEP	individual education plan
IQ	intelligence quotient
IT	information technology
LEA	Local Education Authority
LA	learning assistant
LAC	looked after children
MLD	moderate learning difficulties
NLP	neuro-linguistic programme
OFSTED	Office for Standards in Education
OT	Occupational Therapist
PECS	picture exchange communication system
PEP	personal education plan
PRU	pupil referral unit
QCA	Qualifications and Curriculum Authority
SEBD	social, emotional and behavioural difficulties
SEN	special educational needs
SENCO	Special Educational Needs Coordinator
SEU	Social Exclusion Unit
SLCN	speech, language and communication needs
SLD	severe learning difficulties
SLT	speech and language therapist
SpLD	specific learning difficulties
SSS	scotopic sensitivity syndrome
TEACCH	Treatment and Education of Autistic and Related Communication Handicapped Children
TES	Traveller Education Services
UNESCO	United Nations Educational, Scientific and Cultural Organisation
VI	visual impairment
VOCA	voice-output communication aid

Professional standards for Higher Level Teaching Assistants (HLTA)

These Standards set out what an individual should know, understand and be able to do to be awarded HLTA status.

1 Professional values and practice

Those meeting the Higher Level Teaching Assistant Standards must demonstrate all of the following:

1.1   They have high expectations of all pupils; respect their social, cultural, linguistic, religious and ethnic backgrounds; and are committed to raising their educational achievement.

1.2   They build and maintain successful relationships with pupils, treat them consistently, with respect and consideration, and are concerned for their development as learners.

1.3   They demonstrate and promote the positive values, attitudes and behaviour they expect from the pupils with whom they work.

1.4   They work collaboratively with colleagues, and carry out their roles effectively, knowing when to seek help and advice.

1.5   They are able to liaise sensitively and effectively with parents and carers, recognising their roles in pupils' learning.

1.6   They are able to improve their own practice, including through observation, evaluation and discussion with colleagues.

2 Knowledge and understanding

Those meeting the Higher Level Teaching Assistant Standards must demonstrate sufficient knowledge and understanding to be able to help the pupils they work with make progress with their learning. This knowledge and understanding will relate to a specialist area which could be subject-based or linked to a specific role (e.g. in support of an age phase or pupils with particular needs). Those meeting the Higher Level Teaching Assistant Standards must demonstrate all of the following:

2.1   They have sufficient understanding of their specialist area to support pupils' learning, and are able to acquire further knowledge to contribute effectively and with confidence to the classes in which they are involved.

2.2   They are familiar with the school curriculum, the age-related expectations of pupils, the main teaching methods and the testing/examination frameworks in the subjects and age ranges in which they are involved.

2.3   They understand the aims, content, teaching strategies and intended outcomes for the lessons in which they are involved, and understand the place of these in the related teaching programme.

2.4   They know how to use ICT to advance pupils' learning, and can use common ICT tools for their own and their pupils' benefit.

2.5   They know the key factors that can affect the way pupils learn.

2.6   They have achieved a qualification in English/literacy and mathematics/ numeracy, equivalent to at least Level 2 of the National Qualifications Framework.

2.7   They are aware of the statutory frameworks relevant to their role.

2.8   They know the legal definition of Special Educational Needs (SEN), and are familiar with the guidance about meeting SEN given in the SEN Code of Practice.

2.9   They know a range of strategies to establish a purposeful learning environment and to promote good behaviour.

3 Teaching and learning activities

The following teaching and learning activities should take place under the direction and supervision of a qualified teacher in accordance with arrangements made by the head teacher of the school. (For further details, see the regulations and guidance under Section 133 of the Education Act 2002.) Those meeting the Higher Level Teaching Assistant Standards must demonstrate all of the following:

3.1 Planning and expectations

3.1.1   They contribute effectively to teachers' planning and preparation of lessons.

3.1.2   Working within a framework set by the teacher, they plan their role in lessons including how they will provide feedback to pupils and colleagues on pupils' learning and behaviour.

3.1.3   They contribute effectively to the selection and preparation of teaching resources that meet the diversity of pupils' needs and interests.

3.1.4   They are able to contribute to the planning of opportunities for pupils to learn in out-of-school contexts, in accordance with school policies and procedures.

3.2 Monitoring and assessment

3.2.1   They are able to support teachers in evaluating pupils' progress through a range of assessment activities.

3.2.2   They monitor pupils' responses to learning tasks and modify their approach accordingly.

3.2.3   They monitor pupils' participation and progress, providing feedback to teachers, and giving constructive support to pupils as they learn.

3.2.4   They contribute to maintaining and analysing records of pupils' progress.

3.3 Teaching and learning activities

3.3.1   Using clearly structured teaching and learning activities, they interest and motivate pupils, and advance their learning.

3.3.2   They communicate effectively and sensitively with pupils to support their learning.

3.3.3   They promote and support the inclusion of all pupils in the learning activities in which they are involved.

3.3.4   They use behaviour management strategies, in line with the school's policy and procedures, which contribute to a purposeful learning environment.

3.3.5   They advance pupils' learning in a range of classroom settings, including working with individuals, small groups and whole classes where the assigned teacher is not present.

3.3.6   They are able, where relevant, to guide the work of other adults supporting teaching and learning in the classroom.

3.3.7   They recognise and respond effectively to equal opportunities issues as they arise, including by challenging stereotyped views, and by challenging bullying or harassment, following relevant policies and procedures.

3.3.8   They organise and manage safely the learning activities, the physical teaching space and resources for which they are given responsibility.

Source: Department for Education and Skills and Teacher Training Agency, September 2003, *Professional Standards for Higher Level Teaching Assistants*, downloaded from hltaenquiries@teach-tta.gov.uk on 4 November 2003.

The Higher Level Teaching Assistants (HLTA) website is: www.hlta.gov.uk

Recent legislation, Additional Educational Needs (AEN) and inclusion

Sue Soan

Teachers need to be prepared to teach all children, and that this should be understood as both a personal and an institutional commitment.

(Mittler, 2000: 133)

Introduction

This chapter will introduce the recent legislation that has been influencing educational change. It will give a historical insight into how 'special educational needs', 'additional educational needs' and 'inclusion' have evolved and how they are fuelling and directing change.

Historical perspectives

There have been many pieces of legislation passed during the last century relating to disability within the United Kingdom and they do without doubt often reflect the attitudes and beliefs of the society of that era. In the past decade many pieces of legislation have been introduced building upon preceding Acts. It is for this reason that it is necessary to be aware of the chronology of these Acts and Reports so that one has a clear understanding of how legislation has evolved. However, it is not my intention to detail all the Acts and Reports passed, but only to focus on the significant recent ones, that will help guide the reader in respect of this chapter's subject.

First, it is important to remember that it was not until the Education (Mentally Handicapped Children) Act of 1970 that ALL children were made the responsibility of the local education authority (LEA). From the Education Act of 1944 until the Act of 1970, 'handicapped' children 'had been the responsibility of the health service as children with a learning difficulty were considered to be impossible to educate' (Tassoni, 2003). It was as a consequence of this 1970 Act that special schools began to be built, giving many children an opportunity to receive an education for the first time.

Eight years later in 1978, what was to become a very important and influential Report for the education of disabled children was published. This was the Warnock Report (DES, 1978), written by a committee that was chaired by Mary Warnock. It is this report that suggested introducing the title of 'special educational need' (SEN) to any child needing extra support. Other key proposals included recognising the need for early diagnosis and pre-school support, the *integration* of children into mainstream schools wherever possible and the need for greater parent involvement. It was hoped that in this way children with relatively minor short-term needs would be helped alongside those with more complex long-term difficulties. Importantly it also wanted professionals to focus on children's potential and the help they needed to achieve this, rather than on their disability or condition. In an attempt to prevent the labelling of children according to their medical condition the Warnock Report introduced the terms:

- speech and language disorders;
- visual disability and hearing disability;
- emotional and behaviour disorders;
- learning difficulties; specific, mild, moderate and severe.

Many of these recommendations formed the basis for the Education Act of 1981, in which the responsibility for providing support for children with special educational needs was firmly placed with LEAs. It also introduced the 'statementing' process through which a child was given a legally binding statement of special educational needs, committing a LEA to providing specific resources for the child.

Discussion

Looking at all the proposals and terminologies introduced by the Warnock Report, how influential do you think it was in shaping future changes? Do you know of any guidance or legislation this Report may have helped to shape? Why?

The 1990s

Throughout the 1980s other significant education legislation was passed, but for the purpose of this chapter the next significant Education Act was passed in 1993 (section 160), and was consolidated in the Education Act of 1996 (section 316) when:

> the general principle that children with special educational needs should – where this is what parents wanted – normally be educated at mainstream schools was enshrined into law.
>
> (DfES, 2001a)

Also it was in 1994 that the *Salamanca Statement* was drawn up at a United Nations Education, Scientific and Cultural Organisation (UNESCO) world conference in Spain. It called upon all governments, including the supportive United Kingdom government '[to] adopt as a matter of law or policy the principle of inclusive education, enrolling all children in regular schools, unless there are compelling reasons for doing otherwise' (DfES, 2001b).

This appears to have been the catalyst for the evolving changes that have been, and are continuing to be, introduced to practitioners and schools through government legislation and guidance. A Green Paper, *Excellence for All Children: Meeting Special Educational Needs* (DEE, 1997) set out a strategy to improve standards for children with special educational needs and promoted greater inclusion. This Green Paper indicates support both for inclusion and for special schools:

> There are strong educational, as well as social and moral grounds for educating children with special educational needs with their peers. We aim to increase the level and quality of inclusion within the mainstream schools, while protecting and enhancing specialist provision for those who need it.
>
> (Croll and Moses, 2000: 1)

The twenty-first century

In 2001 'The Special Educational Needs and Disability Act' (TSO, 2001) amended the Education Act of 1996 and transformed the statutory framework for inclusion into a positive endorsement of inclusion. Quickly following this was *Inclusive Schooling* (DfES, 2001b) and this document is vital for practitioners as it is *statutory guidance*, unlike the Special Educational Needs Codes of Practice (DfE, 1994, DfES, 2001a), and provides practical advice on the operation of the new inclusion framework. Being a statutory document the 'guidance must not be ignored' (DfES, 2001b: 2). Thus, it can be seen how determined the government are to make educational settings inclusive; perhaps as a step towards creating an inclusive society? Most recently the Green Paper, *Every Child Matters* (HMSO, 2003: 9) takes a further step forward, by illustrating how the government intends to integrate the education, health and social services for children, 'within a single organisational focus', 'to achieve better outcomes for children and young people' (ibid.: 69, 5.7). Undoubtedly there will be more legislation within the next few years 'to ensure the barriers to integration are removed' (ibid.: 79, 5.53) as the Green Paper states: 'We therefore intend to legislate at the earliest opportunity in relation to the above proposals' (ibid.: 79, 5.53).

This chapter has explained when and why the term 'Special Educational Needs' (SEN) was introduced. So what does 'Additional Educational Needs' (AEN) mean and how does it differ from the term SEN?

Special Educational Needs (SEN) and Additional Educational Needs (AEN)

Some practitioners, quite understandably, are still unaware of the different meanings of SEN and AEN, many assuming that AEN is just a new term for SEN.

So what does SEN mean?

HLTA
2.8

The Special Educational Needs Code of Practice (DfES, 2001a: 6) defines 'special educational needs' in the following way:

> Children have special educational needs if they have a *learning difficulty* which calls for *special educational provision* to be made for them.

The Code of Practice continues to describe *a learning difficulty* in greater detail and provides explanations of the fundamental principles. It also recognises that there is a wide spectrum of special educational needs that may be inter-related, but that there are four identified specific areas of need:

- communication and interaction;
- cognition and learning;
- behaviour, emotional and social development;
- sensory and/or physical.

It is important to note at this stage that the National Curriculum Inclusion Statement (QCA/99/458) (and this is statutory) states: 'All teachers are teachers of SEN' (QCA, 1999).

What does AEN mean?

An Additional Educational Need (AEN) is the term presently used to define any type of need a learner may be experiencing. It may be that a learner has a SEN and thus he or she can be said to have a SEN Additional Educational Need. However, a learner does not have to have a Special Educational Need to have Additional Educational Needs. An important aspect of providing an inclusive environment for *all* learners, where differences are valued and respected, is recognising that learners may have many different additional needs. It is also vital to acknowledge at this stage that these learners' needs may also change quite frequently, depending on other factors, for example, their age, home situations and peer groups. This means that the learning environment has to be constantly

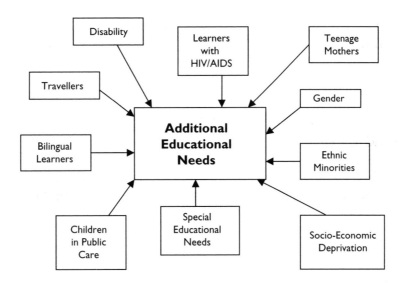

Figure 1.1   Possible reasons why learners may have 'Additional Educational Needs' (AEN)

able to change and adapt to its learners' needs, if they are to be adequately included in the educational setting at all times.

Learners with special educational needs are just one group requiring different and additional support to enable them to access, engage with and participate in learning. There are many other groups of learners that may need specific help and consideration. Examples of possible groups of learners are shown in Figure 1.1 and these are by no means the only possibilities.

Case study 1

This short case study will highlight the need for a school to look at all the learner's additional needs and not assume they will be best dealt with by SEN input.

Fatima arrived at the beginning of Year 5 at her local primary school, speaking very little English. External support was very limited and so the head teacher asked the SENCO to help the class teacher by withdrawing Fatima from the class situation during English lessons. Little formal assessment was carried out initially, everyone assuming that her lack of English meant she had learning difficulties. Fatima became unwilling to attend school and very miserable until her actual ability was recognised by an EAL (English as an Additional Language) specialist teacher, who then helped the school with suitable interventions to aid second language development, without inappropriate SEN support.

The Special Educational Needs Code of Practice (DfES, 2001a: 46) actually states that the 'lack of competence in English must not be equated with learning difficulties'. The class teacher and the SENCO in this case needed to fully assess Fatima's performance in all lessons and to identify how well she spoke and wrote using her first language. From this information additional language rather than learning difficulty support would have been identified as being needed. As Moore (1999: 177) states: 'More inclusive schools will value the presence of a wider range of diversity amongst their pupils, celebrating everyone's contribution within the community.'

Some schools are recognising the distinction between SEN and AEN by altering or adding new roles. There may now be an Inclusion Manager or an Additional Educational Needs Co-ordinator (AENCO), helping the learners with various needs and supporting the teaching staff, as well as or instead of a Special Educational Needs Co-ordinator (SENCO). Indeed, Moore (ibid.) says:

> More inclusive schools will have more inclusive management arrangements with greater sharing of the (SENCO) role. Indeed, the most inclusive schools may have moved away from SEN provision altogether and be fostering more reflective mechanisms which support the development of pedagogy at the classroom/department level.

The National Curriculum 2000 incorporates a statement on inclusion and highlights the need for this change, emphasising the importance of providing effective learning opportunities for all pupils by:

- setting suitable learning challenges;
- responding to pupils' diverse needs;
- overcoming potential barriers to learning and assessment for individuals and groups of pupils.

(DfEE, 2001: 47)

However, to reassure educators, the author believes that the kind of teaching and learning that is good for pupils with AEN is good for ALL children.

> **Discussion**
>
> Look at the learners in your workplace setting. How are their Additional Educational Needs being met, and by whom? Is there a need for a change in roles so that inclusive practice can be developed further? See if you can explain to a colleague the difference between SEN and AEN.

Integration

When asking a group of PGCE students recently what they thought integration in schools meant, they used phrases such as 'fitting various pieces together to make a whole' and 'putting different sections together' (personal account, 2004). It is vital to understand the educational meaning of integration so that the differences between it and the meaning of inclusion and inclusive practice can clearly be distinguished.

Until the late 1990s the medical model of disability affected how children were educated. With this model children with disabilities were seen as 'problems' and were segregated from children attending mainstream schools. They were thought of as 'faulty' and were given labels identifying their 'fault' and frequently, as a consequence of this way of thinking, the educational expectations of these children were lowered and their potential was wasted. With the implementation of many recommendations of the Warnock Report (DES, 1978) in the Education Act (1981) as many children as possible began to be *integrated* into mainstream schools. This was deemed possible if the child could be given enough support and appropriate resources enabling them to fit into the school. With integration the child has to change to fit into the system or otherwise remain segregated. Thus there are three main points to remember about integration:

- The focus still remains on the learner's 'deficit' (and thus the medical model).
- The learner is provided with support to access the curriculum and the school environment already in place. This will not be changed to assist the learner.
- The learner must fit into the system already in place.

Case study 2

This simple case study illustrates the three points described above. For the integration programme to be acceptable to the mainstream school, William had to be fully supported by someone else other than the teacher. He also had to prove he could both fit into the system and cope with the work the teacher had prepared for all the other learners. This is a clear case of the learner having to fit in with the system.

> When William, a boy with learning difficulties, started a part-time integration programme at his local primary school, many discussions took place about what would be needed in order to help him access the curriculum and join in the activities in the classroom. The school agreed to the integration programme only if William always had a Learning Support Assistant (LSA) to help him. It was decided that William could only be integrated during art and music lessons, as the demands of the other lessons would be too much for him. It was felt he could spend more time in the school if he showed he could cope with the work the other children were doing.

In recent years, however, the concept of inclusive education has evolved. Parents and disabled people have lobbied governments to change the education system so that all children can have 'fair and equal access to education' (Tassoni, 2003).

HLTA
1.1
3.3.3

> Consider your own practice. Does the language you use when describing a learner's needs focus on his or her deficits, or their strengths and potential? Do you have lower expectations of some learners than you do of others? If so, why? Consider whether a change in the school system or your practice, as educator, would help some children do better and thus raise your expectations of them.

Understanding the concept of inclusive education

What do you think inclusion and inclusive practice are and how do they differ from integration? When asking the PGCE students what they thought inclusive practice and inclusion were, they immediately commented that this term is freely used in schools. For many of them, following practical experience in classrooms, inclusion meant trying to enable all children to be included within a mainstream classroom. Many difficulties and problems were identified that they had tried to deal with, and this initiated a debate about whether the schools were really including the pupils or integrating them and whether 'inclusion' was seen as being effective for all learners.

> Talk with colleagues about their views of what educational inclusion is. Identify their main positive comments and their concerns. Look at those learners for whom the positive comments are mainly applicable and those for whom the concerns are raised. Why do you think this is? Can you think of anything that could overcome some of the concerns?

I expect you have found that colleagues have very different ideas of what educational inclusion is and that you have recognised it is a very complex subject with the term being open to much confusion. Do you think, for example, that a child with a learning difficulty or with a sensory difficulty is included if he/she is attending a school full-time and is able to work with the whole class, but fails to make friends or learn to his/her potential? This type of question indeed starts discussions about what needs to be considered to enable a school community to become inclusive in its practice. I personally, for example, do not think a school can state they are an inclusive school, because to be able to say this they would have to be able to adapt, probably on a nearly daily basis, to the changing needs of all the children and adults within that community. This would be an immense task and so I believe it is far more realistic and proactive to say that a school is constantly developing inclusive practice through its school development planning, staff training and resources.

There are numerous definitions of inclusive education to be found in the documentation and literature, but the majority of those written within the last four years see 'inclusion as an active, not a passive process' (Corbett, 2001: 55). At a conceptual level, Corbett and Slee (2000: 134) write:

Inclusive education is an unabashed announcement, a public and political declaration and celebration of difference. It requires continual proactive responsiveness to foster an inclusive educational culture.

O'Brien (2000: 5) wrote: 'Inclusive learning is grounded in who you are as a person, your sense of worth and the contribution that you can make to the community now and in the future.'

On a practical level what does this mean for schools, educators and pupils? Hanko (2003: 125) says:

The inclusion debate is no longer concerned merely with the extent to which mainstream schools are able to accommodate all children regardless of need, but increasingly focuses on institutional improvement in understanding the range of their needs.

Thus, inclusive education

signals a significant mind shift. Instead of expecting children to 'come up to standard' or otherwise be segregated, the emphasis is on schools and settings to adapt and be flexible enough to accommodate each and every child.

(Tassoni, 2003: 11)

Unlike integration, therefore, inclusion is not a fixed state, but a process. Inclusion means that ALL the children in a school, whatever their additional educational need, should be able to join in fully with their peers in the curriculum and life of the school.

Whatever an individual's point of view, however, there are a number of definitions that educators need to know and understand, especially when an inspection is imminent. The Centre for Studies on Inclusive Education (CSIE) state that:

While integration may be construed as something done to disabled people by able bodied people according to their standards and conditions, inclusion better conveys a right to belong to the mainstream and a joint undertaking to end discrimination and work towards equal opportunities for all children.

(CSIE, 1989)

Such statements certainly support the social model of thinking rather than the medical model. This model promotes valuing learners and identifying barriers to their learning and developing solutions, rather than focusing on their deficits and giving them labels. It values diversity, and encourages professionals, parents and learners to work together.

The *Index for Inclusion* (Booth *et al.*, 2000) helps schools identify the barriers to learning and participation within their own establishments. It also offers three very clear and vital messages about inclusion:

- Inclusion is NOT another word for integration.

- Inclusion in education is just one aspect of inclusion in society.

■ Inclusion is the process of increasing the participation of pupils in, and reducing their exclusion from the cultures, curricula and communities of local schools.

As well as the National Curriculum Inclusion Statement (QCA/99/458) the statutory document *Inclusive Schooling* (DfES, 2001b: 3) emphasises similar factors about inclusion and inclusive practice. It says:

> Inclusion is about engendering a sense of community and belonging and encouraging mainstream and special schools and others to come together to support each other and pupils with special educational needs. Inclusive schools and local education authorities have:
> a. an inclusive ethos;
> b. a broad and balanced curriculum for all pupils;
> c. systems for early identification of barriers to learning and participation; and
> d. high expectations and suitable targets for all children.

Also, importantly, OFSTED's definition of what an inclusive school is can be found in this document:

> OFSTED defines an educationally inclusive school as 'one in which the teaching and learning, achievements, attitudes and well-being of every young person matter'.
>
> (ibid.)

It continues: 'In order for a school to be satisfactory or better it must be, "inclusive in its policies, outlook and practices"' (ibid.).

Discussion

In the *Inclusive Schooling* (2001b: 3, 21, 22) guidance there are three case studies. Read these and take note of factors you identify as supporting inclusive education. Would any of these help develop further inclusive practice in your workplace setting?

Is inclusive education effective?

As research carried out by Croll and Moses (2000: 1) indicated, education professionals support inclusion as an ideal, but 'Contrasting with support for inclusion was a set of views which stressed the primacy of meeting children's individual needs as overriding an ideological commitment to inclusionist ideals.'

There has, to date, been only relatively limited research carried out to identify whether inclusive education is being effective and, if it is, for whom. Studies carried out prior to 1999 do not endorse or provide clear evidence for the benefits of inclusion (Lindsay, 2003: 6). Indeed, Manset and Semmel's (cited in Lindsay, 2003: 7) conclusions are highly critical of inclusion as an overall policy: 'Inclusive programming effects are relatively unimpressive for most students with disabilities especially in view of the extraordinary resources available to many of these model programmes.'

Lindsay (2003: 10) also discusses other research findings that question the effectiveness of inclusive practice. In conclusion, he writes:

> Inclusion is the policy framework. What is at issue is the interpretation and implementation of inclusion in practice. We need to ensure that there is a dual approach focusing on both the rights of children and the effectiveness of their education. There is a need to develop beyond concerns about inputs and settings to a focus on experiences and outcomes and to attempt to identify *causal* relationships.

Discussion This chapter has hopefully given you a good understanding of how educational inclusion and additional educational needs have evolved and developed over the years. Using the knowledge and understanding gained from this chapter and from your discussions, how do you see inclusive practice and additional educational needs evolving in the next few years? What do you think will be the main driving forces for these developments?

Key issues

It is anticipated that you will now:

- have a good understanding and working knowledge of the terms: special educational needs, additional educational needs, integration and inclusion and inclusive practice;
- be able to understand the need for changing roles and responsibilities of staff within educational establishments;
- have a knowledge of the legislation and documentation that have informed change and developments throughout the last century with regard to special educational needs and inclusive practice;
- have an understanding of the historical implications behind educational changes and developments.

Professional Standards for Higher Level Teaching Assistants (HLTA)

If you can demonstrate your understanding and professional use of the key issues illustrated within this chapter, it is hoped that you will be able to fulfil the following HLTA Standards:

| 1.1 | 2.8 | 3.3.3 |

Useful documents

DEE (1997) *Excellence for All Children*, London: The Stationery Office.

DES (1978) *The Report of the Committee of Enquiry into the Education of Handicapped Children and Young People* (The Warnock Report), London: HMSO.

DfE (1994) *Code of Practice on the Identification and Assessment of Pupils with Special Educational Needs*, London: DfE.

DfEE (2001) *National Curriculum 2000*, London: HMSO.

DfES (2001a) *Special Educational Needs Code of Practice*, Annesley: DfES.

DfES (2001b) *Inclusive Schooling: Children with Special Educational Needs*, Annesley: DfES.

Disability Rights Commission (2002) *Code of Practice for Schools*, London: The Stationery Office.

HMSO (1996) *Education Act 1996*, London: HMSO.

HMSO (2003) *Every Child Matters*, Norwich: The Stationery Office.

QCA (1999) *The National Curriculum Inclusion Statement*, 458, Sudbury: QCA.

TSO (2001) *Special Educational Needs and Disability Act*, Norwich: The Stationery Office.

UNESCO (1994) *The Salamanca Statement and Framework for Action*, Paris: UNESCO.

References

Booth, T., Ainscow, M., Black-Hawkins, K., Vaughan, M. and Shaw, L. (2000) *Index for Inclusion*, Bristol: Centre for Studies on Inclusive Education.

Corbett, J. (2001) 'Teaching approaches which support inclusive education: a connective pedagogy', *British Journal of Special Education*, vol. 28, no. 2, pp. 55–9.

Corbett, J. and Slee, R. (2000) 'An international conversation on inclusive education', in Armstrong, F., Armstrong, D. and Barton, L. (eds) *Inclusive Education: Policy, Contexts and Comparative Perspectives*, London: David Fulton.

Croll, P. and Moses, D. (2000) 'Ideologies and utopias: education professionals' views of inclusion', *European Journal of Special Needs Education*, vol. 15, no. 1, pp. 1–12.

CSIE (1989) Explanatory Paper on the six points in *The Inclusion Charter*, Bristol: CSIE.

Hanko, G. (2003) 'Towards an inclusive school culture – but what happened to Elton's "affective curriculum"?', *British Journal of Special Education*, vol. 30, no. 3, pp. 125–31.

Lindsay, G. (2003) 'Inclusive education: a critical perspective', *British Journal of Special Education*, vol. 30, no. 1, pp. 3–10.

Manset, G. and Semmel, M.L. (1997) 'Are inclusive programmes for students with mild disabilities effective? A comparative review of model programmes', *Journal of Special Education*, vol. 31, no. 2, pp. 155–80.

Mittler, P. (2000) *Working Towards Inclusive Education: Social Contexts*, London: David Fulton.

Moore, J. (1999) 'Developing a local authority response to inclusion', *Support for Learning*, Tamworth: NASEN.

O'Brien, T. (2000) 'Increasing inclusion: did anyone mention learning?', *REACH, Journal of Special Needs in Ireland*, vol. 14, no. 1, pp. 2–12.

Tassoni, P. (2003) *Supporting Special Needs: Understanding Inclusion in the Early Years*, Oxford: Heinemann.

2 Inter-agency collaboration and partnership with parents: roles and responsibilities

Sue Soan

Introduction

With the inclusion agenda gaining momentum, it seems the most logical action for practitioners in schools is to work closely with colleagues from other agencies, support services, voluntary services and charities. The National Curriculum Inclusion Statement (DfEE, 1999) and the SEN Code of Practice (DfES, 2001) reinforce this statement. The latter of these documents dedicates whole chapters to 'Working in partnership with parents', 'Pupil participation' and 'Working in partnership with other agencies', emphasising the importance now placed on joined-up thinking. In the first section of the 'Working in partnership with other agencies' chapter it states: 'Meeting the special educational needs of individual children requires flexible working on the part of the statutory agencies. They need to communicate and agree policies and protocols that ensure there is a "seamless" service' (DfES, 2001: 135, 10.1). This, to the majority of people, is a reasonable and obvious avenue of development to pursue, to further enhance a holistic support system for children and young people. However, to enable this development to reach fruition it is considered necessary for the government to pass legislation to facilitate such action. Indeed, Bronfenbrenner stated such a necessity in 1970:

> It is a sobering fact that, neither in our communities nor in the nation as a whole, is there a single agency that is charged with the responsibility of assessing or improving the situation of the child in his total environment. As it stands, the needs of children are parcelled out among a hopeless confusion of agencies ... no one ... is concerned with the total pattern of life in the community.
>
> (1970: 163)

Roaf (2002) also supports this point of view and suggests that legislation, organisation, professional practice and resources are the four main factors that contribute to the success of inter-agency work. She writes: 'legislation should also devise effective government structures which do not compartmentalise children and ensure that preventative and proactive work is fully integrated' (ibid.: 146).

However, it was not until the Green Paper, *Every Child Matters* that the government's intention to integrate the key services within a single organisational focus at both local and national levels in England and Wales was demonstrated. At the national level, the government aims to do this through a number of initiatives, such as a new Children's Commissioner who will act as an independent champion, and 'in the long term, integrate key services for children and young people under the Director of Children's Services as part of Children's Trusts' (HMSO, 2003). At the local level the government will *encourage* this joint working by setting out practice standards expected of each agency, ensuring children are a priority across services and involving and listening to children's and young people's views. Three other factors clearly identify the government's determination to ensure that joint working is developed further. They are:

- rationalising performance targets, plans, funding streams, financial accountability and indicators;

- creating an integrated inspection framework for children's services. OFSTED will take the lead in bringing together joint inspection teams. This will ensure services are judged on how they work together.

- creating an improvement and intervention function to improve performance by sharing effective practice, and intervening where services are failing.

(HMSO, 2003)

The practice nevertheless can be very different from the theory, as Lacey's (2001) research on inter-professional work within a special school found. In this situation Lacey concluded that the attempt to collaborate with other agencies caused anxiety and even hostility. Referring to the definitions of 'anxiety' and 'hostility' within the psychology of personal constructs (Kelly, 1955), Blamires and Moore write:

> Anxiety is defined as the awareness of an individual that she may not have the skills, knowledge or understanding required to deal with a forthcoming event or challenge, whilst hostility is the active refusal to adapt to the implications of forthcoming events or challenges.
>
> (2003: 7)

It is, therefore, bearing these factors in mind that this chapter will introduce and provide information about terminology and the roles and responsibilities of agencies that can or should be involved with schools and individual families. It will focus on how schools can play a positive part in developing valuable and worthwhile relationships with these agencies to the benefit of the learners. Work of this nature is always very time-consuming and can also cause a great deal of anxiety for children, young people and their families. The purpose of involving a number of agencies in a child's life therefore must be very clear and the professional must feel confident that inter-agency intervention will have *a positive impact on the child*.

> **Discussion**
>
> Consider a case in your workplace setting where more than one agency has been involved in supporting a child. This may be a speech and language therapist or a social worker, for example. List the positive and negative points of how effective the co-operation between professionals was (a) to foster better relationships between services and; (b) to actually support the child or young person in a positive way, academically, socially or emotionally. Then consider reasons why (a) or (b) was successful or not.

HLTA
1.5

Definitions of terminology – three models

There is now a range of terms that describe professionals working together from different disciplines and agencies. In fact, Leathard's (1994) review of research into inter-professional work, as described by Lacey (2001), found over 52 terms that are used to denote different forms of professional work. Over the years these terms have changed quite considerably and many have been used in an inter-changeable way, causing further confusion about their precise meaning. However, when looking at the development of each term, they have evolved specifically to support the trends and legislation of that particular time.

HLTA
1.4
1.6

There have been four reports over the past nearly 30 years that have influenced the development of, and illustrated the need for, professionals across disciplines to work together. The Court Report (Court, 1976) clearly highlighted the importance of both the parental and professional roles. It stated that there was a need for practitioners to do the following:

- work *with* parents;
- gain specialist guidance and support from other professionals in the interests of the child.

The Warnock Report (DES, 1978), focusing on children and young people with special educational needs, emphasised this need for close working relations between professionals in different services again. Additionally, it clarified the need for inter-professional working through the identification, assessment, monitoring and reviewing of provision for children with special educational needs. Then 11 years later The Children Act (1989) took this need for professional collaboration a step forward by stating:

> A co-ordinated approach helps to create an environment where people with different qualifications and experience can share skills and expertise and ideas in a positive way. It is

important for all departments within a local authority to find ways of encouraging staff to work with this in mind, so that all the appropriate skills are available in all settings.

(DoH, 1989)

The Special Educational Needs Code of Practice (1994) continued to encourage this cross-disciplinary manner of working, actually specifying the agencies with which schools should be working: 'Effective action on behalf of children with special educational needs will often depend upon close cooperation between schools, LEAs, the health services and the social services departments of local authorities' (DfE, 1994).

Multi-disciplinary, multi-agency and multi-professional

These terms do actually mean 'more than one' agency, professional or discipline working with a child, but they do not imply that the professionals are working together across the boundaries. Each professional sees a child separately from any of the other services involved with the family or child and shares only vital information with each other.

Case study 1

This case study is a clear example of multi-agency working, where more than one discipline is involved with Colin's development, but does so in isolation from all others working with him.

Colin is a Year 1 pupil in a mainstream school. He is on the SEN Register and the SENCO has requested a Statutory Assessment due to his significant difficulties. His IEP targets are concentrating on improving Colin's fine and gross motor skills and on trying to help with a severe dribbling problem. Colin visits the speech and language therapist at a local clinic on a weekly basis during school time and also attends an occupational therapist's activity group after school on a fortnightly basis. The school's SENCO had supported Colin's parents in obtaining these services, but has had no direct contact with the other professionals involved since interventions have been started. Therefore the SENCO is not aware of what help Colin is actually being given when he goes to the speech and language therapist and the occupational therapist. This obviously means that a holistic approach to Colin's needs cannot be achieved when planning programmes of work and targets for his IEP or any other aspect of his educational development.

Inter-disciplinary and inter-agency

During the past few years professionals have been progressing from a multi-agency to an inter-agency working model. Inter-disciplinary and inter-agency are the terms used when there is greater cooperation between professionals, although they still work in parallel with each other. In these situations the professionals acknowledge that there is a need for a number of specialists to help the child or family and information is shared with jointly agreed action. Each discipline or profession would, however, still deliver their input in a discreet manner.

Case study 2

Nearly eight years ago this case study occurred and the meeting that took place, an inter-agency meeting, was the first of its kind in the local area in which the author was working at the time. The benefits of such a meeting were immediately recognised and it became standard practice in the area, particularly where input from Social Services and Education was necessary.

Three pupils from one family were having serious problems at school regarding attendance, hygiene issues, academic progress and emotional, behavioural needs. All efforts to support these pupils were having little effect because of the over-riding problems occurring at home. The parents and grandparents were unable to really engage with the school about the children's problems due to their own overwhelming difficulties. The SENCO and other Senior Management Team (SMT) members feared that at least one of these three pupils might have to be excluded from school because of the daily behaviour difficulties. Everyone knew this was not the correct course of action for this pupil, but recognised the school needed support from other agencies. The SENCO contacted the Education Welfare Office, Social Services and the School's Health Department to ask if a representative from their agency would attend a meeting concerning these pupils. Social Services were already involved with the family and they had a named Social Worker who was very willing to collaborate with the school. After persuasion, all attended and the parents were invited to be there for the last half of the meeting. The pupils were not involved in this first meeting, but were on future occasions when it was felt appropriate. At this meeting all the agencies discussed what their roles could be to help the family. No one agency coordinated the provision, but in this way they all knew what the others were doing and could ask for assistance quickly and directly if it were needed. As a consequence of this action, the pupils and parents were able to receive additional help from the relevant services. It also enabled the pupils to function at school more positively as their other concerns were being supported by the other agencies. Importantly, the pupils were also able to see that the adults around them were working together to care for them and to keep them safe.

Trans-disciplinary and trans-agency working

This is considered to be the most developed model, and most effectively supports current philosophies (Wall, 2003), because it clearly recognises that areas of child development cannot be effectively separated, but are tightly interwoven. Thus, it stands to reason that professionals need to work across disciplines to provide effective responses to a child's needs. For this reason one of the professionals from the 'team' becomes a 'key worker' or a 'primary worker', and is supported by the others who act like consultants. The key worker will be given the responsibility of coordinating and managing the child's and his/her family provision. Lacey (2001: 67) vividly clarifies this: 'In this way, the children are not seen as a combination of legs, hands, speech and intellect, but holistically in terms of their education and care.' It is also felt that this system is an effective way of supporting families, because it limits the number of professionals that families need to have direct contact with. It is also thought that it helps families to establish a positive working relationship with the professional who is directly responsible for the management of the provision of services and for the passing on of all the information regarding their child or family. Central to this trans-disciplinary working model are review meetings and case conferences when all the professionals, parents/carers and, if appropriate, the child, discuss progress, comment on all the various provisions in place and plan for both the short and long term.

Case study 3

Susan is physically disabled and as such requires the involvement of many medical specialists, social services and all the professionals directly involved with Susan's mainstream schooling. During an initial case conference it was decided that due to the number of professionals involved in Susan's provision, a key worker would be the most effective method of making sure that her education and care were managed in a holistic manner. It was felt essential that information, provision and appointments were efficiently coordinated. In this particular case it was felt most appropriate that the parent (who fully supported the move) should take on the key worker role with a lot of support from the social service caseworker.

Despite these clear descriptions, there needs to be a word of warning. When working initially with a different agency or discipline, do not assume that the term 'trans-agency' or 'multi-agency' will mean the same to them as it does to you. Make sure that all the terminology to be used is clearly understood by all the individuals involved in any meeting or joint project, whether professionals or parents (see Figure 2.1).

Current legislation and guidance tend to use the term *inter-agency working* and therefore in an attempt to avoid unnecessary confusion this term will now be used throughout this chapter.

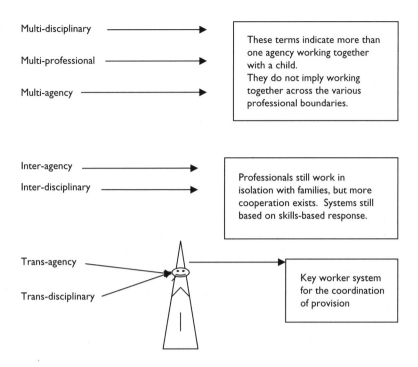

Figure 2.1   The three models

Principles of inter-agency working for children with SEN/AEN

The Special Educational Needs Code of Practice (DfES, 2001) clearly says that ALL services for children with SEN should focus on identifying and addressing the needs of children and enable them to improve their situation through:

- early identification;
- focused intervention;
- continual engagement with the child and parent;
- dissemination of effective approaches and techniques.

Five factors enabling effective inter-agency working are also indicated in the SEN Code of Practice. These are:

- integrated, high quality, holistic support focused on the needs of the child;
- a flexible child-centred approach to service delivery;
- effective collaboration of services involved with the child and with parents;
- based on a shared perspective;
- built whenever possible on mutual understanding and agreement.

Therefore, there needs to be a multi-level approach to interventions, starting on every occasion at looking at what the individual pupil's needs are. As stated earlier in the chapter, the purpose of any intervention needs to be at the centre of all decisions. If there is not going to be a positive outcome for the pupil, then the work should not be continued.

When is there a need for inter-agency working?

The multi-level approach can be used to illustrate how educators can constructively utilise inter-agency working so that most effective use is made of:

■ time

■ professional expertise

■ resources

■ funding.

At the centre of this issue is the individual pupil. The educator needs to see if there is anything she/he can do to improve the pupil's immediate educational environment to increase her/his access, participation and engagement in both the curriculum and the social life of the school. This may require the educator looking at factors such as the times, the places, the people and the curriculum areas when the pupil is successful and also when difficulties arise. At this level the educators in the classroom or tutor group and the pupil will be involved in trying to find solutions. The parents or carers may well also have a positive and supportive role to play at this stage, especially if difficulties are of a behavioural or emotional nature.

Often interwoven with the individual pupil's needs are whole-class factors that have to be considered. This may necessitate the incorporation of group or individual support from teaching assistants, and assistance on whether discussion, observation or actual practical support from the SENCO or SEN teacher is required. At this point the other pupils may need to be included through activities such as Circle of Friends or Circle Time and a 'Buddy' system. The educator needs to make sure that the parents/carers and pupil are fully involved in any course of action taken.

All of the above are suggestions that can be implemented when educators first identify an individual pupil's needs. However, even at this level of intervention, there are certain protocols that need to be known and understood. If, for example, a pupil tells you something that you think could be a child protection issue, do you know what you should do or who to go to for advice and assistance?

Important points to remember

■ It is usually through staff members, such as the SENCO, that external agency involvement is initiated.

■ Never promise a pupil anything that you cannot guarantee will happen. It is vital to maintain trust and honesty at all times.

- If a child protection issue is disclosed to you as an individual, always make sure that the pupil knows you will have to share this information with the Child Protection Coordinator who may need to take further action.

- When reassuring pupils in certain situations that confidentiality will be upheld at all times, IT IS VITAL that the adult always follows this up with the proviso that they will not be able to comply with this if a child protection issue is mentioned. This could occur in a Circle of Friends or Circle Time session, for example, and if the proviso has not initially been mentioned, issues of trust and honesty are immediately put in jeopardy.

- When a possible child protection issue is mentioned, do support the pupil by making sure the necessary people are informed, but DO NOT question the pupil about the specific issue. This could have negative implications for any follow-up course of action by social services.

- Involve the pupil throughout the process.

Discussion

Can you name all the people in your educational setting who fulfil the following roles?
- SENCO;
- designated Child Protection Coordinator;
- designated Teacher for Looked After Children;
- the Inclusion Manager;
- others e.g. the Family Liaison Officer (FLO) or the Children's Liaison Officer (CLO).

Do you know the situations when you would seek their support and expertise? Make sure that you have all the information about these roles particularly for use within your educational setting.

HLTA
1.4
1.6

Whole-school involvement is the next level of the approach and at this stage support may be sought from LEA support services and other educational departments. It is at this point that an evaluation of practice and intervention already implemented is a valuable exercise. This might include making sure that:

- Individual Education Plan (IEP) targets and reviews have been carried out;

- enough time for interventions to take effect has been given;

- the pupil has been fully involved throughout the process;

- the parents have been fully involved throughout the process;

- all expertise in the school has been fully utilised.

HLTA
1.4
1.5
1.6

Following this evaluation process it may be considered that inter-agency expertise is necessary and indeed might begin to include whole community issues.

What do you think schools should consider prior to making a referral to an external agency? The most important factor is, in this writer's opinion, that there is a clear idea of what the school hopes to achieve for the pupil from involving external agencies. This also implies that the school, all educators, parents, pupil and all other professionals are very willing to work in a partnership to really implement the term 'inter-agency working'.

Partnerships

It is important therefore that all those involved in any partnership fully understand what this really means and involves. Mordaunt (2001: 131) constructed a model called 'the Web', based on the proposed SEN Code of Practice (DfEE, 2000) (Figure 2.2) to demonstrate 'a more developed understanding of partnership, one which depends on the interconnected policies of all the players involved in the procedures and implies a greater sense of equality between all players'.

The SEN Code of Practice (DfES, 2001: 4,1:7) adds a further dimension to the idea of partnership. In the section entitled 'Strategic Planning Partnerships' it says:

Meeting the needs of children and young people with SEN successfully requires partnerships between all those involved – LEAs, schools, parents, pupils, health and social services and other agencies. Partnerships can only work when there is a clear understanding of the respective aims, roles and responsibilities of the partners and the nature of their relationships, which in turn depends on clarity of information, good communication and transparent policies.

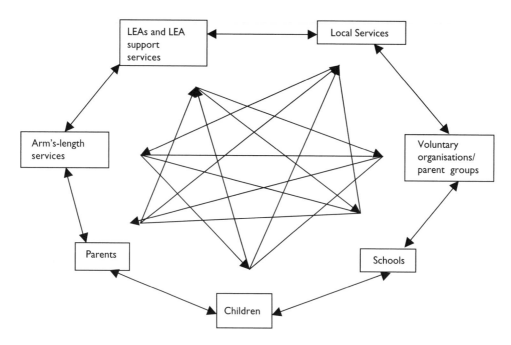

Figure 2.2 The Web
Source: Mordaunt (2001:131)

Understanding the roles and responsibilities of the partners and the nature of the relationships is of paramount importance if the risk of feelings of anxiety and hostility, as well as ineffectual interventions, is to be greatly reduced. Wall (2003: 71) agrees with these warnings: 'Sometimes confusions arise or misconceptions exist because of a lack of coordination and collaboration which can compound a child's difficulties.'

The roles of professionals

In this section of the chapter a brief overview of the roles of the professionals most frequently involved with schools will be introduced. Levels of involvement and actual working practices will vary within individual Local Education Authorities, but having the knowledge about what advice and support the different professionals may be able to offer is what is felt to be important here.

The local education authority or department

The support services within an authority may include the following specialists:

- cognition and learning teachers;
- educational psychologists (EP);
- behaviour teachers;
- early years advisory teachers;
- Visual/hearing/language impairment support;
- Pre-school SEN teachers;
- SEN Assessment Officers;
- Inclusion Officers;
- early years SENCOs.

The support staff listed above will generally all be experienced teachers and may have further qualifications within their specialist field. They all have very different roles, but within their specific area of provision they may do the following:

- offer staff training;
- give practical support to the class teacher or directly teach a group of pupils;
- provide additional specialist assessment;
- either provide or offer advice regarding suitable specialist resources or provision;
- act in an advisory capacity to a school;
- support referrals/complete written reports.

Health professionals

The SEN Code of Practice (DfES, 2001: 7), and SEN Toolkit (DfES, 2001a), Section 12 clearly state that:

> The local Health Authority (HA) needs to ensure that there are clear methods for collaboration with the LEA and social services departments in meeting their joint responsibilities under section 322 of the Education Act 1996 and section 27 of the Children Act 1989, and that they are known by the relevant officers.

There is also a need for the Health Authority to 'designate a medical officer for special educational needs' (DfES, 2001: 7). The SEN Code of Practice (DfES, 2001), in Section 10.26, lists what a designated medical officer should do in regard to inter-agency working with education and social services.

The health professionals that may be included in inter-agency meetings in schools could include:

- health visitors (HV)
- paediatricians
- school health service
- speech and language therapists (SLT)
- physiotherapists
- occupational therapists (OT)
- clinical psychologists (CP)
- audiologists and ophthalmologists
- child mental health team.

They may provide specialist assessment and diagnosis and it is important here to note that the designated medical officer should: 'make sure that there are appropriate mechanisms so that health advice is provided for annual review meetings and transition planning when appropriate' (DfES, 2001: 8).

A health professional will be able to give advice and any relevant training to school staff, in liaison with the parent/carer and the pupil, on the management of a pupil's medical condition. They may also provide input outside of the school context, for example, in a clinic for speech and language therapy or a hospital. It is in this kind of situation that inter-agency planning is vital if a pupil is going to be able to receive a holistic education plan that considers aspects such as missed schooling and medical needs.

Agencies with statutory duties

The Education Welfare Service works within a statutory and non-statutory frame-work and it is essential that good relationships and effective working practices are built up and maintained between a school and its Education Welfare Officer

(EWO). There are also times when schools need to work collaboratively with the police force or the probation service to meet a pupil's needs. This can be very complex, but if a good understanding of the roles and the structures of the different professions are respected within an inter-agency approach and the main purpose, support for the pupil, is focused upon, effective and positive outcomes for the pupil and the services can be achieved.

Social services

As with the Health Authority, social services should designate an officer who is responsible for working with schools and LEAs on behalf of those pupils with special educational needs. Social services may also be involved with children and young people in public care or those 'in need'. The SEN Toolkit, Section 11: The role of social services (DfES, 2001a: 7) also states that at a strategic level, social services departments with NHS bodies should make sure: 'that school and early education settings are aware of the full range of local services they provide'. It is perhaps with this service that the misunderstanding of roles and the services options to be offered, can cause situations that are unhelpful or even damaging for a pupil. This is undoubtedly due to the emotional and attachment issues that can 'cloud' judgements when social service support is required, especially in an emergency situation. Clarifying structures and procedures to be adhered to prior to a child protection incident, for example, may ensure that a pupil requiring emergency support will find professionals working together in a coherent, supportive and effective manner.

The role of voluntary agencies

The voluntary agencies often have charitable status and certainly have an important role to play in helping to meet the needs of pupils with special or additional educational needs, whether they are locally or nationally based. They can offer support, advice, training, library resource loan services and, in some cases, their own provision to practitioners, parents/carers and pupils. They can provide an advocacy service, research databases, links to other agencies and can represent groups on committees. According to the SEN Code of Practice:

> It is essential that schools and local authorities seek to work actively in partnership with the voluntary sector to meet pupils' needs. LEAs and schools should demonstrate a willingness to work with and value the contribution they can make.
>
> (DfES, 2001: 142, 10:38)

It is therefore useful for a school to have contact with local voluntary agencies and to welcome their input, even if the advice given means alternative practice or resources might need to be put in place. It is also essential for perhaps the Special Needs Coordinator (SENCO) to have leaflets and names and addresses of voluntary agencies to give to parents so that they can be correctly informed about the needs of their child. This can only add to openness between the various parties that encourages discourse and thus hopefully a better provision for pupils. Importantly voluntary agencies can offer their services to practitioners, parents/carers and young people and therefore can gain a broad overview of how support or resources can be both gained and then maintained.

Parental partnership and pupil participation

Parents and pupils are now considered to be invaluable members of any inter-agency framework.

Pupil participation

Many practitioners would question how valuable a pupil's voice is in situations where decisions need to be made about their own future educational needs. Children's involvement in their own meetings can also make many professionals feel very awkward. However, Roaf (2002: 49) writes: 'Children have benefited from, and contributed to, the more holistic agency approaches to their care and education developed during the past decade.' Clough and Barton (1995) also illustrate how the voice of the child has been heard due to research and pressure groups. Indeed, the author has known situations where children as young as 8 have been able to play a full role in determining their own education and care futures. By being given relevant information, being listened to and given a voice, pupils can, in many cases, make sound judgements or at least offer valuable contributions that enable successful outcomes.

Case study 4

Child A was in an out-of-county placement and had been for the past few years. Due to county policies and financial concerns the home county's social services and education department wished Child A to return 'home'. This caused considerable concern for Child A's local carers and educators, as progress was, after a long settling in period, actually being seen. Information about the possible options was shared by the social worker with Child A. At a statutory review meeting Child A eloquently told the large group of adults her views and the reasons for the request to stay where she was. The meeting in real terms ended there, because as the social worker said, the child's voice had to be listened to and acted upon, if at all possible.

This was in accordance with Articles 12 and 13 of the United Nations Convention on the Rights of the Child:

Children, who are capable of forming views, have a right to receive and make known information, to express an opinion, and to have that opinion taken into account in any matters affecting them. The views of the child should be given due weight according to the age, maturity and capability of the child. (DfES, 2001: 3, Section 4)

HLTA
1.2

Discussion

- ■ **In how many ways are pupils, within your educational setting, encouraged to participate?**
- ■ **Do the pupils feel that they are listened to and that their voices are heard?**
- **If your answer is yes – how do you know this?**
- **If your answer is no – why not?**

A word of caution is also given regarding pupil voice in the SEN Code of Practice Toolkit, Section 4 (DfES, 2001a) when it includes from the Children Act 1989 Guidance and Regulations, Vol. 6. Children with Disabilities (1991):

The SEN Code of Practice (2001: 3) recognizes that there is: a fine balance between giving the child a voice and encouraging them to make informed decisions, and overburdening them with decision-making procedures where they have insufficient experience and knowledge to make appropriate judgements without additional support.

Parental partnership

Parents have in the past been seen as the 'partners' without professional knowledge and therefore were expected to be merely willing to only listen and agree with the practitioners' decisions. Fortunately during the past decade the value of the information parents have about their children is being treated as a vital element of any programme or course of action. Parents are now considered to be an important link between schools and pupils. There are situations where, quite rightly, the parent takes on the role as the key worker for a pupil within an inter-agency support programme.

Local Education Authorities or departments have particular duties to fulfil, to ensure that parents have access to partnership services. These services are particularly focused at providing information for those parents who have children with special educational needs. The Education Act of 1996 said that: 'LEAs must take whatever steps they consider appropriate to make parent partnership services known to parents, head teachers, schools and others they consider appropriate' (Section 332A(3)). The SEN Code of Practice, Toolkit (DfES, 2001a: 7, section 2) adds that: 'LEAs *must* inform parents and schools in their area about the parent partnership service.' These are very important, but it is the relationship between all parents and an individual school that is so imperative at times for all pupils. Schools have undoubtedly started to include parents more in aspects of their school day and activities, but how many actually ask a good proportion of their parents what they would like implemented to enable them to feel more confident and comfortable within the school environment? A simple question, but how many initiatives for parents do you know are introduced with perhaps only very little consultation, if any at all?

Time spent on establishing good methods of communication and working together on various tasks will improve relationships, trust and cooperation. As Beveridge comments:

> The concept of partnership is based on the recognition that parents and teachers have complementary contributions to make to children's education. Accordingly, it is central to the notion of partnership that schools should demonstrate that they not only listen to, but also value, parents' perspectives.
>
> (1997: 56)

Again, Hurst (1997: 108) reinforces this view, emphasising that professionals must not assume that they know what parents want so that they can feel valued partners with the professionals: 'It is the awareness of parents' needs and the willingness to be adaptable in developing ways of meeting these needs which are the most important.'

> **Discussion**
>
> How does your educational setting involve and include ALL parents?
> What methods are used to find out how parents can play a greater role in the education their children receive?

Inter-agency case studies

In this section three case studies are given to aid discussion about actual situations. One case in particular looks quite a minor problem, but is it? What does it tell you about the relationship between the school, outside agencies and parents?

Case study 5

> A Year 4 girl, pupil D, is unable to run in a straight line or skip and is generally very awkward at school, always knocking into objects and people. Her peers have started to laugh at her and refuse to accept her into their team games. Additional support and particular exercises are incorporated into PE and games sessions to try to improve her skills, but this additional input is making little difference after two terms. The girl is becoming less willing to participate in sport and will frequently be found hiding inside the school at break times.

Discussion

What does the school need to do? Is external agency input required? Who else needs to be involved in helping pupil D?

Case study 6

A distressed parent asks to see the SENCO of a primary school saying that her son is never free of head lice, despite constant treatment. The mother reinforces the fact that every time she clears her son's head lice, he catches them again from another pupil within a few days.

Discussion

How can this parent be supported? What does the school need to do?

Case study 7

A Year 5 boy, pupil Q, has been in the school since the Reception class. Over the years there have been minor behaviour difficulties, but these have been easily addressed using the generic school behaviour policy.

After the first few weeks in Year 5, pupil Q's behaviour began to deteriorate. He was very disruptive in class, rude to adults and extremely aggressive in the playground to his male peers. The midday supervisors found him very difficult to deal with and lunchtime incidents regularly began to be carried over into the afternoon school session. Recently it was also noted that there had been an increased number of absences, without clear reasons. Pupil Q's mother had attended a meeting, but attributed the change in his behaviour to a clash of personalities between pupil Q and his class teacher. She also stated that her son had been ill a lot as well. A number of other parents have complained to the school about pupil Q's aggression towards their children.

Discussion

What does the school need to do next? Who needs to be involved in helping pupil Q?

Key issues

It is anticipated that you will now:

- have a good understanding and working knowledge of the terms used to describe relationships with other professionals;
- understand how important it is to develop effective working practices with other professionals;
- understand the roles and responsibilities of other professionals;
- have an understanding of the historical implications behind inter-agency working;
- have a knowledge of the legislation and documentation that inform and support inter-agency practice;
- be able to identify with colleagues when it is necessary to involve outside school support for an individual pupil;
- know who to go to for specific information and support;
- value the need to listen to and respond appropriately to the voice of the child;
- value and respect parental views and contributions given regarding their child's education.

Professional Standards for Higher Level Teaching Assistants (HLTA)

If you can demonstrate your understanding and professional use of the key issues illustrated within this chapter, it is hoped that you will be able to fulfil the following HLTA Standards:

1.2	1.4	1.5	1.6
2.8	2.9	3.3.3	3.3.7

Useful documents

DfE (1994) *Code of Practice on the Identification and Assessment of Pupils with Special Educational Needs*, London: DfE.

DfEE (2000) (Proposed) *SEN Code of Practice on the Identification and Assessment of Pupils with Special Educational Needs*, London: DfEE.

DfES (2001) *Special Educational Needs Code Of Practice*, Annesley: DfES.

DfES (2001a) *SEN Toolkit*, Annesley: DfES.

HMSO (2003) *Every Child Matters*, Norwich: The Stationery Office.

South East Region SEN Partnership (undated) *Working Positively with Parents*, Filsham Valley School: Michael Phillips.

United Nations (1989) *Convention on the Rights of the Child*, New York: United Nations.

References

Beveridge, S. (1997) 'Implementing partnership with parents in schools', in Wolfendale, S. (ed.) *Working with Parents of SEN Children after the Code of Practice*, London: David Fulton.

Blamires, M. and Moore, J. (2003) *Support Services and Mainstream Schools: A Guide for Working Together*, London: David Fulton.

Blamires, M., Robertson, C. and Blamires, J. (1997) *Parent-Teacher Partnership: Practical Approaches to Meet Special Educational Needs*, London: David Fulton.

Bronfenbrenner, U. (1970) *Two Worlds of Childhood: US and USSR*, New York: Sage.

Clough, P. and Barton, L. (1995) *Making Difficulties: Research and the Construction of SEN*, London: Paul Chapman.

Coulling, N. (2000) 'Definition of successful education for the "looked after" child: a multi-agency perspective', *Support for Learning*, vol. 15, No. 1. Tamworth: NASEN.

Court Report (1976) *Fit for the Future: The Report of the Committee on Child Health Services*. Cmnd 6684, London: Department of Health and Social Services.

Dale, N. (1996) *Working with Families of Children with Special Needs: Partnership and Practice*, London: Routledge.

Department of Education and Employment (DfEE) (1999) *The National Inclusion Statement*, London: HMSO.

Department of Education and Science (DES) (1978) *The Report of the Committee of Enquiry into the Education of Handicapped Children and Young People* (The Warnock Report), London: HMSO.

Department of Health (DoH) (1989) *The Children Act*, London: HMSO.

Department of Health (DoH) (1991) *The Children Act Guidance and Regulations*, vol. 6, *Children with Disabilities*. London: HMSO.

HMSO (2003) *Every Child Matters*, Norwich: The Stationery Office.

Hurst, V. (1997) *Planning for Early Learning: Educating Young Children*, London: Paul Chapman.

Kelly, G. (1955) *The Psychology of Personal Constructs*, New York: Norton.

Lacey, P. (2001) *Support Partnerships: Collaboration in Action*, London: David Fulton.

Leathard, A. (ed.) (1994) *Going Interprofessional: Working Together for Health and Welfare*, London: Routledge.

Mordaunt, E. (2001) 'The nature of special educational needs partnership', in Riddell, S. and Tett, L. (eds) *Education, Social Justice and Inter-agency Working*, London: Routledge.

Roaf, C. (2002) *Coordinating Services for Included Children: Joined Up Action*, Buckingham: Open University Press.

Wall, K. (2003) *Special Needs and Early Years: A Practitioner's Guide*, London: Paul Chapman.

Cultural issues and schools

Sue Soan

Culture is dynamic, active, changing, always on the move. Even within their native contexts, cultures are always changing as a result of political, social and other modifications in the immediate environment.

(Nieto, 1999)

Introduction

This chapter is very closely linked to the issues discussed in Chapter 4 regarding bilingual learners. However, it was decided to look at cultural issues and bilingualism separately, because, although they are interlinked in daily working terms, it is felt that due to busy working environments it is all too easy to 'forget' the importance of really understanding the diverse backgrounds that many learners in our schools now present.

It is first of all important to recognise that the majority of schools and hence educators have traditionally functioned in a way that reflects society's main cultural group's social values and ideologies. An example of this is reported by Wright *et al.* (2000) who wrote that one teacher felt that black children were so different from her that she didn't know how to deal with them.

> Such antiquated views are probably not unusual. They are part of a cultural and historical legacy which continues not only because many of the teachers in our schools have had very little contact with 'ethnic difference' in both their upbringing and training, but also because they continue to have little if any knowledge of their students' lives outside of school.
>
> (Wright *et al.*, 2000, in Blair, 2001: 7)

It is perhaps time to recognise that many of the practices schools have traditionally relied upon are no longer the best or most appropriate because of the number of learners who are now linguistically and culturally outside this main cultural group. Consequently it is important to look again at many of the 'traditional' aspects of schooling so that educators can be properly informed, enabling appropriate responses to be achieved for all their learners within their community. It is hoped that the information presented in this chapter will initiate discussion and ideas so that daily practices can be re-examined to ensure that the needs of all the learners, whatever their cultural background in whatever educational setting, are met.

Before reading further briefly write down what you think the term 'culture' means to you. Do you feel that your own understanding of culture may influence your practice within the educational setting in which you work?

What is culture?

This term can be problematic, because the word 'culture' means different things to every individual, but undoubtedly it can be agreed, I believe, that it is both 'complex and intricate' (Nieto, 1999: 48). It is something that all human beings have in common, because everyone has a culture and in general all cultures are neither totally 'good' or totally 'bad', embodying 'values that have grown out of historical and social conditions and necessities' (Nieto, 1999: 58). Additionally, as illustrated in the quotation at the beginning of the chapter, it needs to be understood that cultures are not static and are changed as a result of people from different cultures coming into contact with one another. A good example of how one culture influences another is Rap music. The style of dancing, speak, dress and movement that accompanies Rap is seen in young people from many diverse cultural backgrounds currently. Thus, for the purposes of this chapter, I am going to use the definition Nieto gives to describe culture:

> the ever-changing values, traditions, social and political relationships, and worldview created, shared, and transformed by a group of people bound together by a combination of factors that can include a common history, geographic location, language, social class, and religion.
>
> (Nieto, 1999)

If you accept the points above, it can be seen how complex it is to fully understand culture and thus cultural diversity.

What are the issues for schools?

Responding to ALL learners' needs

Having gained practical experience teaching immigrant children, Cristina Igoa (1995) recognised she needed to acknowledge:

- the importance of listening to the children;
- the importance of the feeling of having roots;
- the importance of understanding cultures;
- the importance of belonging.

(ibid.: 10)

Four very short sentences, but these incorporate a number of substantial issues for schools and other educational settings re-examining their ability to respond to the cultural needs of their learners. This is a vital issue and one that is of growing significance:

> The 2001 Census has shown that nearly one in eight pupils comes from a minority ethnic background. By 2010, the proportion is expected to be around one in five. Their school achievement will determine their success in later life.
>
> (DfES, 2003a: 7, 1.1)

It is also important to state at this point that culture issues are dominant factors for all learners. Recently in an article entitled 'Focus on Needs of London's white boys', a panel member from the Home Office's Community Cohesion Unit said, 'It had been pressing the DfES to introduce a strategy for white children as a follow-up to its Aiming High campaign for ethnic-minority pupils. But officials were hesitant because they feared it could be perceived as racist' (Shaw, 2004). The DfES responded by saying that there were no such fears and that a pilot scheme for white European boys would be running in London. Importantly the Commission for Racial Equality (CRE) supported this campaign, saying that, 'Schools and local authorities are obliged not to discriminate against children because of their racial background – not just ethnic minority groups – particularly if they are underperforming' (Shaw, 2004). All these comments thus agree that it does not matter which so-called 'cultural group' the learners come from, it is their learning needs that must now be recognised as the most important issue. Recent government research findings (July 2003) also support this need to be alert to all learners' individual requirements as learners' cultural backgrounds do NOT explain all the variations in how they perform at school:

> the largest discrepancy in attainment between FSM [Free School Meals] and non-FSM pupils is found amongst White pupils indicating that other factors must also be considered in understanding and addressing the achievements of minority ethnic pupils.
>
> (DfES, 08.01.2004a)

It is clear, therefore, that cultural diversity in educational settings is evolving and developing, requiring all those involved in teaching and learning to think about the suitability of the curriculum, the social experiences, the teaching practices and the policies being offered to the learners.

HLTA
1.1

> **Discussion**
> ■ How well prepared do you feel the learners in your educational setting are for the cultural diversity of the twenty-first century?
> ■ What factors do you think influence your feelings/thoughts on these issues?
> ■ Are changes required in schools and, if so, how can these effectively be managed?

The curriculum

Within this developing framework it is evidently not enough just to include festivals, foods or dances from various cultures as 'elements' of culture into the curriculum and life of a school, as a goodwill gesture. Equality and diversity need to be built into all aspects of the curriculum so that all cultures can be valued and utilised in all schools and in all classrooms. Following research by the Birmingham Advisory Service, Birmingham's lead adviser on equalities, Karamat Iqbal commented: 'At the moment the curriculum does not reflect the ethnic mix of the city, or of most schools' (Lepkowska, 2004). Edwards (1998) goes even further in demonstrating the importance of representing cultures equitably by suggesting that all pupils who leave school with only a monocultural perspective are actually ill-prepared to meet the needs of twenty-first-century society.

HLTA
3.1.3

Language

The importance of language needs to be mentioned at this juncture, but the reader will need to consult Chapter 4 to gain a thorough understanding of the vital place language plays in considering the needs of all bilingual learners. Nieto (1999: 60) writes:

> language is deeply implicated with culture and an important part of it. That is, the language, language variety, or dialect one speaks is culture made manifest, although it is not, of course, all there is to culture.

Genesee (2001: 1) also supports Nieto's views saying that, 'Indeed where possible and where desired by parents, use of the home language and incorporation of the home culture into the curriculum and activities of the school are to be strongly encouraged.' However, recent research has indicated that: 'Head teachers saw language as a greater challenge than other aspects of ethnicity' (DfES, 12.12.2003).

- Why do you think that research has indicated that language is the greatest challenge at present in educational settings?
- Is it perhaps because of the daily problems educators may have with trying to educate learners with another language, or not?
- Do you agree with the following statement? 'Language is a daily problem that has to be dealt with, but other cultural issues do not tend to impinge on the daily teaching practices of the educators.' Explain to a colleague how this may affect an educational setting's planning and policies and what it could mean to a learner with a different cultural background from the majority of the school community.

Training for educators

Without question, educational settings are now more ethnically and culturally diverse with second and third generation families of minority ethnic groups as well as new arrivals, such as asylum seekers. However, educators are generally not representative of this growing diversity.

Do you think that it matters if the educators are ethnically representative of the learner population or not? Why?

Recent research findings (DfES, 12.12.2003) indicate that, overall, schools felt the most important need is for quality staff and that 'where schools do not have a staff that matches the ethnic mix of pupils, it is not in itself an issue' (ibid., 2). However, information gained from the DfES (2003b) consultation summary *Aiming High: Raising the Achievement of Minority Ethnic Pupils* reveals that minority ethnic pupils themselves reported that they felt barriers to learning included:

> unequal treatment by some teachers, a perceived lack of of respect, from the point of view of African Caribbean pupils … Within the Gypsy and Traveller communities there was a cultural expectation that young people would not complete their secondary education. Low literacy skills among families, … and racial abuse/discriminatory behaviour by other pupils and staff were some of the reasons given.
>
> (Teachernet, 08.01.2004)

Other respondents including professionals, parents and voluntary groups saw the need for a national strategy to support the raising of the achievement for minority ethnic pupils in schools. Over half listed training for educators as essential, stating that this needed to incorporate anti-racism training, and English as an additional language (EAL) (DfES, 2003b).

These views clearly indicate that educators generally still need to seriously consider how they manage to ensure they have high expectations for all learners. Also, training for educators on cultural and diversity issues needs to remain high on any development plan to enable the adaptation of policies and practices to be effectively evaluated and updated. In this manner the climate of schools can be supported so that conditions for learning are appropriate for learners from diverse backgrounds. As Cline (1998: 160) says: 'a more desirable and attainable goal would be for trainers, employers and staff to ensure that relevant professionals are competent to work effectively with the full range of the ethnic and linguistic groups in their geographical areas'.

Understanding culturally preferred teaching and learning initiatives

It must be acknowledged that learners from some cultural groups are not aware of the way schools and educators in England and Wales expect them to behave or to learn. Actions, behaviours and learning strategies encouraged and fostered in learners in English and Welsh schools may appear inappropriate, rude or disrespectful to learners from other cultural backgrounds. For example, it is thought correct for educators to teach children to be critical thinkers and to ask questions within our school system. However, many Polynesian learners are taught by their families that a teacher, like a priest, is to be respected because they hold valuable knowledge and therefore must not be questioned. An African perspective may be similar in that some families will still expect their children to be 'seen and not heard', because this to them is a sign of good behaviour (Hodson, in May, 1999). This indeed may cause a rift between the school and home, and difficulties of allegiance for the learner, unless collaboration and understanding are established between the educators, the families and the learners.

> **Discussion**
> ■ Can you think of any occasion when a cultural difference may have caused a problem for a learner in your educational setting?
> ■ What do you think a school could do to ensure that they are aware of any similar cultural difference? Who would need to be involved?

Legislation and historical perspectives

Prior to the late 1960s: 'The Black "newcomers" were to be absorbed into a culturally and linguistically homogeneous society. People had to get rid of what they came with, in order to fit into "our" society' (Burke *et al.*, in Acton and Dalphinis, 2000). This was called 'assimilation' and this approach preceded a 'culturally diverse' approach. This is described by Roy Jenkins in 1966 as: 'not a flattening process of assimilation, but as equal opportunity accompanied by cultural diversity in an atmosphere of mutual tolerance' (Acton and Dalphinis, 2000: 159). This 'culturally diverse' approach was meant to lead to educational programmes that focused on minority groups' needs, and also included encouraging the positive use of other languages. However, as Burke *et al.* say:

> The 'cultural diversity' approach conceived of racism as simply a set of mental prejudices held by a few people, would disappear if we all knew how other people dress and speak. It didn't look at the effects on education of the structural nature of institutional racism.
>
> (In Acton and Dalphinis, 2000: 15a)

The Bullock Report (1975)

With regard to teaching learners with diverse cultural backgrounds, the Bullock Report suggested to educators that there should be child-centredness in education and that they should evaluate:

> a) what a learner actually has brought with him/her to school;
> b) and then plan and deliver the content of the curriculum on his/her needs and abilities.
> No child should be expected to cast off the language and culture of the home as he crosses the school threshold, nor to live and act as though school and home represent two totally separate and different cultures which have to be kept firmly apart.
>
> (DES, 1975: 286, 20.5)

The Swann Report (1985)

Between 1975 and the Swann Report (1985), it is suggested that an ethnic minority 'deficit model' was instigated by the Callaghan government when it set up a Committee of Inquiry looking into the Education of Children from Ethnic Minority Groups in 1979. This assumed that learners from ethnic minorities needed additional help to achieve the same levels of achievement as their English peers. Mrs Thatcher continued the enquiries, replacing the chair, Anthony Rampton, with Lord Swann. However, the findings did not support Callaghan and Thatcher's assumptions, but they did demonstrate racism in schools. The Swann Report therefore advocated an inclusive, anti-racist 'Education for All'. It was considered quite a controversial report, because although many teachers in England felt it was a genuine endeavour to move towards anti-racism, it did include inadequacies (Acton, 1986) such as 'continuing to use confused racist categories to classify ethnic groups' (Acton and Dalphinis, 2000: 241).

The Race Amendment Act 2000

This Act amended the the Race Relations Act of 1976 and its aim 'is to make promoting race equality central to the way public authorities work'. It continues:

> The general duty says that the body must have 'due regard' to the need to:
> ■ eliminate unlawful racial discrimination; and

■ promote equality of opportunity and good relations between people of different racial groups.

(DfES, 08.01.2004b)

Specific duties were also given to schools to improve the educational experience of all children, but in particular those belonging to ethnic minority groups. These duties are:

■ to prepare a written statement of the school's policy for promoting race equality, and to act upon it;

■ to *assess* the impact of school policies on pupils, staff and parents of different racial groups, including, in particular, the impact of attainment levels of these pupils;

■ to *monitor* the operation of all the school's policies, including, in particular their impact on the attainment levels of pupils from different racial groups; and

■ to take *reasonable steps* to make available the results of its monitoring.

(DfES, 08.01.2004b)

These specific duties can be enforced by a compliance notice (a legal document) issued by the Commission for Racial Equality (CRE). The CRE have produced a Statutory Code of Practice with practical advice and also a guide for schools. OFSTED specifically looks at how well schools are progressing with developing these duties.

> **Discussion**
> ■ Consider how many of these specific duties are in working practice in a known educational setting.
> ■ Were you aware that schools had these specific duties? How many of your colleagues are aware of them?

Aiming high: raising the achievement of minority ethnic pupils (2003)

This consultation, non-statutory document issued in March 2003 by the Department of Education and Skills (DfES) led to the announcement of a national strategy in October 2003 to lift the achievement of under-achieving minority ethnic pupils. The government plans include:

■ training for primary teachers to enable them to better support bilingual learners;

■ the establishment of a national specialist qualification for teachers who work with bilingual learners;

■ focused work in 30 secondary schools to raise African Caribbean achievement.

(DfES, 08.01.2004c)

In the conclusions section of the consultation document the government states:

> Our vision is simple: real equality of opportunity and the highest possible standards for all pupils in all schools. We have argued the case here for seeing the needs of minority ethnic pupils as an integral part of all mainstream policies and programmes, rather than simply an add-on
>
> (DfES, 2003a)

> **Discussion**
>
> Do you feel that the present government's 'vision' as noted above (DfES, 2003a) is in total agreement with the way other bodies such as the Commission for Racial Equality (CRE) see the focus for equality of opportunity in education? Discuss with a colleague, looking at all the information available in this chapter.

Culture, language and learning

This section will briefly comment on two minority groups that should be equally included within our educational system. They are not perhaps the first groups that come to mind, but it is hoped that the information provided will enable focused discussions and the knowledge gained to be transferred and applied to the effective inclusion of other minority groups.

Travellers in Britain

> Travellers represent a small minority within the community and within our schools. But the issues raised when Traveller children go into school are neither minor, nor of relevance only to the minority. They test out the response of the education system at every level in equal opportunities, with respect to access, curriculum, anti-racism and home–school liaison. If a school is sufficiently flexible to respond constructively to the educational needs of Travellers, then it is likely to be doing a good job with most of its other pupils too.
>
> (Foster, in Claire et al., 1993: 54)

Travellers in Britain include Romanies and also Travellers from indigenous communities such as Scottish and Irish Tinkers. Both of these have a nomadic tradition and a wide range of migration. Other communities are called economic and occupational Travellers or new Travellers and these might be circus and fairground workers who have become nomadic due to economic pressures or through a wish for an alternative lifestyle.

As with any group, it is problematic to generalise, but as Foster (in Claire et al., 1993: 54) writes, there are four priorities that characterise the difference between the settled population and (traditional) Travellers. These are:

■ the maintenance of extended family networks and community contacts;

- a positive attitude to mobility;

- a tradition of home education;

- the perpetuation of a shared language.

Educators need to be aware of these factors when establishing a relationship with Traveller learners in school and their families.

It is also part of their tradition to respect educated Travellers and, indeed, formal education is not a threat to their culture. However, those that are not educated are not looked down on as they recognise the fact that formal education is only part of a wider education and does not necessarily affect their survival or economic success. Migration and thus short periods of time in individual schools can mean that learners achieve only limited educational progress.

HLTA
1.2
1.5

> **Discussion**
> Many LEAs now have policies and practices that are specifically in place to meet the needs of Traveller children. Find your LEA policy on providing educational services for Travellers and see how the educational setting in which you work could obtain support and resources for Travellers if required.
> How would your educational setting support Traveller children? Is there a school policy that everyone is aware of and can gain direction from?

Findings from research by the International Centre for Intercultural Studies, the Institute of Education, University of London, suggest that the following practices enable the securing of educational entitlements for Gypsy Traveller children (Bhopal *et al.*, 2003):

- support from the Traveller Education Services (TES);

- a senior management team that is committed to an inclusive ethos and to the equal opportunity and race equality policies;

- effective home–school liaison;

- acceptance and respect for Traveller communities;

- a flexible approach to enable the needs of the pupils to be met;

- it is important that schools have effective anti-racist policies and practices;

- high expectations and accurate assessments leading to additional support if required;

- a curriculum that reflects the reality of Traveller culture, history and language;

- cooperative joint action by the school, the TES and the Education Welfare Services (EWS) can reduce poor attendance.

HLTA
1.1
1.5
1.6
3.1.3
3.3.7

Discussion

What are your views of the findings listed above? Do you think they are statements that could apply to other learners? If so, which and why?

Asylum seekers

The United Nations Convention on the Rights of the Child (1989) and the Education Act (1996) 'require refugee and asylum seeker children to be provided with education' (Spencer, 2002: 8). Also as Stanley (2001: 5) points out, this is applicable 'to all children regardless of immigration status'. It may be significant to know that the estimated number of asylum seekers makes it clear that many schools do now or will in the near future have the opportunity to welcome an asylum seeker into their community. 'It is estimated that approximately 80,000 asylum-seeking children live in the UK, of whom the greatest number, 62,000, live in Greater London' (Rutter, 2002). The number of unaccompanied asylum-seeking children, 'now represent approximately 6 per cent of all children in care, mainly concentrated in London and the South East' (HMSO, 2003: 35, 2.50). Thus it is imperative that the policies and practices of schools enable educators to provide for these learners' educational needs in a practical and understanding manner.

Clarke writes:

> One of the many entitlements often denied young asylum-seekers and refugees is the chance to be 'normal' … the right to be part of a school community and a life … dominated not by the local consequences of bloody international conflicts … but by moaning about exams, sneaking guilty World-Cup-watching revision breaks.
>
> (2003: 177)

There may therefore be a requirement to provide a mixture of learning environments, a variety of group-learning situations and of strategies and skills to meet their varied needs.

So what may asylum seekers experience as barriers to their learning? Clarke (2003) has identified a number of factors that she considers are some of the most common difficulties asylum seekers may experience:

- English language level may be low and this will therefore also affect their ability to concentrate in a classroom;
- obtaining resources for these learners can be difficult as they can arrive from anywhere in the world;
- a difficulty with understanding classroom expectations and protocols, the irrelevance of the curriculum, and poor study skills;

- these children may experience depression and post-traumatic stress syndrome due to past experiences;

- if unaccompanied, the lack of a key adult can make life problematic;

- fear of deportation and dispersal for those who have not been granted at least an Extended Leave to Remain (short-term refuge, usually until their 18th birthday) if not full refugee status;

- inadequate or inconsistent housing does not help establish a routine or a feeling of security and can affect their ability to attend school regularly or to even complete homework, etc.

HLTA
1.2
1.5
3.3.7

> **Discussion**
>
> There are many issues to consider when a learner who is also an asylum seeker joins a school community. How would you, and the establishment in which you work, support this learner so that he/she may experience both a chance to be 'normal' and a positive education environment? Are there any other professionals or agencies you may consider consulting to assist you in this task? If so, which?

Conclusion

The intention of the provision of any education service is to grant all learners access to academic intervention and thus hopefully to academic achievement. Educators teaching learners from various cultural backgrounds thus need to look at them all as individuals and to adapt community practice and policies so that everyone can feel included and valued. Igoa (1995) developed an approach to teach immigrant children that encompasses their cultural, academic and psychological needs. Figure 3.1, entitled 'The Threefold Intervention', illustrates the

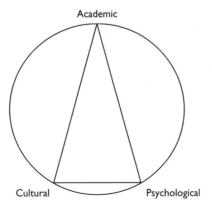

Figure 3.1   The threefold intervention
Source: Igoa (1995: 119)

areas of intervention Igoa focuses on around the circle that represents the whole child. She writes:

> When the child feels in balance with these 3 aspects of herself or himself, the child in school is fully alive. … Sometimes I focus on the cultural, then the psychological, then both, but I always keep the academic clearly in focus, so the child understands the importance of school.

(ibid.: 119)

This example is just one possible approach, but it is one that focuses on all the needs of the individual, and not primarily on their cultural group background.

Finally, therefore, this chapter has hopefully illustrated the need for schools and educators to create positive conditions for learning, where culture, climate and interpersonal relationships, through the revision of policies and practices undergo substantial changes: 'The very climate of schools needs to undergo a critical transformation in order to make it clear that students of diverse backgrounds are expected and encouraged to learn' (Nieto, 1999: 101).

Key issues

It is anticipated that you will now:

- have an understanding of what 'culture' is;
- understand the need to value learners' language and cultures;
- recognise the importance of having high expectations of all learners, whatever their cultural background;
- be able to recognise in a classroom where issues for learners from other cultures may cause difficulties;
- be aware of the need for policies and practices in a school to reflect the cultural diversity of all its different populations.

Professional Standards for Higher Level Teaching Assistants (HLTA)

If you can demonstrate your understanding and professional use of the key issues illustrated within this chapter, it is hoped that you will be able to fulfil the following HLTA Standards:

1.1	1.2	1.5	1.6	3.1.3	3.3.7

References

Acton, T. (1986) 'Reacting to Swann' in *The Swann Report of an ACER/NGEC Conference*, London: University of London Institute of Education.

Acton, T. and Dalphinis, M. (eds) (2000) *Language, Blacks and Gypsies: Languages Without a Written Tradition and Their Role in Education*, London: Whiting and Birch Ltd.

Bhopal, K., Gundara, J., Jones, C. and Owen, C. (2003) 'The achievement of Gypsy Traveller pupils', in Research Report No. 238, '*Working Towards Inclusive Education: Aspects of Good Practice for Gypsy Children*', DfES www.dfes.gov.uk/research/data/uploadfiles/RR238.doc (downloaded on 22.12.2003).

Blair, M. (2001) *Why pick on me?: School Exclusion and Black Youth*, Stoke on Trent: Trentham Books Ltd.

Claire, H., Maybin, J. and Swann, J. (eds) (1993) *Equality Matters: Case Studies from the Primary School*, Clevedon: Multilingual Matters Ltd.

Clarke, L. (2003) 'Supporting asylum seekers in schools', *Support for Learning*, vol. 18, no. 4, Tamworth: NASEN.

Cline, T. (1998) 'The assessment of special educational needs for bilingual children', *British Journal of Special Education*, vol. 25, no. 4, pp. 159–63.

DES (1975) *A Language for Life*, The Bullock Report, London: HMSO.

DfES (2003a) *Aiming High: Raising the Achievement of Minority Ethnic Pupils*, Annesley: DfES.

DfES (2003b) *Aiming High: Raising the Achievement of Minority Ethnic Pupils Consultation Summary*, www.standards.dfes.gov.uk/ethnicminorities (downloaded on 12.12.2003).

DfES (12.12.2003) *Minority Ethnic Exclusions and the Race Relations (Amendment) Act 2000, Interim Summary – November 2003*, Canterbury Christ Church University College. Available on: www.dfes.gov.uk/exclusions/uploads/Minority%20Ethnic%20Exclusions%20Interim%20Findings%20final.doc (downloaded on 12/12/03).

DfES (08.01.2004a) *July 2003: New Research on Minority Ethnic Attainment*, available on: www.standards.dfes.gov.uk/ethnicminorities/raising (downloaded on 08.01.2004).

DfES (08.01.2004b) *Race Relations Amendment Act 2000*, available on: www.standards.dfes.gov.uk/ethnicminorities/raising (downloaded on 08.01.2004).

DfES (08.01.2004c) '*October 2003: "Aiming High": Minister Announces Way Forward*', available on: www.standards.dfes.gov.uk/ethnicminorities/raising (downloaded on 08.01.2004).

Edwards, V. (1998) *The Power of Babel: Teaching and Learning in Multilingual Classrooms*, Stoke on Trent: Trentham Books.

Genesee, F. (ed.) (2001) *Educating Second Language Children: The Whole Child, the Whole Curriculum, the Whole Community*, Cambridge: Cambridge University Press.

Grugeon, E. and Woods, P. (1990) *Educating All: Multicultural Perspectives in the Primary School*, London and New York: Routledge.

HMSO (2003) *Every Child Matters*, Norwich: The Stationery Office.

Igoa, C. (1995) *The Inner World of the Immigrant Child*, Mahwah, NJ: Lawrence Erlbaum Associates.

James, A. and Jeffcoate, R. (eds) (1981) *The School in the Multicultural Society*, London: Harper and Row.

Jenkins, R. (1966) 'Address to a meeting of the Voluntary Liaison Committee' on 23 May 1966, National Committee for Commonwealth Immigrants, London.

Lepkowska, D. (2004) ' "Racist" syllabus hampers children', *Times Educational Supplement*, 6 February.

May, S. (ed.) (1999) *Critical Multiculturalism: Rethinking Multicultural and Antiracist Education*, London: Falmer Press.

Mills, R.W. and Mills, J. (1993) *Bilingualism in the Primary School*, London: Routledge.

Nieto, S. (1999) *The Light in Their Eyes: Creating Multicultural Learning Communities*, Stoke on Trent: Trentham Books.

OFSTED (1996) *The Education of Travelling Children*, London: OFSTED.

Rutter, J. (2002) Including Refugee Children. Notes from 'Including Refugee Children: Education and social inclusion issues facing children of asylum seekers', Conference, National Children's Bureau, April 2002.

Shaw, M. (2004) 'Focus on needs of London's white boys', *Times Educational Supplement*, 6 February.

Spencer, Y. (2002) 'A right to education: schooling for refugee and asylum-seeking children', *ChildRIGHT*, 192, December, pp. 8–9.

Stanley, K. (2001) *Young Separated Refugees in Oxford*, London: Save the Children.

Swann, Lord (1985) *Education for All: The Report of the Committee of Inquiry into the Education of Children from Ethnic Minority Groups*, London: HMSO.

Teachernet (08.01.2004) *Minority Ethnic Pupils in Education: Their Own Views*, available on: www.teachernet.gov.uk/educationoverview/briefing/news/minorityethnicpupils views/ (downloaded, 08.01.2004).

Wright, C., Weekes, D., McGlaughlin, A. and Webb, D. (2000) *Race, Class and Gender in Exclusion from School*, London: Falmer Press.

4 Bilingual learners

Sue Soan

Regardless of how the debate on bilingual education is resolved, bilingual and immigrant students throughout the world require thoughtful and empathetic attention.

(Brisk, 1998: xiii)

[Learners] cannot be treated as empty vessels to be filled, but as containers rich with knowledge to be added and expanded.

(Brisk, 1998: 65)

Introduction

This chapter will discuss issues relating to teaching in a bilingual classroom. The basic principles and research findings on first and second language acquisition will be presented to identify areas for further examination and discussion. The chapter will look at how educators can provide quality education for bilingual learners, particularly focusing on the management of the classroom, resource issues and planning and assessing the curriculum. Supporting needs other than those for academic progress will be highlighted throughout this chapter. Issues discussed in this chapter may also be closely linked to those found in Chapter 3 on 'Cultural Issues and Schools'.

What is bilingualism?

In the 1930s Bloomfield (1933) described bilingualism as full fluency in two languages. By the end of the 1980s, however, the definition had been broadened to include people who were competent in at least two languages, 'to the extent required by his or her needs and those of the environment' (Grosjean, 1989: 6). In *Aiming High: Raising the Achievement of Minority Ethnic Pupils* (DfES, 2003a: 28) the definition for bilingualism is given as:

> Bilingual here is taken to mean all pupils who use or have access to more than one language at home or at school – pupils who are living in and learning in English and one or more other languages. It does not necessarily imply full fluency in both languages.

Other authors, including Brisk (1998) and Wrigley (2000) appear to agree with the same definition. In England, the term, 'English as an additional language' is frequently used in place of 'bilingualism'. Throughout the Special Educational Needs Code of Practice (DfES, 2001a), for instance, the former term is the only one to be mentioned. It must be emphasised at this point that learners with English as an additional language will not be identified as having special educational needs because of this factor. Evidence provided will also indicate that government initiatives, influenced by recent research findings, are trying to ensure that bilingual education models, rather than English-only instruction, are incorporated into mainstream schools to ensure that bilingual learners receive quality education immediately they start school in England (DfES, 2001a; DfES, 2003a).

Why do bilingual/EAL learners require additional educational needs at the present time in England?

According to the Statistics of Education 2002 there are over 632,000 (approximately 9.3 per cent) learners in schools in England who have English as an Additional Language (EAL). The consultation paper *Aiming High: Raising the Achievement of Minority Ethnic Pupils* (DfES, 2003a) not only states that this figure reflects a bilingual population that is growing, but also says that there are over 200 languages being used in England, with varying degrees of fluency by pupils. Bhattacharyya *et al.* (2003) found that 90 per cent of Bangladeshi and Pakistani pupils are registered as EAL learners, 82 per cent of Indian, 75 per cent of Chinese and 65 per cent of Black African. Other legislation and research have alerted the government and educators to statistics that do necessitate whole-school action to ensure bilingual learners' additional educational needs are met. In the Green Paper *Every Child Matters* (HMSO, 2003), the government says that it will raise the attainment of minority ethnic pupils by: 'develop(ing) strategies for supporting bilingual learners' (ibid.: 2.14:28). A further research paper, focusing on the attainments and participation of minority ethnic groups living in England summarises statistics and research to reach its key findings. Of specific interest to readers of this chapter the authors found that:

■ Learners for whom English is an additional language (EAL) perform, on average, less well than pupils whose first language is English.

■ EAL learners generally make better progress between Key Stages.

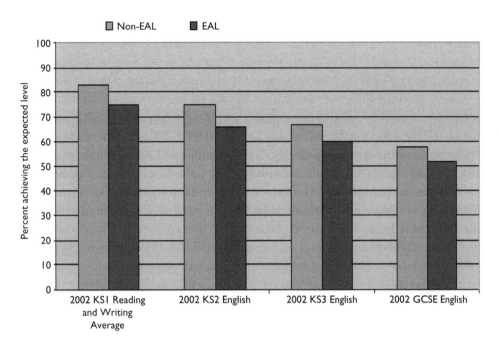

■ Non-EAL ■ EAL

Figure 4.1 Percentage of pupils achieving level at Key Stage 1, 2, 3 and GCSE English by EAL Status, 2002

■ A smaller proportion of EAL learners achieve expected levels at each Key Stage (Figure 4.1). However, the performance of EAL learners does vary across ethnic groups.

(Bhattacharyya *et al.*, 2003)

Further on in Bhattacharyya *et al.*'s paper they include factors they found that potentially may affect the attainment of certain minority groups: 'These include lack of English language fluency ..., racial abuse or harassment, lack of role models, unfamiliarity with the workings of the education system; teaching based on unfamiliar cultural norms, histories and points of reference' (2003: 22).

> **Discussion** How many bilingual/EAL learners are in your educational setting? When a bilingual learner starts at your workplace, do you make inquiries into the learner's previous educational history, cultural experience and English language fluency or not? Would this information be thought valuable for curriculum planning and assessment?

The present debate

When used in public and independent schools bilingual education is accepted as educationally sound (Brisk, 1998: 1). However, in the past 50 years bilingual education for learners with EAL in the state school system has been very controversial, especially as much research completed prior to the 1950s saw bilingualism as a problem to be removed for academic and cultural reasons (Corson, 1998). Since this date, research studies, such as the one carried out by the United Nations Educational, Scientific, and Cultural Organisation (UNESCO, 1953) have reported that the home language (sometimes also called the mother tongue), is the best medium for instruction and for literacy development and should be used for as long as feasible. This, they reported, is because the home language facilitates subject learning and literacy development and is the means through which 'a child absorbs the cultural environment' (UNESCO, 1953: 47) as well as enabling understanding between school and home. It also refuted the following objections:

- native language use impedes national unity;

- native language use prevents learners acquiring the second language;

- some languages do not have a grammar.

(Brisk, 1998)

However, there are others that oppose bilingual education, favouring models that focus on English language development (Brisk, 1998) such as ESL (English as a Second Language). These critics maintain that to be able to access the curriculum, learners with EAL need to have a good grasp of English before they can access all subject teaching in English. Brisk says: 'Proponents of bilingual education believe that students learn faster when they are educated through their native languages while studying English. Opponents maintain that language minorities need English as a precondition to becoming educated' (1998: 2).

Discussion

Discuss the points raised above. Which type of model do you think your educational setting follows? Why do you think this is?

Another issue that requires investigation at this stage is the effect that mainstream press coverage and politics have on teachers' perception of bilingual learners. The following statement was given by David Blunkett, the Home Secretary, in 2002:

Speaking English enables parents to converse with their children in English, as well as in their historic mother tongue, at home and to participate in wider modern culture. It helps overcome the schizophrenia, which bedevils generational relationships. In as many as 30 per cent of Asian British households, English is not spoken at home.

(*Daily Post* (Liverpool), 17 September 2002)

Do you think this statement is supportive of recent legislation and guidance?

As Connors (2003) says, this public discussion seemed to have been informed by a model of second language development that sees the child's first language as a deficit factor, causing a problem for both the child, the family and society. Charity groups and supporters of asylum seekers condemn this and other statements about bilingual children, particularly asylum seekers. 'However, very few of these questioned the assumption that the children's home language was a handicap, a source of problems all round' (ibid.: 2).

Do you think this type of media and political discussion can have ideological effects on what educators think and hence on their assumptions about how bilingual learners should be taught? Give your reasons.

How is current government guidance informing educators' practice?

The National Curriculum Inclusion Statement (QCA, 1999: 32), a legal requirement, informed educators that across the curriculum they must provide effective learning opportunities for all learners, based on the following three principles:

- setting suitable learning challenges;
- responding to pupils' diverse needs;
- overcoming potential barriers to learning and assessment for individuals and groups of pupils.

The Special Educational Needs Code of Practice (DfES, 2001a) gives clear guidance in Chapter 5, 'Identification, Assessment and Provision in the Primary Phase', about what educators need to consider when deciding if learners with EAL have special educational needs or not. It clearly states that lack of competence in English should not immediately be equated with a learning difficulty, but that if progress is not what is expected, then, equally, a learner's language status should not be assumed to be the only reason:

> Schools should look carefully at all aspects of a child's performance in different subjects to establish whether the problems they have in the classroom are due to limitations in their command of the language that is used there or arise from special educational needs.

(ibid.: 46, 5:16)

Further guidance is given about what issues educators should consider when thinking about this question: 'It is necessary to consider the child within the context of their home, culture and community' (ibid.: 46, 5:15). The possible need to plan language support is also discussed: 'At an early stage a full assessment should be made of the exposure they have had in the past to each of the languages they speak, the use they make of them currently and their proficiency in them' (ibid.: 46, 5:16).

The Green Paper, *Every Child Matters* (HMSO, 2003: 28) mentions the need to improve the attainment of minority ethnic pupils, and recognises that the development of strategies to support bilingual learners is a vital part of this. Also of significance is the consultation paper *Aiming High: Raising the Achievement of Minority Ethnic Pupils* (DfES, 2003a). It is in this paper that educators are provided with evidence and guidance about how the government believe teachers should be including bilingual/EAL learners in their schools. Additionally, the government proposed the development of an EAL strand of the Aiming High national strategy which will include:

- training and support for mainstream staff;
- training and support for EAL specialist staff;
- assessment – a national approach;
- meeting the needs of more advanced learners of English.

(ibid.: 29–30)

It also emphasises findings from earlier studies carried out by proponents of bilingual education mentioned earlier in this chapter. For example, it says in Section 3.6 that bilingual learners may demonstrate high standards of achievement, particularly in subjects such as mathematics and other practical subjects, before fluency in English is achieved. Later it also states that EAL specialists generally agree that bilingual learners most effectively learn English in a mainstream situation where they 'are supported in acquiring English across the whole curriculum alongside English-speaking pupils' (ibid.: 3.9:29). Importantly, it also emphasises the need to support the continual development of a bilingual learner's first language, because it supports the learning of English and wider cognitive development (ibid.: 3.12:30). Strategies to support this learning are also briefly mentioned and will be covered more fully in this chapter in later sections.

Finally, in October 2003, following the collation of the consultation findings, the outline of the government's plan was presented as The Aiming High national strategy. Included in this plan is:

- training for primary teachers across 21 LEAs through the National Primary Strategy to help them better support bilingual pupils;
- the development of a national framework to support bilingual learners, including a national specialist qualification for teachers who work with

bilingual pupils to recognise their expertise and progression routes. (www.standards.dfes.gov.uk/ethnicminorities/raising)

A whole school approach

In this part of the chapter a closer examination of what schools and educators can do to ensure that bilingual learners have access to an effective, quality education is provided. As Cummins said: 'Neglect of home language and culture may be significant, but more significant are inadequate teaching methodology, unfair assessment, and lack of communication with the community' (in Brisk, 1998: 34). Ultimately it is the type of education that is provided for bilingual learners that determines whether they are educationally successful or not. However, educators can support bilingual students better if they understand the external and internal factors that can affect the individual learner's progress (Figure 4.2).

How schools use both the bilingual learners' first languages; their cultural experiences and history within the whole curriculum, and how teaching strategies are chosen can all have a vast influence on how well the individual learner's perform. A school's and its staff's attitudes towards bilingual learners can have a great effect on how well the learners are motivated to learn and be successful. Schools need to be constantly questioning their expectations of bilingual learners and their provision for them. The situational factors depicted in Figure 4.2 can influence how learners are viewed by educators and their peers and the personal

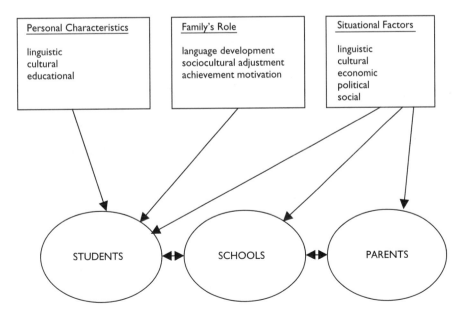

Figure 4.2 External and internal influences on billingual students' education
Source: Brisk (1998: 35)

characteristics of bilingual learners can determine how they actually manage in a mainstream English school. It is quite clear therefore that bilingual learners' families hold an enormous amount of information about their previous educational achievements and situational factors. Schools need to tap into this valuable resource and forge a trusting and supportive partnership with the families so that they are able to understand many of the factors that will help them effectively educate bilingual learners.

In *Evaluating Educational Inclusion* (OFSTED, 2000) the following extract from an inspection report indicates how OFSTED are defining good practice for bilingual/EAL learners.

Case study 1

> The reception teacher and home–school worker use home-visits effectively to find out about each child's language needs. Translators are available to help parents with little or no English. This information is used well to prepare for the child starting school by enabling the school to decide on the level of language support needed … School works closely with local agencies such as speech therapy when needed … The school works hard to promote good attendance. However, it recognises that there are times when families give a priority to the celebration of religious festivals and they ensure that parents and pupils are not stigmatised because of this. The pupils are given extra support to catch up with anything they miss during such times. This pragmatic approach does much to win parents' support and to promote tolerance of different faiths and beliefs.
>
> (OFSTED, 2000: 27)

Discussion

Read the extract above from an OFSTED Inspector's report again closely and compare it to your working practices. How would an evaluation of the practice in your workplace setting compare? Do you agree with the interventions and practices of this infant school? Give reasons why you agree or disagree.

The link with bilingual learners' parents can be supported in many ways already established in the school community, such as coffee mornings and parents' rooms. Bilingual staff, however, can be invaluable to a school, helping support the learners in the classroom by speaking in the family language with them and encouraging the use of their first language. They can also step in to prevent the partnership between home and school becoming tense due to cultural misunderstandings. This can be illustrated in the case study below and highlights the need for constant examination of the way a school presents itself to parents and learners.

Case study 2

> One mother was upset that her children were playing with water and other materials in the nursery. She had expected them to be formally taught the alphabet, because they were at school. The bilingual educators were able to explain to the mother that this was purposeful play – children needed to learn colours and shapes, to develop concepts and vocabulary for heavy and light, full and empty. 'We should explain the purpose of nursery education from the start, rather than assuming a shared understanding'
>
> (Wrigley, 2000: 105).

However, when a school does not have a bilingual member of staff, a great deal can still be achieved by recognising and valuing the learners' home language and culture. If this is managed by the whole-school community with a genuine wish to include all the community, it will foster trust, collaboration and thus success. As Wrigley (2000: 160) says; 'Time and again, when I probed the reasons for the school's success, the head would say "the staff", and the staff would say "the pupils".'

Classroom management

There are many cultural issues that need to be considered and managed positively for bilingual learners when planning the management of a classroom. The four identified below are by no means the only ones, but it is felt that these are the issues that can play a significant role in whether a learner is even initially accepted and therefore included in the teaching, learning and socialisation of a classroom environment:

- Cultures vary in the ways they use *language*, verbal and written and therefore assumptions should not be made by a teacher about whether a bilingual learner will see the value of writing information down for certain activities.

- Different cultures also have rules about the way adults and children *interact*, both verbally and non-verbally. When a learner averts their eyes away from the educator speaking to him or her, it may not be a sign of rudeness or lack of attention, but a sign of respect. If unaware of this type of cultural difference, educators can do great harm and create isolation for a bilingual learner.

- *Disciplining strategies* can again be a reason for miscommunication between educators, learners and the home. Clarity and discussion about behaviour and management of inappropriate learning behaviour all need to take place prior to or when a bilingual learner starts at a school. Cultures vary a great deal with regard to how they discipline the young and all parties need to be fully aware of schools' rules and the reasons for them.

HLTA 2.9

■ Finally, even the way the *school day* is organised can cause problems for bilingual students and, again, differences and clarity are fundamental to ensure a positive start to a new school (Brisk, 1998).

HLTA
1.1
1.2
1.5
2.9
3.3.2

A classroom needs to reflect the value placed on the languages and cultures of the learners and educators. The provision of opportunities to engage in purposeful language interactions can be achieved in a language-rich environment. This also encourages and develops production skills and comprehension. An organisational structure that is consistent, uses visual strategies to support learning, has a routine and is predictable, is good practice for many learners, including bilingual learners. The opportunity to respond to and learn from peer role models can also be very effective for monolingual learners as well as bilingual learners.

Teaching and learning

HLTA
3.2.2
3.2.3
3.3.3
3.3.8

When thinking about this, it is essential to remember, as Gravelle (2000: 3) says, that: 'Bilingual children have an entitlement to education and a personal need to continue to develop their conceptual understanding. Learning cannot be placed on hold while language catches up.' This places a great deal of responsibility on educators to make sure that bilingual learners can understand the curriculum immediately. It is here that educators need to use nonlinguistic forms of communication to supplement the linguistic ones, through gesture and action, visual materials, practical activities, outings and role play. Repetition, re-wording and expansion of texts for clarification can all be utilised at various stages of bilingual learners' development. 'Vygotsky (1962, 1978) argues that, with the teacher's help, learners can do today what they will be able to do independently tomorrow' (Wrigley, 2000: 18). Wrigley suggests that this applies to language and experience. He thinks that if experience accompanies academic language throughout early bilingual learning and teaching, then gradually bilingual learners will be able to use the language without the experience, in a more abstract way, later on. A great deal of experience is required over and over again especially for new bilingual learners, because they frequently do not have the basic knowledge that English learners have about all the curriculum materials.

Discussion

Take a look at one particular National Curriculum topic area, perhaps in Key Stage 2 or Key Stage 3. To be able to understand the language and the context of the information and material, what do learners need to know already? What does this mean for bilingual learners and how can educators ensure they are not disadvantaged?

For example, look at a history topic covered in Key Stage 2. A lot of the initial discussions on food, shelter, transport, etc., will be built upon work and understanding already gained in Key Stage 1.

The other point to remember here is that although individuals may not have any understanding of English, of England or of the National Curriculum, they often do have rich and extensive knowledge about their own culture and country. Educators can use this to help develop language and joint respect for each other's cultures.

Printed texts

The use and understanding of the printed word can also cause great difficulties for bilingual learners. Technical vocabulary clearly needs clarification, but fictional texts might cause problems for even fluent readers. Such a reader may have no difficulty with literal understanding, but when faced with vocabulary with multiple meanings, such as 'bitter' to the taste and 'bitter', a feeling about something or someone, it can cause a complete breakdown of understanding. Also, if a story mentions black cats and big black, steaming cauldrons, bilingual learners may well not have the past experience to enable them to really grasp the meaning of the words and thus the story. This will apply to all curriculum subjects; for example, bilingual learners may not be able to immediately engage in work unsupported, about 'molten rocks' due to a lack of conceptual knowledge of the word 'molten'. In these incidences teachers need to make the connection between experience and learning for them. In this way, concepts as well as vocabulary can be built.

Planning for bilingual learners

Guidance in ways to support classroom practice for bilingual learners can be provided by the theories of second language acquisition. When thinking about planning for all learners, educators first of all think about what the learners already know and build on this knowledge, devising activities and tasks that enable them to develop. When planning for bilingual learners, educators need to think about what they can bring as individuals from their previous experiences to the task in great detail. This will include their social and cognitive understanding and their linguistic ability. Educators therefore need to have this information available to them and to have a good understanding of the individual learner's culture, previous education and family circumstances.

Next, the demands of the task or activity, on the bilingual learners themselves, have to be considered. How a lesson is to be presented and how the tasks are to be completed, need to be made explicit to bilingual learners. An analysis of the language to be used within text will also enable the educator to ensure that support and engagement in the task are possible. This is, as mentioned earlier, where a good understanding of how a classroom functions, can support the demands of the curriculum, the social interactions and the linguistic development for these learners.

The level and type of support needed are also an important aspect of an educator's planning. This may be supplied to the learners in many different ways, using

	What do learners bring to the task?	What does the task demand of them?	What support needs to be planned?
Social			
Cognitive			
Linguistic			

Figure 4.3　Planning framework
Source: Gravelle (2000: 8)

the strengths of their peers, of effective grouping or additional adult intervention. It may also involve using artefacts, videos or pictures to ensure access and engagement in the curriculum. Repetition, gesture, intonation and role-playing can all be used by educators to support cognitive and linguistic development.

The framework presented in Figure 4.3 is very simple, but can be used to ensure that accurate and appropriate planning is achieved for bilingual learners.

Assessment

The National Curriculum (TTA, 2000) requires teachers to carry out assessments to find out what learners 'know, understand and can do'. Assessing skills is far easier for busy practitioners than trying to find out what learners actually understand and know and so it is these that are more frequently tested. Unfortunately this type of assessing is very incomplete and when considering bilingual learners, can lead to very false conclusions. Bilingual learners who are new to the English language obviously tend not to have gained a high level of language skills, but if assessed by these measures, it can be assumed that their understanding and knowledge are also affected likewise. This can lead to educators focusing on what the learners cannot do rather than what they can do. Special educational needs interventions can therefore be given inappropriately, instead of what really should need to happen. The Special Educational Needs Code of Practice (DfES, 2001a:61) points this out succinctly in Section 6:15: 'Lack of competence in English must not be equated with learning difficulties as understood in this Code.' Educators, in this situation need to look at their own pedagogy and the curriculum, before deciding the solution can be found by providing special needs support. This Code of Practice does, however, warn that full assessments are required to ensure that special educational needs are not hindering the learner's progress. In other words, assumptions must not be made about their background knowledge. Educators should ask questions and find strategies to encourage these learners to demonstrate their knowledge and understanding in other ways than speaking and writing.

Classroom performance assessment is a way of measuring achievement by gathering information, discussions with learners and by systematic observation of how learners engage in the classroom. The information gathered can include posters, audio tapes, models, writing and projects and, alongside the discussions and observations, can indicate to the educators how well individuals are progressing set against their own personal objectives. Drawing, ICT and drama can also be effective methods of assessing bilingual learners' abilities and understanding. This may be the most reliable manner to assess bilingual learners, especially during the initial years of acquiring the second language.

Writers like Brisk (1998) suggest that tests would be fairer if they are presented in the home, first language. However, as Cline (1998: 160) points out, tests are culturally biased and although earlier statutory guidance advocated culture-fair assessment: 'Practice advocates the use of "assessment tools which are culturally neutral", (DfE, 1994, para 2:18)', he says this is impossible. 'The purpose of testing is to make predictions in a cultural context, and a culture-fair test would be empty of useful content' (Cline, 1998: 160).

> **Discussion**
>
> How do you feel bilingual learners can most effectively be assessed? Think about resources available in your educational workplace to support these learners, as well as the information presented in this section.

Genuine respect for languages

How can schools and educators demonstrate that they really do want to foster all learners' first or home language? Allowing and actually encouraging learners to use their first language throughout the school day in all parts of the school can show them that their language is considered of value and needs to be developed and utilised. Posters and signs can be written in home languages, in appropriate places throughout the school, so that all the learners accept that there are many languages within the school, all of which are positively accepted. Courses in the various languages within the community can be offered to parents, learners and educators alike. It is also vital that school libraries and the classrooms include books and other material in the bilingual learners' languages. Alongside these it is important, for two reasons, to include bilingual books. For beginners learning English as their second language they are particularly useful, as they also can be for English speakers who want to learn a friend's first language. It is easy to see that if bilingual learners enter an educational environment where this level of support is freely and positively interwoven into the school day, the learning and their surroundings, they are going to begin at least to feel welcome, secure and valued.

HLTA
2.9
3.1.3

The way forward

Bilingual learners have 'Additional Educational Needs' that are frequently misunderstood and mismanaged by educators. This is mostly due to a lack of training, knowledge and support and it is especially hard to manage when a school has only several bilingual learners. It is undoubtedly difficult on many occasions to separate this field of study from other cultural issues that may arise in a school. However, it is essential that educators understand what bilingualism is, and why it requires particular focus and attention. Without the willingness to spend time and energy on planning for the needs of bilingual learners, their opportunity to receive a quality education will be greatly hampered. As Mimi Met (in Genesee, 2001: 178) says: 'Language cannot stand apart from content learning; rather, language should be acquired through content learning just as content may be learned through language.' If successfully achieved, bilingual learners and English speakers can all benefit greatly from bilingual education.

Key issues

It is anticipated that you will now:

- recognise all the issues relating to teaching bilingual learners in a classroom;
- understand the basic principles and theories of first and second language acquisition;
- be able to manage a classroom in a manner that enables bilingual learners to be effectively included socially and cognitively;
- be able to appropriately support bilingual learners when planning interventions and assessments.

Professional Standards for Higher Level Teaching Assistants (HLTA)

If you can demonstrate your understanding and professional use of the key issues illustrated within this chapter, it is hoped that you will be able to fulfil the following HLTA Standards:

1.1	1.2	1.5	2.9	3.1.3
3.2.2	3.2.3	3.3.2	3.3.3	3.3.8

Useful documents

Bhattacharyya, G., Ison, L. and Blair, M. (2003) *Minority Ethnic Attainment and Participation in Education and Training: The Evidence*, Annesley: DfES.

DfE (1994) *Code of Practice on the Identification and Assessment of Pupils with Special Educational Needs*, London: DfE.

DfES (2001a) *Special Educational Needs Code of Practice*, Annesley: DfES.

DFES (2001b) *Inclusive Schooling: Children with Special Educational Needs*, Annesley: DfES.

DfES (2003a) *Aiming High: Raising the Achievement of Minority Ethnic Pupils*, Annesley: DfES.

DfES (2003b) *Aiming High: Consultation Summary*, available on: www.standards.dfes. gov.uk/ethnicminorities/raising_achievement, (downloaded, 08/01/2004).

HMSO (2003) *Every Child Matters*, Norwich: The Stationery Office.

OFSTED (2000) *Evaluating Educational Inclusion: Guidance for Inspectors and Schools*, London: OFSTED.

QCA (2000) 'A language in common: assessing English as an additional language', *National Curriculum 2000*, London: QCA.

Teaching Training Agency (2000) *The National Curriculum*, London: TTA.

References

Bloomfield, L. (1933) *Language*, New York: Holt.

Brisk, M. (1998) *Bilingual Education: From Compensatory to Quality Schooling*, Mahwah, NJ: Lawrence Erlbaum Associates.

Cline, T. (1998) 'The assessment of special educational needs for bilingual children', *British Journal of Special Education*, vol. 25, no. 4, pp. 159–63.

Connors, B. (2003) 'Constraints on effective interaction when English is an additional language', unpublished paper presented at the BERA conference, Edinburgh, 2003.

Corson, D. (1998) *Changing Education for Diversity*, Buckingham/Philadelphia: Open University Press.

Genesee, F. (ed.) (2001) *Educating Second Language Children: The Whole Child, the Whole Curriculum, the Whole Community*, Cambridge: Cambridge University Press.

Gravelle, M. (ed.) (2000) *Planning for Bilingual Learners: An Inclusive Curriculum*, Stoke on Trent: Trentham Books.

Grosjean, F. (1989) 'Neurolinguists, beware! The bilingual is not two monolinguals in one person', *Brain and Language*, 36, 3–15.

QCA (1999) *The National Curriculum Inclusion Statement*, 458, Sudbury: QCA.

UNESCO (1953) *The Use of Vernacular Languages in Education*, Paris: UNESCO.

Wrigley, T. (2000) *The Power to Learn: Stories of Success in the Education of Asian and Other Bilingual Pupils*, Stoke on Trent: Trentham Books.

5 Young people in public care

Sue Soan

Children in public care are our children. We hold their future in our hands and education is the key to that future.

(DfEE and DoH, 2000:1)

Introduction

In the past 25 years there has been research on care-leavers and also national cohort studies that have provided evidence that children in care under-achieve educationally. The Short Report of 1984 highlighted these difficulties, but by 1995, when the joint inspection by OFSTED and the Social Work Inspectorate (SSI) reported its findings, little had improved for this group of young people across England and Wales (Borland *et al.*, 1998: 40). More recent surveys and research, discussed in greater detail later in this chapter, also demonstrate similar conclusions. In response to these findings the government has, since 1998, launched a number of initiatives that are aimed at supporting and promoting the education of children in care. The latest of these, the Green Paper, *Every Child Matters* (HMSO, 2003: 13) states:

> The educational achievement of children in care remains far too low ... We need to ensure we properly protect children at risk of neglect and harm within a framework of universal services which aims to prevent negative outcomes and support every child to develop their full potential.

The term 'children in care' is used to describe children and young people who are 'looked after' by local authorities in England. This means that social services have responsibilities as a corporate parent to support these young people, whether they are in foster placements, residential provisions or in their own families. This chapter will outline these initiatives and explain the reasons why young people are in public care. It will also illustrate ways in which schools can positively and successfully include these young people in their communities.

Discussion

- Do you know how many young people in your school setting are in public care?
- Would you be told if you were to work with a young person who is in public care? If not, why not? Do you think this information should be shared with all members of staff?

Definition of terms

Public care or 'looked after children' (LAC)

The term 'looked after children' (LAC) was introduced by the Children Act of 1989 and is interchangeable with the term 'public care'. The latter has been chosen for the purposes of this chapter as recent guidance and consultations indicate that this is the preferred term of young people. Young people in public care are either 'accommodated' or are subject to a 'care order'.

Accommodated

These are young people who are looked after away from home, but were admitted to care under a legal arrangement on a voluntary basis. When young people are accommodated, their parents retain the primary parental responsibility, but the local authority still has responsibilities as corporate parent (DfEE and DoH, 2000: 9, 3.2).

Care order

A local authority will seek a legal care order when it is considered necessary in the interest of a young person's welfare that they are removed from their home. In this situation the local authority takes on the role of main carer with responsibility for the young person. However, it is good practice, as the Children Act states (1989, 22, (4) (b)), for the local authority to continue working in partnership with the parents concerned.

However, whether young people are accommodated or are subject to a care order, many remain in contact with their family and will return home after an appropriate period of time in care.

Secure accommodation

A young person may be placed in secure accommodation for his/her own safety and welfare. They may also be either on remand or awaiting trial, or have been given a custodial sentence. 'Secure accommodation' could be a Local Authority Secure Unit, a Young Offenders' Institution, a prison or a Secure Training Centre.

Corporate parenting

The term corporate parenting 'emphasises the collective responsibility of local authorities to achieve good parenting ... it is the duty of the whole local authority to "safeguard and promote his [a child's] welfare" (1989, Children Act 1, S22 (3)(a))' (OFSTED, 2001: 4.3). The 'whole authority' includes social services, schools and the Education Department. The responsibility of the corporate parent continues until the young person is 21, or 24 if in higher education or training. Depending on the needs and circumstances of the young person, there may be a considerable number of professionals involved in the maintenance of this role. The *Guidance for the Education of Young People in Public Care* (DfEE and DoH, 2000: 14,4.4) lists the majority of professionals that may be included in delivering corporate parenting:

> They include: elected members, senior officers and managers of the LEA and social services department; representatives of the Health Trust/Authority; head teachers; school governors; social workers, residential social workers and foster carers; education social workers; teachers and learning support assistants; educational psychologists and education support personnel; Career Advisers; Personal Advisers: fostering/family placement managers and parents. A local authority may also have a Children's Rights Officer, Independent Visitors, Mentors and Guardian ad Litem.

It is therefore essential that all the adults involved are fully aware of the importance of education and are committed to helping the young person achieve academically and socially in an appropriate educational setting. Sonia Jackson (1989), an influential figure in highlighting the educational needs of children in public care, agrees with this view. Jackson (1994) and Ward (1995) are very critical of past policies, particularly those of the 1970s, when carers and social workers were encouraged not to have high educational expectations of children in public care because of fears of reinforcing feelings of failure. In a study of young people who had grown up in care, but who still had managed to be educationally successful, Jackson wrote: 'their ability had not been recognised or their achievement recognised by social workers and residential care workers' (Borland *et al.*, 1998: 74).

■ Are the terms defined above known and understood by the teachers and support staff in your educational setting? Why do you think that is the case?
■ Do you think all educators in schools should be aware of this information or do you feel only a selected few require this knowledge?

Are young people in public care 'welcomed' into mainstream schools?

When asked to accept a young person in public care onto their school roll, some educators may give a negative response or offer an immediate excuse. One excuse I have personally heard on many occasions is that the year group is completely full. Thoughts of a low-achiever, a learner with emotional, behavioural and social difficulties (EBSD) and extra paperwork can make it difficult for young people in public care to be given a supportive and welcoming introduction to a new school. As with any other 'labelled' group, a small percentage of the total number of young people in public care will require a substantial amount of resources and help. However the vast majority will only require the staff of a school to provide an inclusive educational environment. Borland *et al.* (1998: 39) support this view, emphasising the need to consider schooling when planning for a young person's future:

> School is an important element in the lives of children who became looked after, providing substantial support and care and a forum where children can develop skills and abilities to cope with adversity. There is evidence that teachers' responses to emerging difficulties have a bearing on how effectively children can be sustained:

They conclude: 'School is thus an essential element in equipping children to survive the turbulence of being "looked after" away from home' (ibid.). Coulling's (2000: 30) study which looked at how 'a shared understanding of what counts as successful practice for each agency in relation to the education of "looked after" children', also emphasises how important it is to find a school with a supportive ethos, that 'encourages the child to be assimilated into the life of the school allowing for good liaison with carers and birth family' (ibid.: 33). She acknowledges that it is not only the relationship between the carer and educational establishment that is vital, but that the social worker and home-finding officer should be actively supportive in matters such as attendance and progress achieved.

HLTA
1.5

Why are young people in public care?

There are many reasons why young people are in public care, but the main cause is due to families experiencing some form of hardship, upheaval or break-down. Other children or young people are placed in public care because their families cannot adequately care for them, or because a parent has an illness or has died. Also many have been affected by suffering physical and sexual abuse and neglect. It is important to realise that less than 2 per cent of young people were in public care in 1999 (DoH, 1999: 26), because of offences that they had committed.

The issues – education in care

The report, *Outcome Indicators of Looked After Children* (DoH, 2003) by the Department of Health, covers all young people 'looked after' by English local councils who had been 'looked after' continuously for at least 12 months on 30 September 2002. This stated that there were 44,100 children in public care, 700 more than the figure given for the previous year. Of this group of young people, 34,500 were of school age. Clearly, from these statistics alone, it is vital that all educators should be well informed about and understand the needs of young people who are educated while in care. Further statistics from this report also highlight the educational difficulties children in public care are still experiencing, compared to their peers. On average, 50 per cent of those children in public care, at the end of Key Stage 1, age 7 (in the appropriate age group) achieve National Curriculum (NC) Level 2, compared to 85 per cent of all children. Some 40 per cent achieve NC Level 4 at the end of Key Stage 2 (age 11), compared to 78 per cent of all children and at the end of Key Stage 3 (age 14), only 22 per cent reach NC Level 5, compared to 66 per cent of all children. This under-achievement continues into Year 11 (age 16), where only 53 per cent of children in public care obtained one GCSE or GNVQ compared to 95 per cent of all school children and 42 per cent did not even sit either of these examinations. Given this percentage, it is unlikely, despite all the government initiatives and resources, that the target set out in 2000 in the *Guidance for Young People in Public Care* will be achieved. This target was to: 'Improve the educational attainment of children looked after, by increasing to 75% by 2003 the proportion of children leaving care at 16 or later with a GCSE or GNVQ qualification' (ibid.: 6, 2.8).

The new target decided upon following research carried out by the Social Exclusion Unit (SEU) (SEU and Office of the Deputy Prime Minister, 2003) aims to 'substantially narrow the gap between the educational attainment and participation of children in care and that of their peers by 2006'. The measures of success for this target are:

- 'outcomes for 11 year olds in English and maths are at least 60 per cent as good as those of their peers;

- the proportion who become disengaged from education is reduced, so that no more than 10 per cent reach school-leaving age without having sat a GCSE equivalent exam; and

- the proportion of those aged 16 who get qualifications equivalent to five GCSEs graded A*–C has risen on average by 4 percentage points each year since 2002; and in all authorities at least 15 per cent of young people in care achieve this level of qualification' (SEU and Office of the Deputy Prime Minister, 2003).

The SEU research also found that 6 out of 10 children in public care have been bullied and 'that they are 13 times more likely to be permanently excluded than their peers' (ibid.: 1). Not surprisingly, therefore when compared to national figures for all children, those in public care are almost nine times more likely to hold a Statement of Special Educational Needs. For the school year 2001/2002, it is estimated that 9,200 (27 per cent) of young people in public care held a Statement of Special Educational Needs (DoH: 2001, OC1). Alongside these issues of low achievement, bullying, special needs and exclusions, another recent report focused on 'The mental health of young people looked after by local authorities in England' (ONS, 2003). This report found that young people in public care, aged between 5–15 years old are four to five times more likely to have a mental disorder compared with children from private households. The report focused on emotional disorders, hyperactivity disorders, and conduct disorders, and found that the difference between young people in public care and those from private households is greatest in the case of conduct disorders (Including Special Children, 2003: 30, 156).

Undoubtedly during the past few years government legislation, policies and surveys from the Departments of Health, Education, Social Services and National Statistics Office, have produced a number of significant and focused developments identifying and evaluating issues, so that action can be taken to tackle the stigma and drawbacks often associated with being in public care. A collaborative approach to care for these young people by all the agencies involved is clearly essential, but the government recognises that it is through education that life-long achievements and improvements can be met. As David Blunkett, then Secretary of State for Education said: 'We want to change attitudes towards education and foster a realisation that education matters to everyone' (The Who Cares? Trust *et al.*, 1999: 4).

Case study 1

Joanna lives in a residential care home and is waiting for a foster family to be found for her. She is attending a local mainstream secondary school and is in Year 9. Her home authority is looking for a foster placement within their county boundaries, but Joanna wants to stay where she is so that she can still attend her school. She has made friends, has a good support system in place and is making outstanding academic progress. Joanna, her carers and the teachers at the school attend a Statutory Social Service Meeting (including the review of Joanna's Personal Education Plan) during which they discuss the reasons why they feel Joanna should remain at her present school. They therefore feel a foster family should be sought that lives within the school's catchment area.

Discussion

- Do you think Joanna should remain at her present school? If you do, list the reasons why you think it is beneficial for her to remain.
- The following describes what happened as a result of this meeting. How do the reasons below match with the ones you considered important? Discuss.

It was agreed at the meeting that in the interests of her education and social development Joanna should remain within the catchment area of her present school. The reasons given were:

- Joanna had made a number of good, supportive friendships.

- Being in Year 9 she had just selected her options for GCSEs and was beginning focused course work.

- She needed a stable, well-established learning environment for Years 10 and 11 (GCSE work).

- The teachers and support staff were effectively supporting her emotional, social and academic needs. A specific member of staff was always available to support Joanna if she had peer issues or other concerns. In the past two years Joanna had built a strong relationship with this member of staff and trusted her.

- The staff also worked collaboratively with the carers and social services in a positive manner, again making Joanna feel safe and cared for.

HLTA
1.4
1.5
1.6

This is an example of how colleagues can work collaboratively in the interest of the young person's social, emotional and educational needs.

> **Discussion**
> - How do the young people in public care fare in relation to all the children in your educational setting?
> - Why do you think the achievement of young people in public care is low compared to all children of the same age?
> - Why are the statistics high for the number of young people in public care with a Statement of Special Educational Needs, who have been bullied and have been excluded?
> - Do you think schools and/or the government or local authorities could do more to improve the barriers to learning and achieving for this specific group of young people?

Recent educational implementations that aim to support young people in public care

Special Educational Needs Code of Practice (2001)

This revision of the original Code of Special Educational Needs (DfE, 1994), includes a quite brief resumé of information for schools and in particular, Special Educational Needs Coordinators (SENCOs), about the roles professionals have in supporting 'looked after' Children. Section 5:29 clearly states that 'The *designated teacher* for "looked after" children should work closely with the SENCO when the child also has SEN' (DfE, 1994: 49). However, many of the other references within this Code identify ways that the LEAs *do not* have the responsibility to provide education for young people in public care in certain situations. This could be when a young person is in a community home that provides education, with an independent fostering agency providing education, or under a court order in secure accommodation (DfES, 2001, 8:98–8:103). However, it has been my own personal experience in the past few years that with the developments and legislation enhancing inter-agency working and inclusion, LEAs are paying heed to guidance, research information and inspection criteria and are accepting responsibility for providing suitable education provision for these young people.

The need for close working with other agencies and with parents or carers is emphasised in Sections 2:5, 2:9, 9:16 and 9:25 of the Code of Practice (DfES, 2001). In Section 9:27 the Code informs teachers that every young person in public care will have a Child Care Plan, 'as required under the Arrangements for Placement of Children (General) Regulations 1991 made under the Children Act 1989' (ibid.: 126) arranged by the local authority social services department. This Care Plan must include information about the arrangements for the education of the young person and must incorporate a *Personal Education Plan* (PEP). At this point joint review meetings are also suggested. A pathway plan is also required for young people who reach the age of 16 and are still in public care. The Code of Practice states: 'This plan will build on the Care and Personal Education Plans, mapping out a pathway to independence, including education, training and employment' (ibid.: 133, 9:68).

Throughout the Code of Practice (DfES, 2001) terms are used that are not clearly described within the document, notably 'designated teacher' and 'Personal Education Plan'. Schools need to have a good understanding of the role a designated teacher should play and the importance of the instigation, monitoring and reviewing of a Personal Education Plan for *every* young person in public care within their educational community. This will require inset, training and close collaboration with other agencies, notably social services.

Designated teacher

So who is appropriate to be a designated teacher and what is their role? *The Guidance for the Education of Young People in Public Care* (DfEE and DoH, 2000) reports that schools that have inclusive policies, robust pastoral systems and good communication with outside agencies are likely to be able to offer effective support to pupils that are 'different'. However, the Guidance continues by stating that 'this does not provide a sufficient safeguard for children in public care. Having a designated teacher who understands about care and the impact of care upon education, in each school is critical to making joint working a reality' (ibid.: 32, 5:28). The Guidance states that a designated teacher should:

- have sufficient authority to influence school policy and practice;
- be an advocate for young people in public care;
- be able to access services and support;

- ensure the school support high expectations for the young people in public care;
- make sure each pupil in public care has a Personal Education Plan;
- be responsible for transferring educational information speedily between agencies and individuals;
- ensure a home–school agreement is written with the primary carer;
- keep a list of the pupils in public care in school with contact numbers;
- ensure that each pupil in public care has a member of staff in school they can talk to.

In some schools this could be quite a significant role and needs the support of the rest of the school, other agencies and the LEA. Time for training needs to be provided for the designated teachers so that they have the knowledge about the Children Act and associated regulations, the role of the school and all aspects of the care system. The summary section 5:34 of the Guidance (DfEE and DoH, 2000: 33) says:

> Schools should designate a teacher to act as a resource and advocate for children and young people in public care. LEAs and Social Service Departments (SSD) should co-ordinate suitable training for them and maintain an up-to-date list of designated teachers in schools in their area.

Case study 2

The young person, who will be known as Brian, was placed in a residential care home with attached educational provision, outside of the home authority's boundaries. Brian started at the educational provision on site at the care home, but within six months it was felt that he would benefit from being in a LEA mainstream school. Brian was a Year 1 pupil and academically able to cope within a mainstream classroom. Collaborative discussions took place involving all parties, including Brian, and a local school able to take Brian was sought by the designated teacher from the care home educational provision. Both LEAs were involved, as were the two schools, the carers, the social worker and Brian. All had the joint aim of successfully including Brian in a mainstream school to enable him to reach his academic potential and to give him the opportunity to continue to make social relationships with peers and adults outside of the care system. Close regular consultations and understanding of each other's roles, and a supportive staff enabled Brian to be fully included. During Year 1, Brian was placed on the SEN Register on School Action, to monitor his literacy progress and initial problems of inappropriate physical touching were soon resolved due to the cooperation and joint working of the team. Personal Education Plans and Individual Education Plans (IEPs) were written with full consultation and were also discussed at the social service Statutory Care Reviews, as was Brian's general progress. All agencies were fully involved in the decision-making and the benefits of this became imperative when the home social service department wanted to withdraw Brian from the care home and the school and to return to the home authority and possibly to a member of the family. The mainstream school was very clear as were the carers at the care home that Brian, now in Year 3, needed to remain at the school to consolidate his skills and maintain consistency, during the time he was receiving help and therapy to readjust to the possibility of returning to a family member. Importantly Brian also wanted to settle and remain at the same school for the present. Following reports and further consultation Brian's views and his educational needs were considered to be of paramount importance. Brian remained in the stable environment of the care home and the mainstream school. Without this joint working approach and understanding of roles, such as the designated teacher, the outcome could have caused unnecessary disruption to Brian's educational and emotional progress.

Personal Education Plans (PEP)

Personal Education Plans are important as they are intended to promote and prioritise the education of young people in public care, as a vital part of the care plans and statutory reviews. Again the *Guidance for the Education of Young People in Public Care* (DfEE and DoH, 2000: 28) highlights their purpose:

> Every child and young person in public care needs a Personal Education Plan which ensures access to services and support; contributes to stability, minimises disruption and broken schooling; signals particular and special needs; establishes clear goals and acts as a record of progress and achievement.

Personal Education Plans are very similar to IEPs in that they need to include targets and objectives for the young person to achieve within a set time frame and with specified resources. They may relate to academic achievement or social, personal or behavioural targets. They also need to state who will actually be responsible for seeing that the plan is actioned, monitored and reviewed. Local authorities and independent special residential schools have produced their own Personal Education Plan documents, but model plans have been produced by voluntary sector child care organisations such as the National Children's Bureau *Personal Education Plan for Children and Young People in Public Care* (Sandiford, 1999). They should encompass the following areas:

- an achievement record;
- the identification of developmental and educational needs;
- short-term targets;
- long-term plans and aspirations.

It is a requirement that PEPs are reviewed and rewritten at least twice a year, to coincide with the Social Services Statutory Review of the young person's care plan, but many schools feel that they are more successfully monitored if, like

IEPs, they are rewritten on a termly basis. PEPs will indeed reflect IEP targets or Statement of Education Needs' objectives, if the young person has special education needs, but if not, they may remain focused on ensuring that all resources and support are in place to enable access to and engagement in the curriculum and school life for the young person. Undoubtedly as well as supplying essential information, they necessitate inter-agency dialogue, as can be seen from the case study illustrated above. The importance of the young person's education is also expounded by the PEP to everyone involved in any type of corporate parenting. However, it is the social worker's responsibility to manage the statutory review process of which the PEP forms a part.

> **Discussion**
>
> 'The introduction of PEPs was also an issue for schools. Many teachers felt strongly that where a school has effective monitoring systems PEPs were unnecessary. Many teachers also explained how difficult it is to complete PEPs, due to the number of people involved in the process' (Thomas, 2003). What reasons can you think of that support the need for PEPs? Use the information gained from this chapter to help you. How can schools maintain a consistent approach to PEPs?

Understanding the needs of young people in public care

Hopefully with good inter-agency and whole school systems in place, such as a designated teacher and Personal Education Plans, young people in public care will receive not only the curriculum access they have a right to, but also the support and understanding required to enable them to be full members of a school's community.

So what are the 'different' or 'additional' needs of this group of young people? The Code of Practice (2001) describes these terms as when interventions are provided that are: '*additional* to or *different from* those provided as part of the school's usual differentiated curriculum offer and strategies' (School Action) and when advice or support is provided from outside specialists 'so that alternative interventions *additional* or *different* strategies to those provided for the pupil through School Action can be put in place' (School Action Plus) (DfES, 2001:206). Like all other young people, those in public care are all individuals and hence they respond and react to experiences in very different ways. However, in 1996, Sandiford tried to encourage teachers to be aware of pupils' survival strategies and to respond to challenging behaviour, bearing in mind that it may reflect the following:

■ sense of loss;
■ lack of trust in adults;
■ feeling of rejection;
■ feeling of isolation;
■ feeling of confusion;

- feeling of being stigmatised;
- lack of personal advocacy;
- fear of bullying;
- feelings of being left behind

(Borland et al., 1998: 49).

The report, *Raising the Achievement of Children in Public Care* (OFSTED, 2001), offers a number of useful vignettes describing some good and bad experiences of young people in public care in school. Of particular value is Section 7.8 (p. 21) where ten factors affecting achievement as viewed by pupils are described. Young people in public care may have a problem with attending school regularly for a variety of reasons, including negative past experiences of school, a fear that their siblings or carers will not still be at home when they return from school or a lack of commitment to education from carers, to name a few. They may not be able to establish a good homework timetable because of poor studying environments or lack of adult support and encouragement, or they cannot value their own work or achievements. All of these difficulties can be solved with cooperation between the carers, other teachers and/or emotional support from other adults and peers. It may be that offering individual support during a homework club, once or twice a week, may be enough to help give the young person a method of organising homework and the realisation that the school does want to help him/her to succeed. It also means that there is an adult monitoring the child's progress and ability to cope with the curriculum, to give helpful feedback to both the carers and the teachers. It is important to try to see the problem from the young person's perspective, so that the support the school puts in place allows learning to take place, because emotional issues are recognised, discussed and managed.

HLTA
2.5
3.1.2

Case study 3

Jan, a Year 6 boy, found concentrating on his lessons extremely difficult and he would demonstrate very challenging behaviour in the classroom. During discussions with the SENCO, Jan informed her that he could not concentrate because he was extremely worried that his Mum would not be able to cope with his younger brothers and sisters without him. His Dad had recently been sent to prison and had left him 'in charge' of the family. With this knowledge, and following discussions with Jan's mother, it was agreed that Jan could ring his Mum from school at break and lunch time to check she was fine so that he could resume lessons without concern. A member of staff was also made available for Jan to go to if he was worried at any time. Mum also played a role in helping Jan to see that she was the adult in charge now and that she was going to look after him. Improvements were not sudden, but gradually with reassurance and understanding Jan was able to concentrate on his learning, knowing that his family would be fine.

HLTA
3.3.2

Some head teachers do not willingly accept young people who are in public care onto their school roll because they fear that they will exhibit challenging behaviour and cause many other difficulties. It is at this initial stage that it is vital that planning from all involved in the life of the young person in care is thoroughly considered and action carried out prior to the commencement of a placement (if the behaviour is already known about) to ensure that the school, the parents or carers, the teachers, the other pupils and the pupil him or herself feel supported and encouraged. This is not an easy task, but it is one that, when achieved, can quite simply alter the life chances of the young person.

Treating young people in public care in the same way as the other pupils and expecting as much of them also is perhaps the most important aspect according to the young people themselves, especially if they are of secondary age, when asked about school support. It is therefore essential that all the adults respect this wish, while at the same time recognising that they may well need additional monitoring or a different discipline approach if difficulties are encountered. As one head teacher commented:

> We go the extra mile with the children who are looked after, to send them out of school can destroy their foster placement, can leave them roaming the streets. We are aware of why they try our patience and therefore work harder to avoid the situation or to make alternative provision within the school.

> (OFSTED, 2001: 13)

Case study 4

Provision of positive support

Claire had settled into a mainstream secondary school with only a few minor difficulties that the school had worked with her to solve. However, the school and the carers had noticed that on Thursday mornings Claire had been attempting to miss school or had not attended her lessons when she was taken to school. After discussions with the designated teacher, Claire and the carers it was found that Claire had to change for PE in front of all the other girls. Due to past experiences Claire was finding this extremely difficult to cope with. The school felt that they could not allow Claire to change individually in a private room as it would be seen as providing preferential treatment. It was therefore decided that she would wear the PE kit under the school uniform on that morning, meaning that she would only have to take off her outer garments in public. Changing back was able to be coped with using skilful manoeuvres!

Case study 5

Negative support

Daniel is an able pupil living in a residential care home due to the fact that his mother is unable to look after him. He wants to be treated in the same way as all the other pupils. However, despite close consultation with the school's SENCO, the Inclusion Manager and the Head of Year regarding his background and past experiences, an English lesson was nearly enough to cause what could have been a very confrontational and damaging event. Daniel was asked to write a detailed history of the family he was living with and then verbally present this to the group. Daniel did not wish to inform the whole class or the teacher in this setting about his situation, but was not allowed to tackle another issue. This could have caused enough stress to provoke very challenging behaviour or a severe loss of confidence and self-esteem, all of which prevent learning and could in certain situations lead to detentions, depression or even exclusion.

Fortunately Daniel was very hopeful about his future at that time and therefore decided to 'invent' a family for the lesson. This in itself could have been detrimental to his emotional status, but in this circumstance allowed Daniel to maintain his 'normality' with his peers. Daniel was able to alert his key worker to this situation and discussions took place that ensured that this situation did not reoccur.

Supplying all the parties with the information they may require, while still paying the necessary heed to confidentiality, is essential. This may well include lunchtime supervisors and administration staff. Without this all-round blanket of knowledge, incidents can occur unwittingly, that can have devastating effects on the life of a young person in public care. Hopefully, if this is achieved, there may be more young people who say: 'I thank God for this school every day when I walk through the door' (15-year-old girl, OFSTED, 2001).

> **Discussion**
>
> How well does or would the educational setting in which you work support a young person in public care? Consider the government initiatives, such as Personal Education Plans and designated teachers and discuss how successful you feel they may be in promoting and enhancing the educational opportunities of these young people.

Key issues

It is anticipated that you will now:

- understand which children are included under the umbrella term of 'young people in public care';

- recognise the educational and social issues that cause barriers to learning for young people in public care;
- demonstrate an awareness of the legislation and guidance that inform professionals about the needs of these young people;
- recognise the importance of inter-agency working, including parents and carers, and of the need for frequent dialogue and collaboration;
- acknowledge the rights of the young person to be as fully involved in the decision-making as is possible;
- understand the need for training to enable the effective instigation of the role of the designated teacher and the implementation of meaningful and valuable Personal Education Plans;
- understand the reasons why young people in public care may demonstrate difficulties with aspects of a school's community such as attendance, homework, bullying, curriculum issues and conforming to acceptable behaviour.

Professional standards for Higher Level Teaching Assistants (HLTA)

If you can demonstrate your understanding and professional use of the key issues illustrated within this chapter, it is hoped that you will be able to fulfil the following HLTA Standards:

1.1	1.2	1.3	1.4	1.5	1.6	2.5
3.1.2	3.2.3	3.2.4	3.3.2	3.3.3	3.3.7	

Useful documents

DfEE and DoH (2000) *Guidance for the Education of Young People in Public Care*, London: DfEE.

DfES (2001) *Code of Practice on the Identification and Assessment of Special Educational Needs*, London: HMSO.

DoH (1998) *The Quality Protects Programme: Transforming Children's Services*, London: HMSO.

HMSO (2003) *Every Child Matters*, Norwich: The Stationery Office.

References

Bhabra, S., Ghate, D. with Brazier, L. (2002) *Consultation Analysis: Raising the Educational Attainment of Children in Care*, London: Policy Research Bureau.

Borland, M., Pearson, C., Hill, M., Tisdall, K. and Bloomfield, I. (1998) *Education and Care Away from Home*, Glasgow: The Scottish Council for Research in Education.

Coulling, N. (2000) 'Definitions of successful education for the "looked after" child: a multi-agency perspective', *Support for Learning*, vol. 15, no. 1, Tamworth: NASEN.

DfE (1993) *Special Educational Needs Code of Practice*, London: DfEE.

DfEE (1999) *Social Inclusion: Pupil Support*, (10/99) London: DfEE.

DfES (2001) *Code of Practice on the Identification and Assessment of Special Educational Needs*, London: HMSO.

DfEE and DoH (2000) *Guidance for the Education of Young People in Public Care*, London: DfEE.

DoH (1998) *The Quality Protects Programme: Transforming Children's Services*, London: HMSO.

DoH (1999) *Bulletin*, 26, London: HMSO.

DoH (2002) *Educational Qualifications of Care Leavers, Year Ending 31 March 2002: England, Statistical Bulletin, 24*, London: HMSO.

DoH (2003) *Outcome Indicators of Looked After Children*, London: HMSO.

Hibbert, H. (2003) 'Closing the gap', *Including Special Children*, vol. 156, p. 34. Birmingham: Questions.

Including Special Children (2003) 'Could do better', 156, p. 30, Birmingham: Questions.

Jackson, S. (1989) 'The education of children in care', in Kahan, B. (ed.) *Child Care: Research, Policy and Practice*, London: Hodder and Stoughton.

Jackson, S. (1994) 'Education on residential child care', *Oxford Review of Education*, vol. 20, no. 3, pp. 267–79.

OFSTED (2001) *Raising the Achievement of Children in Public Care*, London: HMSO.

OFSTED/SSI Report (1995) *The Education of Children Who Are Looked After by Local Authorities*, London: HMSO.

Office of National Statistics (ONS) (2003) *The Mental Health of Young People Looked After by Local Authorities*, London: HMSO.

Sandiford, P. (1996) *Improving Educational Opportunities for Looked After Young People: A Good Practice Guide for Teachers*, London: National Children's Bureau.

Sandiford, P. (1999) *Personal Education Plan for Children and Young People in Public Care*, London: National Children's Bureau.

SEU/Office of the Deputy Prime Minister (2003) *A Better Education for Children in Care: The Issues*, available on: www.socialexclusion.gov.uk (accessed 12.08.2003).

The Who Cares? Trust, Equal Chances Project and Calouste Gulbenkian Foundation (1999) *Practice Guide: Developing Services to Improve the Educational Outcomes of Looked After Children and Young People*, London: The Who Cares? Trust.

Thomas, N. (2003) 'Breaking down barriers', *Including Special Children*, 156, pp. 32–3, Birmingham: Questions.

Ward, H. (ed.) (1995) *Looking After Children: Research into Practice*, London: HMSO.

Therapeutic education

John Cornwall and Sue Soan

Introduction

The past three decades performance and curriculum content and delivery have been the main driving forces in education, and therapeutic approaches have not been felt to be effective methods, producing measurable results. However, at the start of the twenty-first century government guidance, such as *Every Child Matters* (HMSO, 2003) has suggested the need for educators to develop a more therapeutic approach to learners, to the curriculum and to school ethos. The overall aim of this chapter therefore is to positively support educators in their work with learners who lack motivation, inspiration and engagement.

> **Discussion**
>
> Write a list of at least five words describing what you think therapeutic education is. Then write another list stating what you think the needs of the young people are who are placed in a therapeutic school. If possible, ask a few colleagues to carry out these two short tasks as well. What do you find? What aspects of teaching and learning do the lists mostly refer to? How does this link in with the educational changes of the past 30 years?

Common characteristics of therapeutic education

The common characteristics of therapeutic education are basically related to the human side of teaching and learning rather than the mechanical or technical process of the so-called 'curriculum delivery'. Educators, policy-makers and politicians have asked, and continue to ask, for simple solutions to issues such as challenging behaviour; thus, a way of teaching that incorporates a number of approaches is not seen to be useful. However, as is presently being recognised by many educators, there are actually no simple solutions to the complex problems that are encountered on a daily basis within classrooms. Additionally, when thinking about what makes good, motivating and inclusive teaching, many factors are mentioned that do not just involve the transaction of knowledge between the educator and learner. These other factors will most likely involve sophisticated human relationships and they will have an enormous impact on the effectiveness of the educator's teaching. This, of course, is nothing new to educators, as for thousands of years it has been recognised that the inter-personal transaction between educator and learner is fostered by a therapeutic and nurturing ethic. All adults in a classroom want the best for every pupil, but without doubt there are some children who are very difficult to like, to build a relationship with and thus to motivate. It is for these children that simple solutions are constantly sought, but their needs are complex and therefore the solution will out of necessity be complex and will require a variety of approaches. Thus, therapeutic education is essentially about this educator–learner relationship and the various ways it can be developed and enhanced to improve *engagement, motivation* and *learning* for children with significant social, emotional and behavioural difficulties (SEBD). It is the quality of this relationship between educator and learner that has an enormous impact on the learner's ability to learn and access the appropriate curriculum so that his or her true ability can be released. This is not easily achieved, because the learner's defences built up to protect him or herself, perhaps over a number of years, mean that it is immensely difficult for the learner to form and maintain relationships with both adults and peers that are conducive to learning and education in the school context.

Case study 1

When meeting Dillon for the first time to discuss coming to the special school that was on the same site as his residential home, he stood at the other end of the room with his key worker for a few minutes, with his head lowered, swaying from side to side. Without warning he took off, running out of the house and then up on to the roof of an out-building from where he chucked available objects down at his key worker and myself. After a little while trying to encourage him to come down and talk or play a game with me, it was clear that he was too anxious to even think about school. I therefore left, but before I did I told Dillon I would return the next day at a certain time and that I was really looking forward to talking to him. On that occasion, his parting cry was 'I don't do school.' This flight response to my arrival occurred a number of times, but gradually Dillon began to accept my presence with the help of his key worker and I was eventually able to start establishing a relationship with him – and thus was able to start helping him with the massive task of facing school and learning. Dillon needed to know that I was reliable, consistent and constant in what I said before he would even risk talking to me about his education. Children with such severe SEBD need to accept and build a relationship with the educator before any 'curriculum delivery' can even be considered. When starting to access learning, the activities chosen were based on his favourite football team and other hobbies and involved many different approaches. He was supported in all activities so that failure was not encountered until a sound learning ethos was established. An extreme case, but one that clearly identifies the importance of the trust required between educator and learner before successful learning can be achieved.

HLTA
1.2
3.3.2

Discussion

Can you think of a situation when your intervention or support has enabled a child to complete a piece of work or have a go at a new activity? What did you need to do or say to enable the child to take the risk? Were the decisions you took based on the relationship you had built up with the child or about the actual learning task?

The case study and discussion clearly show that educators need to compensate for children's difficulties in forming and developing relationships to enable them to access education. They need to have the ability to implement a range of approaches to their teaching and learning and it is these that come under the umbrella term of 'therapeutic education'. Educators must be willing to change their behaviour first, if they want the children to change theirs. The usual carrot and stick behaviour approaches will not be effective ways of helping the children with complex SEBD. Important characteristics of therapeutic education can be expressed using the following words:

- enjoyment
- inspiration
- motivation
- engagement
- inclusion.

Therapeutic education – the main messages

- Therapeutic education is about developing and making explicit well-established therapeutic strategies and *not* about turning educators into therapists.
- To acknowledge that simple behavioural approaches (e.g. rewards and sanctions), even when applied on a whole-school basis, will not develop confidence or deal with a significant number of children's difficulties.

■ It is possible to develop a therapeutic and humanistic approach to learners and to the curriculum, by changing the school ethos and creating a more interactive curriculum.

So how is this achieved?

To actually be able to motivate, inspire and engage learners with these significant difficulties there is a need for educators to do the following:

■ develop strategies that better inform daily lesson delivery and planning;

■ be more flexible and creative in planning and delivering the curriculum;

■ use positive relationships to counter the insecurity of current educational challenges;

HLTA
2.5

■ be more sensitive to learners' individuality;

■ listen better;

■ recognise and contextualise the learners' characteristics and work more effectively with them;

■ move beyond simple behavioural technologies and into more holistic, nurturing and therapeutic approaches.

> **Discussion**
>
> Using the list of objectives above, consider how the educational establishment in which you work could develop specific areas to enable the development of a more therapeutic environment.

How do the therapeutic approaches to education fit in with the current education system overall?

Since the 1970s the view of education has been based on 'performance', 'outcomes', 'target setting' and 'curriculum delivery'. The emphasis has therefore until recently mostly been placed on the teaching and learning of static knowledge and on the disciplinarian approach to teaching. However, with government statements on inclusion and inclusive practices predominating currently, therapeutic education may once again be considered a valuable educational method, encapsulating the best aspects of the humanistic approaches to education.

What does it mean to the educator?

It does *not* mean that educators are not firm, assertive, directed, focused and skilful in group management and dynamics. It is also *not* a soft option, but it is an approach that seeks to achieve cooperation and appropriate compliance through responsible teaching approaches and not coercion.

Positive relationships

⇩

Increase in:
SKILL
KNOWLEDGE
UNDERSTANDING

More control of the world around the child

Increase in self-esteem

Figure 6.1 Effect of positive relationships

HLTA
1.6

Thus, educators need to have a great deal of confidence in their own teaching and to have developed particular skills and personal resources before they can attempt therapeutic approaches through education. The approach does not pass the buck by allocating blame and in doing so dismiss the problem encountered. The educator carrying out this approach must take responsibility for their own part they play in the interactive process and not try to ignore their own, sometimes unsuitable behaviour and actions.

Therapy and education do involve separate specialised training and are different disciplines, but it cannot be denied that the edges of both are very blurred. Due to this fact, the principles and practices of teaching, learning and therapy are sometimes significantly intertwined, recognising the reality that children's lives cannot be separated into the various components of professional endeavour. Also, the children who have education and therapy at the same time do not experience these activities in isolation, but will put them together in a holistic way in their own thinking. If the children are not able to do this, then the educator and therapist are not achieving the necessary/desirable outcome.

Undoubtedly, therefore skilful educators form relationships with children and young people that not only enhance their learning and social and emotional development, but they are in fact crucial to them as is demonstrated in Figure 6.1.

Case study 2

HLTA
1.2
2.9
3.3.1

When I first worked with Carrie, a 10-year-old girl, she only printed words in a very slow, precise manner and she refused to write sentences as she said she could not spell. She had just joined a residential home and school, after being taken into public care. Carrie had missed quite a bit of schooling due to her behaviour, but was clearly an able learner. When meeting Carrie for the first time I spent a great deal of the time listening very carefully to what she said about her difficulties and why she felt she could not succeed at reading and writing. During the next few weeks before she started at the school, I taught Carrie on a one-to-one basis, spending the time getting to know her and developing her skills, self-esteem and self-confidence. Gaining her trust and maintaining her interest were paramount and then modelling new skills to help develop her handwriting into a neat cursive script had massive positive effects. When a relationship had been built and her self-esteem was beginning to rise, I then began to tackle Carrie's spelling difficulties. With a specific scheme, individual attention and encouragement, her progress was amazing. When Carrie joined a class, the transference of these new skills was understandably very slow and cautious. However, our individual lessons continued and we were able to work together with the teacher to continue building both the skills and the self-esteem until Carrie had enough confidence to risk making mistakes in the classroom situation. Her progress was rapid and has continued to grow.

Without the time and effort given to establishing a good trusting relationship Carrie would probably not have been able to lower her defences to let herself learn, because to learn you have to be willing to experiment and risk making mistakes. To be able to do this, a learner has to have good self-esteem and confidence in his or her own ability; if a learner has not got this inner security, then it is frequently much easier to mess around, refuse to work or even refuse to attend school than face the risk of failure. This case study clearly illustrates the factors described in Figure 6.1. Through this positive relationship, an increase in skill, knowledge and understanding should, as in the case of Carrie, lead to an increase of control of the world around the learner and a subsequent improvement in self-esteem.

The ecology of behaviour

When considering this it is important to remember that a great deal of human behaviour is in response to the behaviour of other human beings. Many learners with social and emotional difficulties in schools have experienced negative and sometimes abusive child rearing. It is therefore not surprising that these learners' behaviour may be a reaction to the events in their past. It is *very* important for educators to recognise that this behaviour is also a response to the way they perceive themselves, the way others see them, their history of success or failure at school, and the list could continue.

When thinking about the needs of a learner with social and emotional needs using a therapeutic education approach, it is important to remember that behaviour is either a response to the surroundings or is the result of what he or she has learned or both. A learner's behaviour cannot be erased by a quickly implemented 'behaviour programme', because to change behaviour new patterns have to be taught. This process needs to be well planned and will nearly always involve changes in behaviour by adults as well. Very occasionally the 'key' to a learner's problems is quickly solved, but usually it is a slow learning process, especially if the behaviour is well embedded, perhaps being used as a means of self-protection over a number of years.

The social web

In the therapeutic approach to education, pupils are seen as existing in a social web that includes the home, the family, religion, the culture, the sub-culture and the community as well as the school. A learner's behaviour and development are influenced by, as well as an influence on, the behaviour and development of others with whom they interact in this web. It is clear therefore that human behaviour is the product of an ongoing interaction between the social environment and internal motivations (gained from previous social experiences). There are always interconnected elements between all these systems and hence any alteration in one part of the web can have repercussions in the others.

> **Discussion** Think of a situation in which one system within a learner's social web (e.g. the home) changes. Does this change just affect that one part, or could it affect the whole social system? Bearing the answers in mind, do you think that all the solutions to learners' problems experienced in the classroom can be solved through school-based actions?

Maslow's hierarchy of needs

Maslow's theories of motivation (1970) give some insight into the relative importance of 'survival' needs and growth needs. According to Maslow, there are seven levels of human needs:

- Biological: air, water, food, shelter, sex, sleep.
- Safety: protection from the elements, disease, fear.
- Love and belongingness.
- Esteem: self-esteem and esteem by others.
- Cognitive: knowledge, meaning, enquiry, order.
- Aesthetic: beauty, balance, form.
- Self-actualisation: realising potential, becoming everything you can be, having 'peak' experiences of being.

What educators want to do in classrooms relates to the last three points listed, but it is obvious that unless the basic needs of the learners are met, these latter areas are less likely to be successful. This would be true for any child, young person or adult. A child or young person who feels unloved, unwanted and/or has low self-esteem will understandably, I suggest, find it harder to concentrate on school work.

Due to the often hidden influences, therefore, it is crucial to therapeutic education approaches that plans and procedures are shared among everyone involved with the learner and that these are all *reviewed* and *regularly evaluated* so that strategies can be swiftly altered in response to changes and developments, from any part of the social web.

Unpredictability

Every problem will be different and thus a new solution will be required for each learner's problem. It is important that an educator does not try to apply an old solution to a new problem, because it most probably won't work. Why? Two problems are never exactly the same. Also learners' behaviour does different things to different people and learners behave differently in response to different adults. Added to this is the fact that the various educators that any one learner has contact with will have differing expectations.

Consistency

When working with learners with emotional and/or behavioural difficulties, an educator needs self-confidence and well-thought-out strategies as well as a positive approach. There is definitely no room for impatience or a judgemental attitude. An educator needs to be sure of where his or her own boundaries are, as well as the behavioural boundaries for the learners. It is therefore important that within his or her own particular work context an educator can rely on something to provide some *consistency*. This can be supplied through a well-thought-out structure or framework for both solving problems and getting to a variety of solutions that suit the educator's context. The concept of 'therapeutic education' can provide such a framework that is ethically acceptable to educators and workable in a variety of school contexts. This is where an educator can begin to look at the skills he or she might develop and the confidence generated by the thought that a well-considered, strategic and therapeutic approach is being followed. The consistency is achieved through the systemic steps approach, not the solutions being generated by the educator for him or herself and the learner(s) in his or her charge.

Why is challenging behaviour such a problem in schools?

Learners with challenging behaviour may do the following:

■ have low self-esteem and poor self-image (identity and feelings);

■ lack a useful language of social interaction (capability/skills);

■ be unable to respond assertively rather than aggressively (capability and feelings);

■ lack 'emotional intelligence' or sensitivity to their own feelings (capability/skills);

■ have experienced a series of academic failures and have poor self-belief (beliefs);

■ have developed a set of 'habitual' conflict-laden behaviours (beliefs and behaviour);

■ be very vulnerable and lack 'resilience' (despite external toughness) (identity).

They may also find:

■ a greater level of conformity and cooperation is expected at school (environment);

■ academic pressures need to be sensitively managed (environment).

O'Connor and Seymour (1990) identify how challenging behaviour can affect learners' life-long learning opportunities as well as the occasions when challenging behaviour is exhibited: 'Behaviour is often taken as evidence of identity or capability and this is how confidence and competence are destroyed in the classroom.' An incidence of challenging behaviour is rarely just a matter of conflict originating solely between two people at that one moment in time. There is nearly always a range of background factors, social, educational and personal, involved. If an educator has a working knowledge of 'possible additional influences' in the learner's life, then, it is suggested, there is a better chance of achieving a change in the present state from the challenging behaviour to a more desirable state. Engaging the learner and others involved in the problem-solving may also be a starting point for change. Resources will always be required when finding a solution to a learner's challenging behaviour. Sometimes these may involve physical or financial support, but equally these resources may be skills, persistence (personal skills) or knowledge. This is where the problem-solving is frequently required, because the necessary resources may not always be those of the school, the system or the adult. To make the present state change permanently to a more desirable state, considerable resourcefulness on the part of the learner is necessary as well.

So how can an educator help a learner with challenging behaviour?

First, the educator needs to build up an ecological view of the learner, looking at the relationship between the learner, their circumstances and their surroundings. Then the educator should look for clues and opportunities to solve the problems that face the learner. Importantly, this should not be a catalogue of negative evidence, but a professional analysis of the situation where clues are found that can help the educator and learner find solutions. This will involve gathering information that will help the educator build bridges to the school and the curriculum for the learner, not just concentrate on the 'bad behaviour'. The learner MUST be involved in this process so that he or she is also consciously working on changing his or her behaviour; without this involvement any intervention is really just behavioural manipulation. Figure 6.2 identifies the possible sources of a problem and clearly illustrates a broader view of an incident of challenging behaviour.

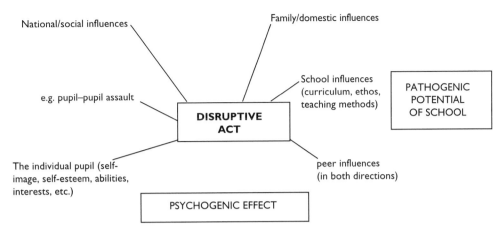

Figure 6.2 Influences on challenging behaviour
Source: McGuiness (1993)

Recall an incident of challenging behaviour. Did the educators involve the learner as well as other adults in trying to find solutions? Was the larger picture researched appropriately, gathering broad and balanced information? Could the situation have been handled differently, perhaps resulting in a more positive solution for the learner?

HLTA
1.3
1.4
1.5

What next?

Following the assessment and problem-solving period, it is necessary for educators to share and use the information gathered successfully, so that the learner's behaviour is not just temporarily adjusted. If there is an over-reliance on 'behavioural strategies', this can happen. However, in busy schools, this is not easy, and spending time on developing positive relationships is often seen as peripheral to the process of teaching. A therapeutic approach to education does actually mean working with the relationships involved and in fact, socially and psychologically, it is central to the whole process. Emotions and feelings are inextricably tied up in the process of learning and teaching and cannot be ignored. Robert Dilts' Unified Field Theory (O'Connor and Seymour, 1990) (Figure 6.3) provides a useful model for considering how educators interact with learners when teaching.

O'Connor and Seymour (1990) explain the terms used by Dilt as:

■ *Behaviour* is the outward manifestation of our inner thoughts, feelings, identity, beliefs and spirit.

■ *Capability* is the range of personal or emotional, social, academic, physical and practical skills we bring to bear on life events.

■ *Beliefs* are inner maps we use to make sense of the world – they give stability and continuity.

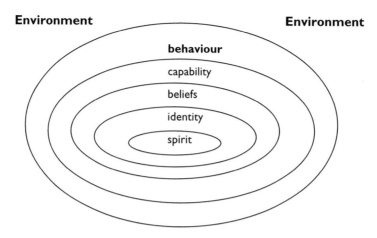

Figure 6.3   Robert Dilts' Unified Field Theory
Source: O'Connor and Seymour (1990)

- *Identity* incorporates all of the outer levels and such things as self-esteem, confidence, security, etc.
- *Spirit* is the deepest intangible levels of our being or personality – what we sometimes call 'our hidden depths'.

Change at the higher (or innermost) levels will always affect lower (outer) levels. The impact of change at higher levels is greater than at lower levels. Developing new skills will change a whole range of behaviour. For example, enhancing self-esteem will change many behaviours and spiritual vision may change a person's whole life and most of the behaviours in it.

Teaching strategies

Having explored some of the underpinning causes of emotional difficulties and challenging behaviours and some principles that might underpin practice, it is now appropriate to consider how educators can use a curriculum to impact on the personal and social development of these learners. It is important to recognise, however, that unlike learners with obvious disabilities or learning difficulties, those with social and emotional difficulties do not fit into a category or syndrome. There is no set of symptoms, no particular recognisable features of an individual. In fact, they are as diverse as the general population and different from each other. They are categorised therefore solely by the effect they have in the classroom, on others in the classroom and on the traditional school system of managing learning.

Many learners with SEBD are socially immature and have not had the opportunity to reflect on their personal development. Understandably this leads to a lack of knowledge, skills and understanding in the social and inter-personal domain. Access to the curriculum means making the broad national curriculum meaningful and relevant to learners who are either socially immature, may have differential abilities, who are disaffected or who are experiencing emotional difficulties in their lives.

Motivation

The level of motivation of learners is an important indicator of the quality of learning as an emotional experience. Learners who are emotionally involved in their study will deepen their learning, increase their attention span and adopt many other recognisable features of good learning. Stimulating and maintaining motivation for learners with SEBD are frequently the main problems for educators. So how can this be achieved? Figure 6.4 presents some ideas and indeed these can be utilised in all Key Stages and in all subject areas.

Social skills

Social skills are defined as specific strategies used by an individual to perform a social task effectively and thus be judged socially competent. They can be split into two categories:

- *environmental social skills*: These are skills that are essential to perform tasks in both an educational setting and the workplace, such as listening, following instructions, appropriate work habits etc.
- *Social interaction skills*: These are skills that facilitate any positive social interaction, such as starting and maintaining a conversation, complimenting others, resolving conflict, etc.

Learners with SEBD in school are delayed in their personal, social and emotional development, and this may be for a variety of reasons. They may have been deprived of satisfactory adult models or may not have been given sufficient opportunity to learn from those around them or from their surroundings. However, this social

Stimulating interest	Maintaining interest
✓ Using novel, incongruous, conflicting or paradoxical events to arouse attention and stimulate curiosity ✓ Allowing learners to explore, experiment and therefore sustain interest ✓ Relating new material to existing knowledge ✓ Presenting different perspectives to promote reflection, puzzlement or explanation ✓ Use of colour; movement; sound; movies; animation; simulations; working models; questions; attractive design; problem-solving approach; novel events; cognitive conflict; challenges to the users; guided exploration	✓ Giving examples that link individual preferences to the content of an application ✓ Stating and re-stating the relevance and end result ✓ Create opportunities for the learners to achieve standards of excellence with small risk factor ✓ Providing positive and constructive feedback ✓ Allowing choice and responsibility

Figure 6.4   How to stimulate and maintain learners' interest

immaturity, although developmental, is not necessarily something that cannot be compensated for or accelerated by an appropriate social and emotional environment both at home and at school. When considering involving inter-agency working it is also important for educators to remember that although a learner's home environment may be challenging at times, if it is generally secure and loving, then it is likely to go further to solving a learner's problem than a school environment can. Cornwall and Tod (1998) clearly explain how lack of early guidance can affect a learner's opportunities when entering school.

Similar strategies are applied to enable their child to develop social skills needed for school. Their child is encouraged to play with same age peers and social behaviours such as listening, turn taking, sharing, etc. are made explicit and rewarded 'Here's some sweets – give one to Martyn and one to Peter – good boy, for sharing.' These behaviours are developed in a supportive safe setting for the child so that the chances of success are maximised. The important point to note is that these behaviours are explicitly taught and learned during the years prior to school entry. If a child does not have these experiences, and arrives in school without the appropriate 'learning behaviours' then he/she will not only make slower academic progress and have more peer-related problems but will have to acquire these behaviours in a group setting where failure is public. For some children this 'developmental delay and/or impairment' can be addressed in school by using an available adult and selected peers to recreate home-type situations as described above so that the necessary behaviours can be developed initially in a safe setting. Children seek to make sense of their environment and protect themselves from further failure and rejection. To do this they develop particular ways of thinking and behaving, e.g.:

- If not given sufficient attention from a parent during the early years, they may constantly seek attention even if it results in an uncomfortable experience, i.e. being shouted at or smacked.

- If they are not allowed to succeed, they may decide not to attempt to do anything in case they fail.

- They may adopt a style of thinking, i.e. 'everyone hates me' to protect themselves from rejection and then behave in such a way as to confirm that their belief is correct.

- They may believe that they are the cause of events (i.e. they caused their parents to split up, etc., they are too 'thick' to be able to do schoolwork). If they believe that they cannot change events, then they stop trying to change, but carry with them the burden of guilt and failure.

> **Discussion**
>
> Discuss learners you have taught that would fall into one of the categories mentioned above. How did the educators at the school support the learners? Do you consider the learners' problems were really solved? If 'yes', how was this achieved? If 'no', why?

In essence, the learners having difficulties at school may simply not have the appropriate behaviours in their repertoire, in which case some behavioural approaches aimed at building up and rewarding new skills may fulfil the need and be successful. However, if the learner has made an active 'adjustment' to his individual circumstances and the consequent behaviour serves a purpose, then simply trying to change that behaviour without reference to the function will not achieve the desired result.

For example, a learner avoids starting work (so that he cannot fail) by chatting with peers. This learner could be 'stopped' from chatting, but the fact that the chatting has stopped does not allow him to lose his fear of failure. He would in fact probably develop another behaviour that serves to protect him from revealing his difficulty with his work.

Educators have an important role, therefore, when deciding which problem-solving techniques to use, whether the learner 'can't' or 'won't' behave and will have to adjust strategies accordingly.

Thus, this kind of behaviour, leads to a lack of knowledge, skills and understanding in the social and inter-personal domain. This means that a learner in school cannot elicit the help, support, sympathy or even guidance that he or she needs and this can mean that he or she responds inappropriately to the questions and intentions of others. Misinterpreting the actions and words of others can lead to negative reactions from them or confusion and there will be an ensuing loss of self-esteem. How many times have you as an educator been involved in sorting out a problem which is basically a learner misinterpreting what another learner has meant?

What could be found in a 'Therapeutic Education' programme?

Remember:

- Relationships are central to the whole process.
- There is not a simple solution approach to teaching and learning.
- Educators are not just 'deliverers of curriculum'.
- Educators' humanity and professional skills are an integral part of the process.
- Therapeutic education approaches recognise the essential humanity of both educator and learner.
- Therapeutic approaches involve all areas of the curriculum and the social environment of school.

Table 6.1 summarises possible teaching and learning strategies. They are ideas to be developed according to an educator's and learner's needs. It is intended to trigger thoughts about where and how developments can take place in individual schools.

Table 6.1 Teaching and learning strategies

Programme content	Group work	Staff involvement	Learning support	Whole school
Social and interpersonal skills at work and in learning	Developing more structured group work/discussion to practise social skills	Teachers and other adults modelling good behaviour	Raising self-esteem – positive strokes in all areas of the curriculum	Whole school approach – input, develop-ment or relationships in school
Scripts for educators and for learners	Developing emotional literacy by exploring literature and poetry	Working with home – links with parents and a forum for parents to share views and concerns	Monitor individu-als carefully and be open about this and sharing observations	Normalisation of anger so it cannot be used as a manipula-tive weapon – everyone involved
Pictorial stories to reflect on showing effect of good and bad behaviour	Increasing aware-ness of feelings by exploring social stories and situations	Adults develop a skilled, firm but empathetic response to learners	Training for educators in developing a therapeutic approach to education	Planning procedures i.e. thinking it through before-hand
Individuals keep-ing diaries – noting problems and good times. Self-awareness of emotional 'patterns' in their lives	Role-play – make up social skills and opportuni-ties for rehearsal of social skills	Practising tone of voice and modelling back learner's behaviour	Teaching learners to express anger without directing it at a person	Celebration or reinforcement of instances where success, management of feelings or social interaction are achieved
Writing down bad feelings to throw away, i.e. developing emotional self-awareness	Give practice in resolving conflicts by generating controlled situations	Developing the language of personal expression and assertiveness in the workplace	Self-assessment and review built into the programme	Planned individ-ual programme of intervention teaching of strategies and skills
Relaxation tech-niques for staff and learners as an 'ambience' in the workplace	Assertiveness – e.g. not being crowded into a corner, saying 'no' etc.	Identified steps and criteria for success	Recognition of the need for 'time out' and privacy	Solution-focused approaches related to whole-school behaviour

Table 6.1 Teaching and learning strategies (Continued)

Programme content	Group work	Staff involvement	Learning support	Whole school
Developing the language/words for emotion and feelings	Circle time and nurturing approaches are intended to develop social and emotional skills	The initial assessment and quality of observation by educators are important. This should be non-judgemental observations	Working with home, peer group, gang identity to explore further incidents	How do we judge success? Evaluation of environment
Using fiction, TV, video clips as a way of depersonalising 'difficult' situations and emotions	Involvement of learners in process of making evaluations about their own behaviour and feelings	Deliberately modelling behaviour to learners – demonstrates control and awareness of feelings	Background information on family and possible abuse or other reasons for excessive 'triggering' of difficulties	Incorporate into whole staff PSE programme

Key issues

- 'Behaviour' is never just behaviour (good or bad); there are always reasons for behaviour.
- Learners cannot always articulate those reasons and often they may not even be aware of them.
- This is why it is hard to change learners' behaviour and it will involve a learning process, called for the purposes of this chapter, the triangle of awareness, where *thoughts*, *feelings* and *behaviour* are all important.
- Understanding the basis of a therapeutic approach to education can open up ways in which schools can be effective in reducing the impact of disaffected and disruptive learners as well as providing a healthy educational culture that will also minimise the problems for individual learners themselves.
- Behaviour cannot be divorced from its underlying thoughts and feelings.
- The triangle of awareness is vital throughout this area of work, because behaviour does not occur without a good reason. The 'good' reason may only exist in the mind of the learner whose behaviour is being looked at, but to them the reasons are good and worthwhile, whatever anyone else thinks. This notion needs to be grasped before problem-solving can commence.
- Remember – acting on 'behaviour' out of context and without an effort to understand the nature of the behaviour is usually a recipe for failure for all concerned, especially the learner.

Professional Standards for Higher Level Teaching Assistants (HLTA)

If you can demonstrate your understanding and professional use of the key issues illustrated within this chapter, it is hoped that you will be able to fulfil the following HLTA Standards:

1.2	1.3	1.4	1.5	1.6	2.5
2.9	3.1.2	3.3.1	3.3.2		

Useful document

HMSO (2003) *Every Child Matters*, Norwich: The Stationery Office.

References

Ayers, H., Clarke, D. and Murray, A. (1995) *Perspectives on Behaviour: A Practical Guide to Effective Interventions for Teachers*, London: David Fulton.

Bovair, K., Carpenter, B. and Upton, G. (eds) (1992) *Special Curricula Needs*, London: David Fulton.

Cornwall, J. (1999) 'Pressure, Stress and Children's Behaviour at School' in David, P. (ed.), *Young Children Learning*, London: Paul Chapman.

Cornwall, J. and Tod, J. (1998) *IEP, Emotional and Behavioural Difficulties*, London: David Fulton.

DFE (1994a) *Pupils with Problems: Pupil Behaviour and Discipline*. Circular 8/94, London: HMSO.

DFE (1994b) *Exclusions from School*, Circular 10/94, London: HMSO.

DFE (1994c) *The Education by LEAs of Children Otherwise than at School*, Circular 11/94, London: HMSO.

DFE (1994d) *The Education of Children with Emotional and Behavioural Difficulties*, Circular 9/94, London: HMSO.

Fogell, J. and Long, R. (1997) *Emotional and Behavioural Difficulties*, Tamworth, NASEN.

Greenhaigh, P. (1995) *Emotional Growth and Learning*, London: Routledge.

Lawrence, D. (1994) *Self-Esteem in Children*, London: Paul Chapman.

Maslow, A. H. (1970) *Motivations and Personality*, 2nd edn, London: Harper & Row.

McGuiness, J. (1993) *Teachers, Pupils and Behaviour: A Managerial Approach*, London: Cassell.

McNamara, S. (1995) *Changing Behaviour: Teaching Children with Emotional and Behavioural Difficulties in Primary and Secondary*. London: David Fulton.

McNamara, S. and Morton, G. (1994) *Changing Behaviour*, London: David Fulton.

Merrett, F. (1994) *Encouragement Works Best: Positive Approaches to Classroom Management*. London: David Fulton.

O'Connor, J. and Seymour, J. (1990) *Introducing Neuro-Linguistic Programming: Psychological Skills for Understanding and Influencing People*, London: Thorsons.

The Elton Report (1989) *Discipline in Schools*, London: HMSO.

Thomas, G. (1997) Inclusive schools for an inclusive society, *British Journal of Special Education*, vol. 24, no. 3. Tamworth: NASEN.

University of Illinois Cooperative Extension Service (1998) *Children, Stress and Natural Disasters*, A set of resource materials for teachers. http://www.ag.uiuc.edu/~disaster/teacher.html – size2K- 5.Dec.95

Varma, V. (ed.) (1996) *Coping with Children in Stress*, Aldershot: Arena.

Warden, D. (1997) *Teaching Social Behaviour: Classroom Activities to Foster ...*, Donald Warden and Donald Christie.

Watkins, C. (1997) *Managing Behaviour*, ATL.

Watson, J. (1996) *Reflection through Interaction*, London: Falmer Press.

Zarkowska, E. and Clements, J. (1994) *Problem Behaviour and People with Severe Learning Disabilities: The Star Approach*, London: Chapman and Hall.

7 Social, emotional and behavioural difficulties (SEBD)

Sue Soan

Behaviour is never found in a vacuum. It is always functional for that individual. Some behaviour can be ambiguous, so STOP and think of a plausible hypothesis for the behaviour and then decide what intervention is required. The better the questions you ask, the better the solutions/interventions will be.

(Long, 2003)

Introduction

This chapter will provide an introduction to the theoretical understanding and the knowledge that underpins all aspects of behaviour. It is intended that by the end of this chapter the reader will be able to develop approaches that pay regard to their theoretical understanding and will also aid motivation, academic improvement and concentration for the learners. It will discuss the purposes of behaviour and the circumstances that affect behaviour. This chapter also includes a section that focuses on gender issues and learning behaviours. In these ways it is hoped that the reader will begin to learn how to question the implementation and evaluation of interventions and targets in a manner that will benefit the needs of all learners, including those with ADHD and ADD.

Definition of terms

SEBD: Social, Emotional and Behavioural Difficulties

This term has been selected as the chapter title because the social and physical environment in which a young person lives and learns is considered to have an enormous effect on emotional development and consequently on behaviour. However, the abbreviations EBSD (emotional, behavioural and social difficulties) and BESD (behavioural, emotional and social difficulties/development) are also commonly used in documentation and legislation. The Professional Standards for Qualified Teacher Status say, for example, that teachers must demonstrate that: 'They identify and support more able pupils, those working below age-related expectations, those who are failing to achieve their potential in learning, and those who experience behavioural, emotional and social difficulties' (TTA, 2002a, Section 2, Sub-section 4). The Special Educational Needs Code of Practice (DfES, 2001) also uses the heading 'Behaviour, emotional and social development', as does the National SEN Specialist Standards (TTA, 1999).

Behaviour

So what is behaviour? It is important to understand that: 'Behaviour always has a purpose, whether it is interpreted as appropriate or inappropriate and it is learned and determined by antecedents and consequences (ABC of behaviour – Antecedents, Behaviour and Consequences)' (Crisp and Soan, 2003: 153). Thus if looked at in this way, a complete picture of what caused the behaviour, the behaviour itself and what happened following the behaviour, can be constructed. It is also important that the behaviour is interpreted by the educator with all the information gained from asking and answering the questions above, to ensure that an appropriate solution or intervention is implemented. Learners' behaviour does not therefore just occur; it is the result of a learner's relationship with him or herself, with others, including all adults and peers and with the curriculum. Brofenbrenner (1979) agrees that these relationships are the three most influential factors that affect any learner's ability to achieve.

Behaviour management

In educational settings behaviour management applies to the management of resources, the curricula and the classroom environment in a way that enables learners to access and engage with the curriculum. Behaviour management also includes, as a response to the Statement of Inclusion and the social and academic aims of the National Curriculum, learners' ability to develop positive outcomes for the future and the development of social skills (DfEE/QCA, 1999).

Learning behaviour

'Learning behaviour' is a term that, it is believed, presents a more positive image to both educators and learners than that of 'behaviour management'. This is because behaviour management can frequently be identified as a reactive process. This view is supported by the fact that usually behaviour management is not addressed as part of subject knowledge throughout a course, but only as an 'add-on' if teaching and learning are disrupted. Training is also often presented in the context of Additional Educational Needs, again suggesting that it is 'additional to' normal provision. This, whether intentional or unintentional, has the effect of separating learning from behaviour and can mean that individual educators and school policies and practices can adopt either a fragmented or a 'control' approach to behaviour management. As a result of this, learning can be negatively affected and relationships can break down between educators and learners. Unfortunately many teachers still make assumptions about learners' academic ability based on their behavioural difficulties. If this happens, then a situation where the learner experiences a lack of both self-esteem and success is created, producing an environment that allows under-achievement, disaffection and disruption to control the learning and teaching. Over a period of time, this type of environment created by the separation of learning and behaviour may build up cumulatively, producing additional problems for those who are already disadvantaged. Following research, Feinstein (cited in HMSO, 2003: 19) illustrated how anti-social behaviour can deepen through a learner's school life.

> **Discussion**
>
> Consider whether educators as individuals or school policies and practices within your own workplace setting think about learning and behaviour as separate entities? Would you describe the behaviour management in your school setting as a reactive process or one that is really trying to connect learning with behaviour? From the information discussed above, how could you perhaps suggest ways of improving practice?

HLTA
1.4
1.6

So why is learning behaviour felt to be a more appropriate term than behaviour management? Powell and Tod (forthcoming: 38) write: 'Learning and behaviour should be linked via the term "learning behaviour" in order to reduce perceptions that "promoting learning" and "managing behaviour" are separate issues. Powell and Tod's conceptual framework for understanding learning behaviour in a school context supports Brofenbrenner's "triangle of influence", but also links outside factors such as family structures, cultures, agency involvement, the community and policies to their model (Figure 7.1).

The way in which educators respond to and communicate with learners is felt to be imperative for the establishment of high self-esteem and self-confidence, especially if outside influences have not been supportive of a learner's educational development. Barrow *et al.* (2001) support this view by saying that the way in which an individual feels about himself (self-esteem) is built up from early childhood experiences. Crisp and Soan (2003: 154) explain this in greater detail:

> By interpreting the way others respond to him, the learner creates a view of himself that is directly interpreted from his perception of the way he has been treated. This is further set within a cultural framework where certain ideals are promoted as valuable and desirable. The greater the link between what the learner thinks of himself and his ideal of what he should be, the greater level of self-esteem will be established.

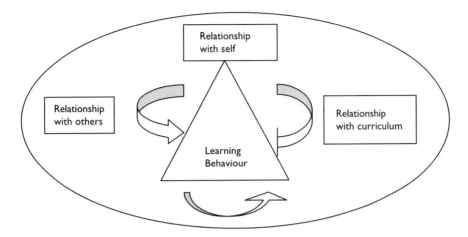

Figure 7.1 Conceptual framework for understanding learning behaviour
Source: Powell and Tod (forthcoming)

Elmer (2000) warns the educator, however, that the self-esteem of a learner will fluctuate depending on the context and the situation they are in, and this again requires consideration and reflection by the educator to maintain a positive and successful environment for the learner. The following case study illustrates such an occasion and finally, following reflection and consultation, shows that a mainstream placement for this particular pupil is not enabling him to feel confident and included.

Case study 1

Pupil A attends a special school for learners with SEBD. Substantial progress has been made and it is considered by all agencies involved, including social services, LEA officers, teachers and carers that pupil A should be able to attend and maintain a mainstream placement. Pupil A is included in the discussions but is not quite so confident of success as the adults. A mainstream placement is arranged as quickly as possible, after consultation with all involved and visits to the school for pupil A are arranged. Everyone is very positive and encouraging and the placement of full inclusion commences. Very quickly pupil A starts to disrupt lessons he is not enjoying and although individual support is available for him within classes, relationships with the new peers encourage his inappropriate behaviour. Additional support and discussions about how pupil A feels he is managing are quickly put in place, but despite great efforts, the school feel they cannot disrupt the rest of the class for this pupil. Pupil A is withdrawn from the school and following a few days of reflection and time to talk, he returns to the special school and once more becomes a model pupil.

HLTA
1.2
1.5
3.3.2

Mistakes regarding pupil A's ability to build and maintain peer relationships and manage to learn in a larger educational environment were made. The behaviour pupil A demonstrated clearly illustrated to the adults around him that he was struggling to manage on a number of fronts. Efforts to support these aspects were not enough at that particular time and it was clear that his self-belief was not yet strong enough to defend him against all the difficulties he encountered. This experience was not responded to in a negative way, but used to continue developing pupil A's self-belief and to design programmes to continue to encourage social and educational skills. Learners with complex needs, including physical disabilities, can also display behaviour that is just unreasonable or puzzling. It might not always be very negative destructive behaviour, but nevertheless appears to the educator to be totally inappropriate and unnecessary, but as with all other exhibited behaviour: 'Puzzling behaviour seems meaningless. Try interpreting it rather than setting out to eliminate it. It is probably serving a purpose' (Orr, 2003: 48). Thus, it is vital that learning and behaviour are planned and thought about together and not as separate units, brought together only as a reactive response to negative behaviour.

Behaviour that challenges educators

When first considering this problem, an educator might think of those relatively still rare occasions when a learner throws a chair or turns tables over or hits the teacher. However, as research has revealed, the behaviours that cause educators most concern are:

- answering back;
- using offensive language;
- continuous talking;
- constant interruptions;
- refusal to start work independently;
- preventing others from working.

This research was completed for a DfEE survey (1989) and it found that both primary and secondary educators agreed on this list of particularly irritating behaviours shown above. In fact, 70 per cent cited answering back and the use of offensive language as the worst problems. These behaviours can occur very frequently and cause continuous disruption to the learning context. If this is achieved, then further behaviours can occur involving other learners who experience disrupted lessons and raised levels of anxiety, and a bigger problem can begin to emerge. At the same time these behaviours can engender in the educator feelings of failure, stress, anger and great anxiety. It is clear from this illustration that if such a situation arises then both learners and adults will begin to feel the learning environment is insecure and unsafe, and the teaching–learning process will be interrupted.

> Discuss how you would try to solve such a difficult development. Use the questions below to help you think carefully about all the issues involved:
>
> ■ Would you tackle these problems by dealing with the behaviours of a few of the learners or not?
> ■ Can you see any links between learning and behaviour?
> ■ Who would need to be involved in supporting the changes needed?
> ■ Would you need to consider training or extra support/monitoring for the educator? If so, why?

Hopefully this exercise will have enabled you to see clearly the interwoven nature of learning and behaviour and why it can make matters far worse if attempts are made to solve behaviour difficulties without considering the learning environment. To become independent learners, young people have to know and understand what behaviours they need to master to be efficient learners. If this is not demonstrated to them in their educational settings, the path to life-long learning immediately, it is feared, becomes far more difficult and uninviting.

How can educators encourage effective behaviour for learning?

How a school, as a whole establishment, approaches behaviour for learning is vital, taking into consideration the 'triangle of influence' as promoted by Powell and Tod (forthcoming) and Brofenbrenner (1979). Educators 'need to construct learning environments in which school is thought of as a place where learning, understanding, improvement, and personal and social developments are valued and in which social comparison of a student's ability is de-emphasised' (Kaplan *et al.*, 2002). To enable this to happen, school educators first of all need to have a productive, consistent and supportive relationship with their learners. Within this type of environment self-motivation will be encouraged and learners will develop independent learning skills and adopt positive behaviours from role models and through clear guidelines produced by the school. It is clear from this that as Cooper *et al.* (2000) say, the way a school community responds to a learner's difficulties is imperative for that learner's future and should never be under-estimated. Crisp and Soan (2003: 155) reinforce this when writing: 'Many problematic situations can be solved, or at least improved, when school educators, parents and learner work together to alleviate the barrier(s) to learning.'

When recently discussing the development of learning behaviours with post-graduate teacher training students, the one factor they felt they needed in the classroom was the respect of the young people. Strategies such as involving learners in their own setting of learning objectives are not new, but do allow an

HLTA
1.2
1.3
1.4
1.5
2.9
3.3.2

ethos of mutual respect to be established between educator and learner and can 'contribute to improved confidence and self-image' (DfES, 2001: 3:14). The Qualified Teacher Status Standards also state that teachers must demonstrate that: 'They know a range of strategies to promote good behaviour' (TTA, 2002a, Chapter 2, Section 7). Educators also need to value learners' individual achievements and to develop an environment that does not encourage competitive cultures within the classroom. By taking into consideration such factors, educators are not only considering the learning environment but are also developing the relationship between themselves and the learners. This is vital if appropriate learning behaviours, motivation and confidence are to be promoted in a manner that actually reduces the challenging behaviour of a school's learners (Thacker *et al.*, 2002).

> Reconsider a previous situation in which you had to deal with a learner's difficult behaviour. Were you able to use the school systems to support you and did you investigate the learning environment as well as the behaviour?

Behavioural theories

Can theories help to explain learning behaviour in a school context?

This is an important question to ask and to answer. This section of the chapter will introduce four of the main behavioural theories that are used in English schools. Their importance and actual impact on learners and whole-school establishments will be examined. Many practitioners feel it is unnecessary to understand and know about behaviour theories, saying that experience and common sense provide far more reliable day-to-day strategies for dealing with difficult or challenging behaviour. Indeed, it must be acknowledged that in practice interventions for learners with behaviour problems are usually chosen using this approach and not on any evaluated effectiveness (Olsen and Cooper, 2001). Those that respond in this way, though, frequently do not understand the reasons why and for what purpose they have acted in a certain way. Without this, educators' methods of supporting behaviour for learning may become inconsistent and unfair. This final statement alone does not match what the *Handbook of Guidance on QTS Standards and ITT Requirements* (TTA, 2002b) suggests assessors judging trainee teachers should look for as appropriate practice: 'Can the trainee identify, with the pupils, clear classroom rules and routines and apply them fairly and consistently? (ibid., Chapter 3, Section 3, Sub-section 9). Thus, it is imperative that educators do understand why they select certain methods to help develop behaviours for learning.

The four behavioural theories to be examined in this section are:

- the behaviourist theory
- the psychodynamic theory
- the cognitive-behaviourist theory
- the eco-systemic theory.

Discussion

Honestly examine how you choose interventions to help learners with behaviour difficulties. Do you use any theoretical understanding to make your decisions, or do you just use school systems and personal experience?

Behaviourist theory

Behavioural approaches are undoubtedly the ones that presently underpin class-room management strategy and most discipline policies such as 'assertive discipline'. Wheldall, Watson and Skinner are all behaviour theorists (cited in Olsen and Cooper, 2001) who believe the most effective way to help learners with behaviour problems is by teaching them new behaviours through the use of rewards and sanctions. Encompassed in the philosophy of this theoretical approach is the reasoning that the most powerful means of shaping behaviour is that of rewards and sanctions. Thus, if a school's behaviour policy adopted this theoretical stance, a learner would be rewarded for appropriate behaviour and sanctioned for any inappropriate behaviour. Decisions about what rewards and sanctions are implemented are most consistently reached through observations, documentation and analysis of the specific behaviour in question. It is considered that in this way rewards will shape and reinforce desired behaviour, while at the same time making the negative behaviours that receive sanctions less attractive.

Case study 2

A Year 2 pupil, X, is unable to participate in a whole outside playtime without hitting and hurting his peers. Pupil X's teacher, TA and SENCO all observe playtime behaviour over a two-week period looking for clues for the change in X's behaviour. Factual information is correlated regarding X's offences and analysed as carefully as possible looking at factors such as friendship groups, teachers on playground duty and next lessons. X's parents are also consulted and agree to support the school by offering rewards at home if the hitting stops at school. A reward programme is designed for X, giving extra choosing time if hitting does not occur during three playtimes. If X does hit another child, an outside play session has to be missed. X enjoys the extra choosing time at school and the additional rewards and praise from parents at home and dislikes missing playtimes. Within a matter of weeks the incidents of hitting decrease and eventually disappear. In this instance the behaviourist approach is successful.

Case study 3

> Pupil Y is also a Year 2 student and displays very similar behaviour to that of pupil X. The school carries out the same assessment process as they did with Pupil X. It was decided to implement a replica of X's rewards and sanctions programme including the parental support. However, after a period of two weeks no improvement in Y's behaviour had been noticed and in fact the majority of the playtimes had been spent inside on his own with an adult supervisor. Y did not respond to or desire extra choosing time and did not seem to wish to please his parents. After another two weeks the programme was stopped as it was only managing to isolate Y further from his peers. Other rewards and sanctions were tried by the school within it's behavioural approach, but Y did not show any consistent positive behaviour change. Another approach needed to be applied to meet Y's needs. In this instance the behavioural approach was not successful. (This case will be revisited later in this section.)

Undoubtedly educators consider the behaviourist approach to be the most straightforward and effective method for the majority of learners. However, it does not take into consideration the percentage of learners who do not value rewards and sanctions. It is for this group that educators frequently want quick fix strategies, not acknowledging that without understanding why a particular intervention is implemented will quite likely make it ineffectual and inappropriate. Vygotsky, Piaget and Bruner also felt that this 'behaviourist' approach was too restrictive and needed to take into consideration the social situation in which the behaviour occurred. As mentioned at the beginning of this chapter, they also felt that behaviour is very dependent on others and on the specific context in which it happens as well as on the self (Olsen and Cooper, 2001).

Psychodynamic theory

The term 'psychodynamic' is used when the study of interacting motives and emotions is discussed. This approach stresses the evolutionary and biological foundations of human behaviour and is closely linked with psychology, psychiatry and socio-biology. The 'Attachment Theory', developed by John Bowlby, is based on psychodynamic theory and it is this that is often implemented in a school that works in a 'psychodynamic' way. Holmes (1995) describes attachment theory as:

> a theory about relationships, based on the idea that human beings evolved in kinship groups and that in the original 'environment of evolutionary adaptedness' (Bowlby 1969) survival was increased by the maintenance of secure bonds between their members, primarily, but by no means exclusively, between parents and children.
>
> (Holmes, 1995: 178–9)

Therefore, according to the psychodynamic theory approach, how learners feel about themselves can determine how they behave. As they seek to make sense of the world, learners' past experiences, as well as their current ones, will shape the way they feel. 'Attachment disorder behaviours' occur when a child has been unable, for any of many reasons, to securely attach to one or a small group of consistent carers, at a young age. O'Connor *et al.* (cited in Bennathan and Boxall, 2001: 124) support this definition following studies of the English and Romanian Adoptees (ERA) project: 'Considered together, available findings on attachment disorder behaviours suggest that the critical causal factor may be the lack of a consistent and responsive caregiver (or small number of caregivers), or the opportunity of the child to form selective attachments.'

A learner who may benefit from this approach may not respond positively to the behaviourist approach. Returning to Pupil Y described in Case Study 3, an example of a psychodynamic approach can be illustrated.

Case study 4

Further observations of Pupil Y by the SENCO took place and a number of additional factors for consideration became apparent. Pupil Y found it extremely difficult to accept praise and if a teacher verbally rewarded him for good work he would tear this work up. To try and prevent this, the teacher had been quickly taking the work away from Pupil Y and sticking it in a scrap book so that his parents could be shown his good work. Pupil Y tried to do everything to prevent this from happening. The fighting in the playground continued and when asked why he thought he had such difficult playtimes, he explained that he was a bad boy. Following further discussions with Pupil Y's parents, it was also clear that he was behaving in the same way at home, especially towards his well-behaved younger sister. His father 'disciplined' him when incidents occurred either at home or at school. The SENCO, with the support of the class team, started to work on a one-to-one basis with Pupil Y. The SENCO started talking to Y about how his behaviour was sometimes not very nice, but that HE was good. Pupil Y did not believe this and once again said he was a bad boy. A visual image of his growing goodness was then set up. After every playtime the SENCO (whatever else was happening stopped!) met Pupil Y and if he had played well, a small coloured line would be added to a growing spiral on a large piece of paper on the SENCO's wall (Figure 7.2). Within a few days Pupil Y trusted the SENCO to turn up at the end of playtimes and then after a couple of weeks he looked at the spiral on the paper, smiled and said, 'Look how good I am growing.'

Pupil Y did not manage to get a line every playtime to begin with, especially when the trust was being built, and on these occasions the bad behaviour (not Pupil Y) was discussed and more positive input was put in place for the next time. Similar interventions were put in place in the classroom. Instead of lots of verbal praise for good work, a simple tick or smiley face was put on the work without further comment. In this way the teacher was able to build up Pupil Y's self-esteem in a slow, steady and consistent manner. Pupil Y's educators also made concerted efforts to tell the parents about all the good work and behaviour Y had achieved. Other than this, the external influences for Pupil Y were beyond the control of the school context (see Figure 7.1), but by using the psychodynamic approach, the educators tried to understand the origins of the behaviour from Y's perspective. They then sought ways of minimising the barriers to learning for Y and put in place interventions that would hopefully encourage behaviours for learning. The educators tackled Y's problems using a whole-school approach and would also have worked collaboratively with other agencies and professionals if they were involved with the learner's family.

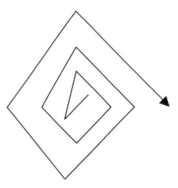

Figure 7.2 Pupil Y's spiral of good behaviour

A similar approach may be required for a learner who avoids independent work or constantly distracts others. The learner may have developed this behaviour because he feels he is going to fail at the task, however hard he tries, because he is a failure. Why, therefore, should he even try, just to receive negative comments from the teacher and hence have it reinforced that he is a failure? As before, the educators cannot know all the reasons why the learner has these feelings, but they can try to remove the barriers and encourage new, positive behaviours for learning.

Cognitive–behaviourist theory

Cognitive theorists such as Seligman (1990) believe it is possible to alter a learner's behaviour by teaching him or her to perceive or think about things in a different way. They think that a learner with emotional and behavioural difficulties needs encouragement to actually change his or her perceptions, by developing the ability to think about situations in different ways.

This cognitive approach necessarily requires the learner, with the assistance of the educator, to engage in a process of analysis so that he or she can think and look at situations in different ways.

Case study 5

> Pupil B was never chosen to be a team football captain at playtimes by his peers. He felt that this was because all the other children disliked him and so he ended up not playing at all. Pupil B was told and shown that the majority of the other children playing football were never chosen by their peers to be captain either. Pupil B learned that just because he was not chosen to be captain did not mean the other children disliked him. As a result of this additional knowledge and understanding pupil B was taught to manage his feelings. He could still really want to be captain, but it did not mean his peers disliked him and therefore was not able to be part of the whole team game.

Eco-systemic theory

The eco-systemic approach differs from the three previous theories already discussed. Interventions implemented using this approach do not teach new skills to a learner by an educator. The eco-systemic theory agrees with the ideas of the behaviourists, but is also concerned with the effect the environment has on the learner. Eco-systemic theorists, such as Olsen and Cooper (2001) support the view that if a learner displays social, emotional and behavioural difficulties, he or she does so as a direct response to the environment. They think that 'behaviours do not occur in isolation, but as a result of the relationship the learner has with self, with others and with the curriculum' (Crisp and Soan, 2003: 161). Therefore, it is through the examination of the school's policies, procedures and methods of communication that an eco-systemic theorist would seek to make suitable changes to the environment to enable more positive relationships and successful learning to be developed. An example of such an intervention would be perhaps the setting up of a nurture group or of weekly circle time. A similar assessment of a situation may result in outside agency involvement being requested. It may also mean looking at the level of work a learner is given in a classroom, to ensure that the educational challenges are set at the appropriate level to support a learner to reach their potential without undue anxiety.

- Using your understanding of the behavioural theories discussed above, discuss how you might use this knowledge to enhance your classroom practice.
- Do the policies in your workplace setting promote behaviour for learning and do they reflect actual practice?

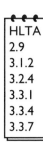

HLTA
2.9
3.1.2
3.2.4
3.3.1
3.3.4
3.3.7

Gender issues

It is considered that gender is an issue when discussing learning behaviours, but it is an area that seems to have attracted only limited study. Whitelaw *et al.*

(2000: 97) suggest that literature does inform educators that gender has a 'substantial effect on the ways in which children negotiate their personal positions in the relationship between academic achievement, school cultures and home/peer culture'. Abraham (1995) also suggests that girls are more passive when it comes to accepting school rules and systems, but Whitelaw *et al.* (2000: 98) think that:

> some girls are far from being passive in their compliance. They may be actively deploying a range of strategies and a degree of flexibility in their approaches and responses to widely different expectations and experiences. Such flexibility may be allowing them to achieve in both academic and social arenas, with peers and adults, skilfully negotiating the inconsistencies of the spheres which they inhabit.

Discuss the issues mentioned above. How do you see girls' behaviour in the classroom? Are their behaviours always conducive to effective learning and do girls incorporate strategies that enable them to be respected by their peers as well as maintain positive relationships with their educators?

Crozier and Anstiss (1995: 44) say that evidence they collected from a study showed that the ways in which pupils were talked about by their educators 'seemed to be determined by their sex and girls were additionally disadvantaged by a concern with their sexuality in teachers' discussions about them'. They found that plans to support problem behaviours in boys were carefully implemented, while proposals to support girls' behaviour were often dealt with on a 'wait-and-see basis'. They suggest that because girls' behaviour generally presents less of a problem in school, even though they are just as prone to problems and are just as needy, the predominant focus about behaviour remains targeted on boys. As a result, girls' needs are often neglected until severe action is required. A report by Susannah Kirkman (TES, 2003) says: 'New research shows a three-fold increase in serious psychological distress among 15 year old girls since 1987, mainly triggered by rising educational expectations.' Crozier and Anstiss (1995: 45) say that educators need to make sure girls' needs are not marginalised and that, 'For schools to redress the balance there needs to be a shift of focus from behaviour and control issues to concern with learning and the variety of factors and events that interfere with it.' A similar view was expressed in an article entitled 'Off the rails' in the *Guardian Education* (Berliner, 2003: 4) about a mother and her two daughters:

> She [the mother] needed it [support] while the girls were at primary school, when things were going wrong, and the response was to control and contain rather than to refer them for specialist appraisal and help. Their problems weren't extreme then but they are now.

Discussion

Take another look at how social, emotional and behavioural difficulties are supported in your workplace setting. Is there a difference, in practice, between how boys and girls are helped or not? Do colleagues feel there is a difference and, if so, why?

ADHD/ADD

Attention Deficit Hyperactivity Disorder (ADHD) and Attention Deficit Disorder (ADD) is also frequently debated within the subject of SEBD. Due to this continuing debate about what causes ADHD, or indeed, if ADHD actually exists, a learner's needs can be lost or sidelined. Cooper *et al.*, (1998) feels that learners with ADHD or ADD, therefore, are just as at risk as learners from ethnic minorities and females, because their behaviours may just be seen as wilful misconduct. Schools, Cooper suggests, need to take the phenomenon of ADHD/ADD seriously and work with medical colleagues so that a combined medical-educational approach to ADHD/ADD can be achieved. In this way the additional educational needs of the learner can be planned and implemented with full awareness of any medical diagnosis or intervention. The educator needs to understand and differentiate for the needs of a learner with ADHD by, for example, planning that he or she should work in a pair rather than in a small group for certain learning activities, to aid his or her ability to concentrate and behave appropriately without too much pressure. The whole school may, following discussions with medical colleagues, change the time of playtimes so that learners such as those with ADHD can demonstrate better on-task behaviour and self-controlling behaviour (Cooper *et al.*, 1998). Thus again by using the 'triangle of influence' (Figure 7.1) learners can have their learning behaviours supported and developed effectively by educators in schools.

Key issues

With the awareness gained from this chapter about the importance of relationships, responsibilities and relevance and an understanding of different behavioural theories, the reader will be able to encourage positive educational experiences with and for all learners, therefore fostering a desire to continue learning throughout life.

It is anticipated that you now:

■ have an understanding of the theoretical perspectives discussed in this chapter and their importance for the promotion of behaviour for learning;

■ understand that educators need to 'know' and have constructive relationships with learners;

■ understand that relationships with learners need to be built on mutual trust and respect;

- know that educators need to encourage and support learners with SEBD;
- know that behaviours for learning is a shared responsibility and one that indeed finally rests with the individual learner. However, the learner is immensely influenced by the treatment and attitudes he receives from the educators;
- recognise the significance of the relevance of the curriculum and learning experiences for learners, especially their appropriateness to the learner's ability and aptitude;
- understand that developing behaviours for learning is a whole-school responsibility and that they should be encouraged and supported in a consistent and positive manner.

Professional Standards for Higher Level Teaching Assistants (HLTA)

If you can demonstrate your understanding and professional use of the key issues illustrated within this chapter, it is hoped that you will be able to fulfil the following HLTA Standards:

1.1	1.2	1.3	1.4	1.5	1.6	2.9
3.1.2	3.2.4	3.3.1	3.3.2	3.3.4	3.3.7	

Useful documents

DfES (2001) *Special Educational Needs Code of Practice*, London: HMSO.

DfEE/QCA (1999) *The National Curriculum for England*, London: HMSO.

HMSO (2003) *Every Child Matters*, Norwich: The Stationery Office.

TTA (1999) *National Special Educational Needs Specialist Standard*, London: TTA.

TTA (2002a) *QTS Standards*, London: TTA.

TTA (2002b) *Handbook of Guidance on QTS Standards and Requirements*, London: TTA.

Websites

DfES 'Improving Behaviour in Schools' http://www.dfes.gov.uk/ibis/index.cfm

http://education.cant.ac.uk/xplanatory

Behaviour4Learning, www.behaviour4learning.ac.uk. A web-based professional resource network for TTT tutors

References

Abraham, J. (1995) *Divide and School: gender and class dynamics in comprehensive education*, London: Falmer Press.

Barrow, G., Bradshaw, E. and Newton, T. (2001) *Improving Behaviour and Raising Self-Esteem in the Classroom: A Practical Guide to Using Transactional Analysis*, London: David Fulton.

Bennathan, M. and Boxall, M. (2001) *Intervention in Primary Schools: Nurture Groups*, 2nd edn, London: David Fulton.

Berliner, W. (2003) 'Off the rails', *Guardian Education*, 25 Feb, pp. 2–4.

Bowlby, J. (1969) *Attachment and Loss*, vol. 1. *Separation*, London: Hogarth Press.

Brofenbrenner, E. (1979) *The Ecology of Human Development: Experiments by Nature and Design*, Cambridge: MA: Harvard University Press.

Cooper, P., Drummond, M.J., Hart, S., Lovey, J. and Mclaughlin, C. (2000) *Positive Alternatives to Exclusion*, London: Routledge Falmer.

Crisp, J. and Soan, S. (2003) 'Managing behaviour for learning', in Alfrey, C. (ed.), *Understanding Children's Learning: A Text for Teaching Assistants*, London: David Fulton, pp. 152–65.

Crozier, J. and Anstiss, J. (1995) 'Out of the spotlight: girls' experience of disruption', in Lloyd-Smith, M. and Davies, J.D. (eds), *On the Margins: The Educational Experience of Problem Pupils*, Stafford: Trentham Books Ltd.

DfEE/QCA (1999) *The National Curriculum for England*, London: HMSO.

Emler, N. (2000) *Self-Esteem: The Costs and Causes of Low Self-Esteem*, York: The Rowntree Foundation.

Holmes, J. (1995) *John Bowlby and Attachment Theory*, London: Routledge.

Kaplan, A., Gheen, M. and Midgley, C. (2002) 'Classroom goal structure and student disruptive behaviour', *British Journal of Educational Psychology*, vol. 72, pp. 191–211.

Kirkman, S. (2003) 'An ABC of emotions', *Times Educational Supplement*, 4 April, p. 32.

Laslett, R., Cooper, P., Maras, P., Rimmer, A. and Law, B. (1998) *Changing Perceptions: Emotional and Behavioural Difficulties since 1945*, East Sutton: AWCEBD.

Long, R. (2003) Paper presented at a NASEN conference held at Canterbury Christ Church University College.

Olsen, J. and Cooper, P. (2001) *Dealing with Disruption in the Classroom*, London: Kogan Page.

Orr, R. (2003) *My Right to Play: A Child with Complex Need*, Maidenhead: Open University Press.

Powell, S. and Tod, J. (forthcoming) 'EPPI Systematic Literature Review: Behaviour Management'.

Seligman, M. (1990) *Learned Optimism*, New York: Pocket Books.

Thacker, J., Strudwick, D. and Babbedge, E. (2002) *Educating Children with Emotional and Behavioural Difficulties: Inclusive Practice in Mainstream School*, London: Routledge Falmer.

Whitelaw, S., Milosevic, L. and Daniels, S. (2000) 'Gender, behaviour and achievement: a preliminary study of pupil perception and attitudes', *Gender and Education*, vol. 12, no.1, pp. 87–113.

Simon Ellis

Introduction

During their school career children experience a number of transition or transfer points. Fabian and Dunlop (2002: 3) define transition as: 'the process of change that is experienced when children (and their families) move from one setting to another'. All transition points mark a progression, a 'moving on' not just in education but through life and it is entirely appropriate that within the new setting there are differences and new experiences and challenges. The challenge for educators is to manage the process of change for the child in such a way that provides support at both a pastoral, social and emotional level and at the level of continuity of the curriculum and progression in learning. At all transition points extra consideration needs to be given to children identified as having additional educational needs as they are likely to require higher levels of planning and support.

Supporting transitions for pupils with Additional Educational Needs (AEN)

All children are likely to bring with them anxieties about how they will cope in a new setting, whether this is the young child concerned at being away from their parent for so long or the Year 7 pupil worrying about getting on the right bus home. Some of these anxieties can be dispelled by proper, accurate information, others require the implementation of supportive structures and processes that span both the leaving of the previous setting and induction into the new one. For the child with AEN the general worries are likely to be compounded by others which might, depending on the type of need, include concerns over the type of support they will receive, access to specialist equipment, not being able to do the work, accessibility of buildings and rooms as well as social concerns about how their need, disability or impairment will be perceived and accepted by other children. In order to support the child with additional educational needs, the current school and the receiving school need to liaise closely, not only to ensure that the support in place is continued, replaced with a suitable alternative, phased out or removed in a planned way but also to support the child pastorally prior to, during and following the transition.

A timely transfer of information that involves collaboration by the present and the receiving school or setting, the parents, the child and any other professionals involved such as LEA support services and external agencies, is likely to lead to a more successful transition. Information transferred should focus on what the child can do, not just on areas of weakness. The information should include detail on strategies and approaches used and the outcomes. In terms of the provisions a school needs to make, it is important to bear in mind that some children with AEN will also have a disability under the Special Educational Needs Act 2001.

The transition points

The transition from home to pre-school setting

As children make the transition from home to a pre-school setting they are entering the Foundation Stage. The Foundation Stage, introduced from September 2000, is a stage of education for children aged from three to the end of the reception year. It is distinct from Key Stage 1 and is an important stage in its own right and in preparing children for later schooling. The emphasis of the Foundation Stage is on making the transition from home to infant school a positive induction into compulsory education.

Macintyre and McVitty (2003: 1) make the point:

> Attending a playgroup or nursery for the first time is an important milestone in the lives of many children and their parents. It may be the first time that parents have entrusted their children to 'strangers' and the first time that these children have had to cope without their parents at their side. Some will anticipate the new venture confidently while others will need more reassurance that good things lie ahead.

For parents of children with AEN, entrusting their child to someone else can assume an even greater significance as there may be concerns over how additional support will be provided and whether this will be sufficient. Sometimes service and agency support that has previously been provided in the home or clinic setting might now be provided in the early years setting. This may be a source of anxiety for the parent as he or she may feel less in control over the interventions that are taking place. Educators and agencies need to be aware of these potential anxieties.

Many children will attend some form of pre-school or nursery soon after their third birthday and some will attend a number of different settings during the Foundation Stage either part-time or full-time. The QCA/DfEE document *Curriculum Guidance for the Foundation Stage* (QCA/DfEE, 2000) gives an example of good practice for transition from home to a nursery. The features identified include:

■ Children start to visit with their parents as babies or toddlers.

■ Parents are encouraged to share their knowledge and views of their child's development and raise any concerns.

■ Displays and resources reflect children's home and community experience.

■ The early years practitioner visits the family and child at home to get to know them.

■ Information about the nursery and how it works with children is given to families in a practical, accessible format.

■ The parent is encouraged to stay with the child as part of the process of transition between home and the nursery.

■ The key practitioner, the child and the parent talk regularly to check how they are all adjusting to the arrangements for settling in, learning and teaching.

■ The family's or child's particular interest and experiences are used in planning work with the child.

(QCA/DfEE, 2000: 12)

The importance of this first transition as the child moves from life at home to the first stage of his/her journey through the education system should not be underestimated. It is vital to remember the importance of emotional security as a necessary element before a child can access the learning opportunities that exist within the setting.

The transition from the pre-school setting to school

HLTA
2.2

During the Foundation Stage there will be a point of transfer for children when they move from a pre-school setting to a school. In supporting the transition to the curriculum of the reception class of infant school it is important that the Foundation Stage curriculum in the pre-school setting is delivered in the knowledge that its contribution represents only a part of the stage and that it will be continued by the receiving school. The stepping stones within the Foundation Stage are not age-related goals and rates of progress will of course vary between children (QCA/DfEE, 2000). It is likely that most 3-year-old children in the Fundation Stage will be better described by the earlier stepping stones, while the later stepping stones will usually reflect the attainment of 5-year-old children. Children will therefore be at different points in terms of progression through the stepping stones and accurate records are essential in ensuring that the teacher of the receiving class can plan for appropriate progression in learning.

At the transition to primary school, it is not just the issue of ensuring curricular continuity and progression in learning that needs consideration, the primary school potentially represents a source of anxiety for the child because of differences in organisational structure.

Table 8.1 identifies some of the differences the child might encounter when starting primary school, together with some possible strategies to address these.

Table 8.1   Differences between Foundation Stage and primary school

Difference	What might you do?
Other children up to the age of 11 are present in the school	■ Year 6 helpers in class ■ Older pupils act as buddies for younger pupils ■ Explore with older pupils in circle time their responsibilities towards the new entrants
Midday supervisors	■ Photos of MDS in the Reception class ■ MDS visit reception class ■ Ensure MDS are aware of new pupils with particular needs
Other teachers who do not work with the child but whom they encounter	■ Photos of staff ■ Make sure the children know who is on break duty ■ Rehearse skills for talking to an adult in school who you don't know ■ Ensure other teachers are aware of new pupils with particular needs

■ Can you add any more differences?
■ Can you add any more strategies?

What might be the child's anxieties/feelings in relation to each difference?

The way the child and parents are introduced to the school setting is important in supporting the transfer from pre-school to school. The following approaches are likely to be helpful:

- The child visits the school either with the early years practitioner from the pre-school setting or with their parents.
- Induction sessions for the child where he or she spends a period of time in the classroom.
- Parents are encouraged to share their knowledge and views of their child's development and raise any concerns.
- Home visits and visits to the pre-school setting by the teacher, TAs, etc.
- The separation of the child and parent is not rushed. Parents are encouraged to come into cloakroom areas and into the classroom when their child first starts school.
- Thought is given to how new entrants are gradually introduced to occasions in school when they will encounter larger groups of children, e.g. whole-school assemblies and the dining hall.
- Where the child has additional educational needs that require specific support, this information is transferred well in advance and, where necessary, external agency advice, additional training for staff and specialist equipment are sought before the child starts.

Much of the effort of the receiving school will be devoted towards developing positive links with parents. Schools will need to consider how they communicate with parents so that the right tone is set for a positive partnership. Consideration of practicalities such as the timing and length of meetings, seating arrangements, availability of refreshments and the level of formality of the event will determine the success of this process.

The transition from Foundation Stage to Key Stage 1

The introduction of the Foundation Stage means that there is a transition point for pupils as they move from this Stage to Key Stage 1. As children move into Year 1 they are likely to experience a more explicit structure to teaching and learning, with higher expectations in relation to aspects such as levels of independence, time spent on a single activity, sustained listening and concentration and time spent in their seat. For many children this is a natural progression that they will adapt to very well but for some, including many with AEN, this change will prove very difficult, particularly where they do not have the necessary underlying skills to reach these expectations. The results can be the emergence of behavioural difficulties or a range of other problems such as withdrawal, lack of motivation, lack of confidence, increasing anxiety and school refusal. Careful consideration will therefore need to be given to the Foundation Stage to Key Stage 1 transition to ensure that there is sufficient pre-planning and support.

The Foundation Stage Profile, completed before the child moves into Year 1, should provide information that supports the transition. In curriculum planning it is important that account is taken of the child's progress on the stepping stones that lead towards the Early Learning Goals. Some pupils in Year 1 will require teaching approaches and a curriculum that support them in working towards the achievement of the Early Learning Goals rather than embarking on Key Stage 1 of the National Curriculum.

Case study 1

In the final term of the academic year the Reception class joins the Year 1 class for story time on a weekly basis. Sometimes this takes place in the Reception classroom, on other occasions it takes place in the Year 1 classroom.

On days in the summer term when the majority of Year 6 pupils are visiting their new secondary schools for 'taster days', all children spend some time in their new classes. This includes the Reception-aged children who get the opportunity to spend two mornings in the Year 1 classroom with their new teacher. As well as allowing the children to experience a range of activities in the Year 1 classroom, the teacher shows the pupils where they will hang their coats and the toilets that they will use and the door that they will need to leave by at the end of the day.

In the final term the Reception teacher introduces elements of the literacy and numeracy strategy. The teacher includes 10–15 minutes of whole-class literacy teaching which may involve sharing a text, shared writing or phonic work. At another point in the day the children engage in a teacher- or TA-led literacy task. For numeracy the teacher includes 10–15 minutes whole-class numeracy teaching which may involve counting, number rhymes, or recognition of numbers. At another point in the day the children engage in a teacher- or TA-led numeracy task. Later in the day the teacher or TA will talk to the children about what they learned when engaged in the literacy and numeracy tasks.

The Reception teacher passes the Early Years Profile to the Year 1 teacher before the end of the summer term. The Year 1 teacher uses this to inform planning for September.

At circle time pupils are given the opportunity to talk about what they are looking forward to about moving to Year 1 and anything that worries them. The Reception class teacher and TA look for opportunities to initiate conversations about transition with children they perceive to be anxious about the move to Year 1. Any anxieties are listened to. The teacher or TA then focuses on solutions. Sometimes this can be in the form of reassurance, other times it requires specific additional actions like arranging for opportunities for the child to visit the receiving class on errands. The child is always reassured that after the transition they can still go to their previous teacher or TA. In certain cases this is set up as part of a specific plan to support the transition, but for the majority it is an offer that is informally made.

Within Case Study 1 identify:

- those actions that are intended to ensure continuity of the curriculum and teaching and progression in learning;
- those actions that are intended to support the personal, social and emotional needs of the child.

Are there other, additional practices that could be adopted by the school to support children in the transition?

The transition from Key Stage 1 to Key Stage 2

This transition is likely to be less of an issue in primary schools where the child remains in the same school even though they are moving up a Key Stage. Nevertheless it is important not to under-estimate that 'becoming a junior' will still be a daunting prospect in some children's minds even if they are not changing school.

If the change is within the same school, then many of the points raised in the section previously considering Foundation Stage to Key Stage 1 will, with certain adaptations, apply.

The KS1 to KS2 transition takes on greater significance where the transition is from an infant to a junior school when the child will be leaving familiar surroundings, familiar staff and on some occasions leaving friendship groups if the infant school feeds several junior schools. Because junior schools do not have infants on site, sometimes the ethos can feel very different to the child.

Where the change is to a separate junior school, useful steps to support the child might include:

- Visits to the receiving school.
- Visits from the teacher(s) from the receiving school.
- Knowing the names of the class teacher and TAs who work in the class.
- Knowing other children who are transferring to the same school.
- Identification of a 'buddy' at the receiving school.
- 'Friendship Stops' in the playground at the receiving school. An area, such as a bench, where a child can go if they have no one to play with. Older children are assigned to visit the area and help the child to find someone to play with.
- Circle time sessions exploring what children are looking forward to or worrying about.
- Practice through role play, puppets and stories of skills such as asking for help and introducing yourself to someone you don't know.
- Planning farewell activities that celebrate past school experiences.

Discussion

Can you identify any other measures that either the infant school or the receiving junior school could adopt to support the transition?

The transition from KS2 to KS3

For many children this transition will represent their first change of school since transferring from their pre-school setting to primary school. It not only represents a major change for the child in the nature of their educational environment, it also coincides with a major change in physical, mental and emotional terms as they move into adolescence.

Casey (2002), citing the earlier work of Maines and Robinson (1988) highlights the following findings about secondary transfer:

- Approximately 30 per cent of pupils transferring from primary to secondary schools show a drop in academic performance.
- Failure to adjust adequately brought about low motivation in some pupils – this proved to be a permanent feature of their subsequent response to schooling.
- Pupils with a poor self-concept found the transition harder.
- Poor readers have greater problems adjusting.
- Projects started in the old school and continued in the new one are useful in helping pupils to make a successful transfer.
- Pupils settle in more easily if they are in a class with their friends.
- Pupils found assembly at the beginning of the first day very threatening.
- Boys are more at risk than girls.
- An informative video about the new school which is shown to leavers prior to transfer is generally found to be well received and perceived as useful by pupils.
- The most effective 'pupil tours' are those with limited numbers of pupils and which maximise pupil–teacher interaction and minimise pupil distraction. The most successful visits are those that pair pupils with peers of approximately the same age.
- Familiarising pupils with minor differences (e.g. presentation, layout, methods) can be reassuring.

(Casey, 2002: 93)

McSherry (2001) identifies the following differences between the primary school and the secondary school for the child to adjust to (see Table 8.2).

Table 8.2 Differences between the primary school and the secondary school

Primary school	Secondary school
Head teacher is usually seen by the pupils each day	Many pupils report not seeing the head teacher from one week to the next
Head teacher often knows all the pupils by name and can talk to them about their families and interests	Head teacher of a large secondary school will know a few pupils well and others hardly at all
Schools are generally smaller than secondary schools. Often Key Stages 1 and 2 are on different sites or in different schools	Schools are often large, many in excess of 1,000 pupils
Pupils have one teacher for the year who teaches the majority of subjects	Pupils may be taught by ten or more teachers in a week, not including their tutor and Head of Year
Pupils stay in the same classroom for most lessons	Pupils are expected to navigate their way around a large building at each lesson changeover
Equipment needed for most lessons is provided and kept in the room	Pupils are expected to bring their own equipment and to remember which day they need to bring it. They are also expected to carry it around with them all day
Pupils in Year 6 are the oldest and most knowledgeable pupils in the school	Pupils in Year 7 are the youngest and least knowledgeable in the school

> **Discussion**
>
> Can you add any others to this list? For each of the items on the list consider:
>
> - What might be the pupil's feelings/concerns in relation to each item?
> - How could the pupil be supported before, during and after the transition in relation to each item?

Commercially available resources to support transfer (e.g. Casey, 2002; Cossavella and Hobbs, 2002; Maines and Robinson, 1988) typically include a mixture of activities that focus not only on different terminology, routines and personal organisation requirements associated with secondary schools and familiarity with the physical layout of the school, but also on particular social skills and coping strategies.

For the child with AEN, the prospect of transition to secondary school will potentially be more daunting than for other pupils. The child is likely to have sufficient awareness of their own needs to be able to predict the difficulties they may encounter. It is therefore important that the child is given the opportunity to voice these concerns and that these are taken seriously.

Case study 2

The primary school has used a 'calm down' area and has successfully reduced the number of angry outbursts from Tony. A lot of work has been done with Tony on both recognising when he is becoming angry and on reframing the way he thinks about the triggers he has identified. Staff are also aware of the signs that Tony is becoming angry and know when to prompt him to 'remember his plan' and when it is better to 'back off' completely and to follow up later.

In preparation for secondary transfer, the school involves Tony in group work that covers many issues related to secondary transfer but also includes an element on keeping your temper. This work incorporates role play activities to rehearse language for apologising for being late or forgetting homework and other similar situations that could lead to conflict with staff. The work explores how Tony's responses can shape the course the interaction takes. Similar techniques are also used to cover pupil–pupil interactions.

A planning meeting is held in the summer term attended by Tony and his mother, the primary teacher, the primary SENCO, the secondary SENCO and the secondary form tutor. During the meeting Tony's views are sought about the progress he has made in primary school in relation to managing his anger and the kind of support he feels he will need in secondary school.

Prior to transfer the secondary school ensures that it has identified both a defined calm down area that Tony can use and a key adult that he can go to at any time. The teachers who are timetabled to teach Tony are all briefed by the secondary school SENCO about his patterns of behaviour. The school revises its 'on call' system so that all staff know who can be summoned should a problem arise. All staff know that if Tony leaves the classroom they should not intervene but should ensure that the school office is aware that he is out of class so that someone can check he has either arrived safely at his calm down area or is with his key adult.

The secondary school provisionally puts Tony on the list to be involved in an anger management group that will start in the autumn term.

Case study 3

The primary school has developed a system where when Michael shows signs of becoming angry he is taken to a calm down area by his TA. The school has become very good at recognising when Michael is getting angry. The primary school staff are worried that it will be hard for colleagues in a large secondary school to develop the same awareness. To try to help secondary staff, the school logs all incidents when Michael loses his temper.

Out of concern for Michael's secondary prospects, the primary school calls a meeting. The meeting is attended by the primary class teacher, the primary SENCO, Michael and his mother and the deputy head from the secondary school. The primary class teacher and SENCO explain that they are worried about how

Michael is going to cope when he gets to secondary school and, summarising the incident log, suggest that the triggers to Michael losing his temper are when he can't get his own way or if he becomes frustrated with the work.

The secondary Deputy Head explains that the school has high standards of behaviour and that the behaviour exhibited in primary school would not be tolerated. The Deputy describes to Michael's mother how the detention system works and how parents are called in if the pupil is at risk of exclusion. The Deputy explains that he personally has little contact with Year 7 pupils and tells Michael that he will get the chance to see his Form Tutor when the Year 6 pupils from the area come for a taster day in July.

The Deputy asks Michael if there are any particular pupils he doesn't get on with as it might be possible to ensure that he is put in a different class from them.

HLTA
3.3.3

Discussion

- Compare and contrast Case Study 2 and Case Study 3.
- Draw out elements from Case Study 2 that demonstrate that both the primary and secondary school are concerned with Tony's personal development and are prepared to look at the interventions and adaptations they can make in order to support this.
- Draw out the elements from Case Study 3 that demonstrate that both the primary and secondary school are concerned with achieving a level of behaviour that allows Michael to fit in with the expectations of secondary school.
- In both case studies, how might the child and parent feel about the prospect of transfer?

Transition from KS3 to KS4

This is a significant transition point in the child's journey towards adulthood. It also has the potential to be problematic. For many children the move into the world of adult life beyond school is not far away and they will have established a view of themselves in relation to what education has to offer them. Some will hold on firmly to the notion that obtaining qualifications will be the route to a better job and provide access to things that are important to them. Others will feel that education has little to offer and through the latter stages of Key Stages 3 and 4 become increasingly disaffected. Many of these will display their disaffection by truanting or misbehaving. Research (Parsons, 1999) shows that the rate of exclusion rises steadily through Years 7, 8 and 9 before peaking in Year 10. There is another group, however, who continue to come to school, do not cause much disruption but who gain very little. This group was termed 'the disappointed' by Barber (1994) and 'passively disaffected' by Parsons (1999). Significant numbers of children do of course exhibit these forms of disaffection long before they make the transfer to Key Stage 4 but it would seem at this point that they are confronted with the stark reality and often make what is sadly a realistic assessment of what the remainder of compulsory education has to offer them. The vulnerability of children already identified as having behavioural, emotional social difficulties is obvious at this transition point. In a surprisingly blunt and succinct pair of sentences the DfES sums up the problem: 'Too many young people truant in their last two years of compulsory education. And the behaviour of some who turn up makes it hard for teachers to teach and others to learn' (DfES, 2002b: 4). In many ways as important as the transition point itself therefore is the need to keep children motivated and engaged during Key Stage 3 so that they feel education still has something to offer and therefore can move positively into Key Stage 4.

As children approach the transition from Key Stage 3 to Key Stage 4 it is essential that they are supported in making informed decisions about their future options. This is a significant period in the child's life as the choosing of options represents the first real academic and career choice they are required to make. The choices made at 14 begin to map out longer-term opportunities such as further study and future employment. Schools can implement a number of measures to support children in making their choices. These might include:

- involving parents/carers in the options process by holding open evenings and careers conventions to provide a forum for questions and concerns;
- producing written materials to assist with discussions at home;
- arranging individual careers interviews where plans for future study, or job interests are discussed in relation to the 'options' being considered now;
- the Form Tutor taking an active role talking through any worries or complications with the child before final decisions are made;
- group talks on career-related topics as part of the school careers education and guidance programmes.

The DfES document *Careers Education and Guidance in England* (DfES, 2003) sets out a Careers Education Programme for Key Stage 3, Key Stage 4 and Post-16 to support schools in helping pupils to make informed decisions and manage transitions.

The Connexions Service Personal Advisors are another resource in the support available to a child at this stage in their school career. The Connexions Service aims to help all children and young people make decisions about their future and offers advice on routes into employment, training, or further education. It has a particular focus on supporting disadvantaged children and young people or those likely to under-achieve, including those with SEN but without statements. It is envisaged that all children and young people in the 13–19 age group will have access to a Connexions Personal Advisor. For some children and young people this will be at the level of careers advice, for others it may involve more in-depth support to help identify barriers to learning and find solutions. Much of the work will involve one-to-one support, especially at times of transition or when decisions have to be made which will affect the child's or young person's future education and training.

Transition plans for children with Statements of Special Educational Needs

For children with Statements of Special Educational Needs, the Code of Practice (DfES, 2001) requires that a Transition Plan is prepared following the Year 9 annual review. The focus of the Transition Plan is on helping the child prepare for a successful transition into adult life.

The procedures for the transition to Key Stage 4 for children with Statements of Special Educational Need are clearly defined but it is important to recognise that there will also be significant numbers of children without statements whose transitions to Key Stage 4 and beyond require careful consideration. The principles and many of the processes outlined (DfES, 2001a, 2001b) for effective transition planning are also relevant to these children.

Beyond Key Stage 4

The end of Key Stage 4 marks the end of compulsory education. Young people at this point will be taking different paths, some will make the transition into the world of work, others will continue with their education in a variety of ways including entering a sixth form in their own school, attending a sixth form college or pursuing their vocational options at a College of Further Education. The diversity of routes means that young people need particular support and guidance related to the path they choose. Some common principles apply and in supporting the young person in making a successful transition to adult life, work undertaken in Key Stage 3 following the programme in the DfES document *Careers Education and Guidance in England: A National Framework 11–19* (DfES, 2003) should be continued using the Careers Education programme for Key Stage 4. Alongside this, work using the Personal Social and Health Education non-statutory guidelines within the National Curriculum (DfEE/QCA, 1999) will help to support the young person gain practical knowledge to help them lead confident, healthy and responsible lives as individuals and members of society. The Connexions Service also continues to offer support to young people through to the age of 19.

For the young person with a Statement of Special Educational Need the regular review and updating of the Transition Plan formulated in Year 9 will be important to ensure that the focus is kept on his/her needs. Years 10 and 11 link programmes, often referred to as Alternative Curriculum Programmes, with Further Education Colleges can be of particular benefit for a young person with special educational needs (DfES, 2001b:15). Such links can 'provide opportunities for integration, extensions to the school curriculum and offer an induction into the more adult environment of further education'.

Conclusion

As outlined within this chapter, in their school career the child will encounter a number of transition points. At each point there is scope for work both at a planning and administrative level and at the level of direct work with the child and his or her family that will help to make this a positive experience.

It is through the adoption of a coordinated, planned approach to transition that the child will be enabled to see progression to the next stage of their education as an opportunity to extend both their learning and their personal, social and emotional development.

Key issues

It is anticipated that you will now:

- have knowledge of the main transition points within children' school careers;
- understand how important it is for transitions to be planned for and supported;
- have an understanding of general issues related to all transitions and specific issues related to some transition points;
- have knowledge of some general strategies and approaches that can be used to support pupils of different ages at transition points;
- understand that in supporting transitions attention needs to be given to practical and pastoral aspects of transfer and to progression in learning and continuity in the curriculum.

Professional Standards for Higher Level Teaching Assistants (HLTA)

If you can demonstrate your understanding and professional use of the key issues illustrated within this chapter, it is hoped that you will be able to fulfil the following HLTA Standards:

1.5	2.2	2.8	3.3.3	3.3.7

References

Barber, M. (1994) *Young People and their Attitudes to School*, Keele: University of Keele.

Casey, J. (2002) *Changing Schools*, Bristol: Lucky Duck.

Cossavella, A. and Hobbs, C. (2002) *Farewell and Welcome*, Bristol: Lucky Duck.

DfEE/QCA (1999) *The National Curriculum*, London: DfEE/QCA.

DfES (2001a) *Special Educational Needs Code of Practice*, Annesley: DfES.

DfES (2001b) *SEN Toolkit Section 10: Transition Planning*, Annesley: DfES.

DfES (2002a) *14–19: Extending Opportunities and Raising Standards*, Annesley: DfES.

DfES (2002b) *14–19 Opportunity and Excellence*, Annesley: DfES.

DfES (2003) *Careers Education and Guidance in England*, Annesley: DfES.

Fabian, H. and Dunlop, A. (eds) (2002) *Transitions in the Early Years*, London: Routledge Falmer.

Macintyre, C. and McVitty, K. (2003) *Planning the Pre-5 Setting*, London: David Fulton.

Maines, B. and Robinson, G. (1988) *The Big School*, Bristol: Lucky Duck.

McSherry, J. (2001) *Challenging Behaviour in Mainstream Schools*, London: David Fulton.

Parsons, C. (1999) *Education, Exclusion and Citizenship*, London: Routledge.

QCA/DfEE (2000) *Curriculum Guidance for the Foundation Stage*, London: QCA.

9 Gifted and talented education

Richard Bailey

We do not have so many talented children that we can afford to make it difficult for them to emerge.

(Rowlands, 1974: 25)

Introduction

Recent years have seen a radical change in both policy and practice related to the education of our most able pupils. The issue of education for the most able pupils in schools has moved from the margins of the educational arena towards centre stage. Central government has introduced a series of initiatives aiming to raise the profile and substantially improve the quality of experience of these children, and it has made clear its expectation that schools and local authorities will support the education of their able pupils (Dracup, 2003). These changes are, in part, in response to calls from schools and parents that there was a group of children – the most able – whose needs were not being met, and also following on from inspection reports that have indicated that, in general, talented pupils were not being sufficiently challenged (OFSTED, 2001).

Thinking about the gifted and talented

Who are the gifted and talented? Traditional conceptions of giftedness have focused on single measures of ability, most commonly the famous intelligence quotient (IQ). Simply put, the higher one's score on an IQ test, the more able one is. Underpinning notions like IQ is the assumption that ability can be related to a 'general intelligence factor', which relates to an individual's ability to reason and make connections (Koshy, 2002).

The appeal of this type of approach is obvious, and the opportunity to reduce a child's ability to a single number was so attractive to teachers and policy-makers that it continued to dominate educational assessment until relatively recently. Over time, however, there has developed a consensus that it is not possible to capture giftedness with a single measure like IQ. Critics have shown that a high IQ is not a good predictor of later success (Winner, 2000), and that creative or divergent thinkers may perform poorly in such tests (Koshy, 2002). Nowadays, almost all educational theories of high ability tend to favour what is called 'multi-dimensional models' (Ziegler and Heller, 2000).

Perhaps the best-known multi-dimensional model is Gardner's Multiple Intelligence theory (1983). Although it, too, has its critics (White, 1998), Gardner's theory has won massive international recognition. Its key notion is that ability manifests itself in numerous ways, and that children possess multiple talents that ought to be acknowledged. In its most recent formulation, Gardner (1999) suggested nine forms of intelligence, as follows:

1 *Linguistic Intelligence*: including sensitivity to and love of words, spoken and written language.

2 *Logical-mathematical Intelligence*: logical and special mathematical thinking skills.

3 *Spatial Intelligence*: conception and perception of space, including spatial memory.

4 *Bodily-kinaesthetic Intelligence*: psychomotor abilities, coordinated movement and athletic performance.

5 *Musical Intelligence*: skills in producing, composing, performing and appreciating music and sound.

6 *Intrapersonal Intelligence*: self-awareness and sensitivity to one's own actions, motivations and feelings.

7 *Interpersonal Intelligence*: social intelligence, and sensitivity to others' actions, motivations and feelings.

8 *Naturalistic Intelligence*: the ability to discern patterns in the living world.

9 *Existential Intelligence*: reflection on the fundamental questions of existence.

The case has also been made that giftedness and talent represent more than just academic ability. Renzulli (1973), for example, argues that giftedness is the coincidence of creativity and motivation (or task commitment, in his terms). His 'three ring' model (see Figure 9.1) offers a framework for parents and schools to ensure that children's abilities are nurtured and supported through fostering motivation and creativity.

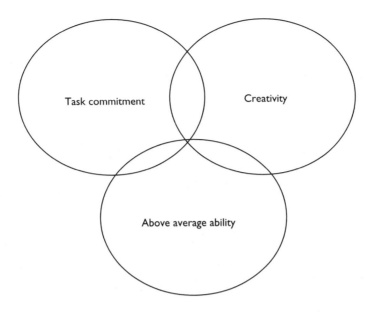

Figure 9.1 'The three ring model'
Source: Renzulli (1978)

The nature and nurture of gifts and talents

Closely related to these discussions of conceptions of giftedness and talent is the question of the source of such high ability. For many people, the most able pupils in schools are those who have been fortunately endowed by genetics. However, while it is very difficult to discount the role of innate abilities, there is mounting evidence that acquired personal and environmental factors contribute significantly.

Recent research increasingly highlights the central role of practice in the realisation of high ability. At one level, this seems a perfectly obvious finding, but many people seem to hold an implicit, unquestioned theory that talented individuals are qualitatively different from the rest of the population, so that they appear to realise extraordinary achievement without the hard work and effort required by the rest of us (Howe, 2001). Shermer (2001) calls this the 'Amadeus Myth', which he defines as 'the belief that genius and original creations are produced by mysterious mental miracles limited to a special few' (ibid.: 263). In fact, nowadays, we are more likely to attribute such powers to genetics than to miracles, and the appearance of extremely high level performers like Mozart is often explained away in terms of some convergence of innate mechanisms (Winner, 1996).

Empirical research does not support the Amadeus Myth. This is not to deny the contribution that genetics makes to human development. However, rather than determining outcomes, genetics seems to provide 'a range of possibilities' (Shermer, 2001: 95), and the scope for development within this range is potentially vast. In this context, gifted and talented education plays a vital role in creating the conditions that will allow individuals to realise their biological potential.

Perkins (1981) claims that the appearance of certain individuals acquiring skills at a faster rate than others is more readily explained by sustained but unobserved practice. He is supported in this claim by studies showing a pattern in the time necessary to progress from beginner to expert in an activity. Hayes (cited in Abbott et al., 2002) demonstrated that all major composers without exception have required at least ten years of concentrated training in order to reach their high level of mastery. And Raskin (cited in Abbott et al., 2002) reviewed the careers of important scientists, poets and authors, and concluded that an average of ten years elapsed between first work and best work.

If practice of an activity is so fundamental to the development of high levels of ability in that activity, one would expect that personal and environmental factors facilitative of practice would also be significant. This does seem to be the case. So, we find that many children showing signs of high ability in the early years do not achieve high levels of performance in later life (Tannenbaum, 1992), and this seems to be often due to an inadequate or inappropriate social environment (Perleth et al., 2000).

One aspect of the talented child's environment that has been the focus of a considerable amount of research from a wide variety of domains is the family (e.g., Freeman, 2001). In his study of 120 musicians, artists, athletes, mathematicians and scientists, Bloom (1985: 3) found

> strong evidence that no matter what the initial characteristics (or gifts) of the individuals, unless there is a long and intensive process of encouragement, nurturance, education and training, the individuals will not attain extreme levels of capability in these particular fields.

As Kay (2000: 151) sums the matter up, within the context of elite sport, 'Children are simply much more likely to achieve success if they come from a certain type of family.'

There are other variables, too, that can increase or decrease the likelihood of the emergence of gifts or talents, such as schooling, the formation of friendship groups and socio-economic status (Ziegler and Heller, 2000). If chance means that such factors are fortuitous, the likelihood of developing one's abilities is increased significantly. If they are not, then one's gifts and talents may go forever unrealised. Atkinson (1978: 221) captured the situation nicely when he wrote that all human accomplishment can be ascribed to 'two crucial rolls of the dice over which no individual exerts any personal control. These are the accidents of birth and background. One roll of the dice determines an individual's heredity; the other his formative environment.'

There is a positive side to this situation, too. It is that, genetics aside, there is a great deal that can be done to improve children's life chances. School, in particular, and the adults that work there, can play important roles in searching for individuals' (often hidden) gifts and talents, and then supporting and fostering them. Indeed, the assumption that schools can play such a role is implicit within a great deal of recent government policy in the area of gifted and talented education.

HLTA 1.1

Policy development

> In the past too many of our most able children have not done as well as they should, especially those from disadvantaged backgrounds. We want to explore ways of making sure we do better for those pupils.
>
> (DfES, 2001a, unpaged)

Formally beginning in 1999, the government has developed a range of closely related initiatives to support the education of the most gifted and talented pupils from 5–19 years. These schemes include intensive area-based programmes for the most able in each school, through localised 'Excellence' initiatives, such as 'Excellence in Cities', 'Excellence Clusters', 'Excellence in Cities Primary Pilot' and 'Excellence Challenge', and national opportunities and resources for the most able across the country, through a National Academy for Gifted and Talented Youth (Dracup, 2003).

The Excellence in Cities (EiC) initiative is particularly relevant in this context, as its main principles reflect the wider gifted and talented agenda that is impacting on schools across the country. The scheme was introduced by the UK government in March 1999, and represented a series of strategies aimed at honouring earlier commitments to raising educational standards in urban areas, promoting educational partnerships and disseminating good practice to the wider educational community (DfEE, 1997). In practice, the initiative was made up of seven 'strands', including the appointment of learning mentors (specialists who, together with teaching and pastoral staff, assess, identify and work with those pupils who need extra help to overcome barriers to learning), and the establishment of Learning Support Units (providing separate short-term teaching and support programmes for pupils at risk of exclusion), City Learning Centres (providing state-of-the-art ICT facilities and technology to a network of partner schools), Beacon Schools (representing models of successful practice that can be shared with others), and specialist schools (such as Technology and Sports Colleges) (DfES, 2002). A further strand focused on the gifted and talented education.

> Schools will take a robust and consistent approach to the identification of their gifted and talented cohorts, making use of available test and assessment data alongside a range of other evidence such as subject-specific checklists of high ability indicators and analysis of

pupils' work. They will need to take care to identify and include able children who are currently underachieving, as well as those who are already relatively high attainers.

(Education and Employment Committee, 1999: v)

**HLTA
3.3.3**

It is worth stressing that the new agenda for gifted and talented pupils was explicitly located within the broad content of inclusive schooling, 'which provides a broad, flexible and motivating education that recognises the different talents of all children and delivers excellence for everyone' (DfEE, 1997). The inclusive ideal has frequently been interpreted by teachers and policy-makers in terms of special educational needs provision, but the White Paper sought to broaden this interpretation by stressing the needs of very able pupils, too: 'The idea that all children had the same rights to develop their abilities led too easily to the doctrine that all had the same ability. The pursuit of excellence was too often equated with elitism' (DfEE, 1997: 11). Through new initiatives like these, the government aimed to bring about 'the largest culture shift of any part of the programme' (DfES, 2001a: 16), towards an education system in which excellence and outstanding achievement were identified, developed and celebrated.

> **Discussion**
> - Is there a tension between the goal of excellence and the principle of equity? In other words, is the policy of identifying a small group of pupils who may receive additional support fair?
> - Is there a danger that gifted and talented provision simply reproduces inequalities already experienced by many children in schools?

Many teachers and teaching assistants report mixed messages from above, which has led to a wide range of interpretations of department and school responsibilities. 'Who do we identify?', 'How do we identify them?', 'How many pupils do we identify?', 'Which curriculum areas?', 'What do we do with them, once we've identified them?'

To begin to address these issues, it may be useful to consider recent policy in terms of four main themes:

- rarity
- achievement
- value
- excellence (Bailey and Morley, 2002).

These are not terms used in government publications, but they capture the essence of what is required of schools.

Rarity

In order to be labelled as gifted or talented, a pupil must possess a level of ability in some area that is rare relative to peers. The guidance suggests that schools select a cohort comprising between 5 and 10 per cent of pupils in each year group within Key Stages 3 and 4, and sixth form, if one is present (DfES, 2002), and good practice dictates that a similar figure is identified in primary schools, too. It is acknowledged that there is no scientific reason for this figure; it merely 'represents a manageable target population for provision, monitoring and evaluation purposes' (DfES, 2002).

The constitution of the gifted and talented cohort in terms of areas of ability is at the discretion of schools, however, it is significant that schools are directed that those with ability in so-called 'academic' areas (English, Mathematics, Science, History, etc.) 'should form at least two-thirds of the cohort in each year group', and may make up the total cohort (DfES, 2002). In practice, this means that the number of pupils identified as gifted or talented in any area of the curriculum will inevitably be very small (certainly smaller than the number of pupils identified as having special educational needs), and this has led many schools and authorities to plan their provision for gifted and talented pupils across clusters of schools or authority-wide.

Achievement

Schools are advised not only to select pupils who are currently achieving at an exceptionally high level, they should also strive to identify pupils who are under-achieving and who have the potential to achieve (OFSTED, 2001). This would seem to suggest that schools ought not limit themselves to selecting pupils on current performance alone (such as whether they perform best on formal tests). Instead, they should take a broader perspective, encompassing the potential to excel. This is entirely in keeping with the original intentions of the programme, which were explicitly concerned with removing barriers to excellence and opportunity (DfEE, 1997).

In this regard, Montgomery (2003) offers a useful framework for identifying under-achieving pupils. She suggests that they fall into at least one of three groups:

- Members of the first group have some high scores on ability tests, but have underlying difficulties that can be uncovered and given support.
- The second group is made up of those pupils for whom a disability or learning difficulty masks their potential to excel in an area of study, and who require specialist support to help them realise their gifts.
- The third group are the disengaged, the disaffected or those with social or behavioural difficulties.

Value

Recent policy documentation makes a strict distinction between the so-called 'academic subjects' (English, Mathematics, Science, History, etc.), and 'art, music, PE, or any sport or creative art' (DfES, 2002), with pupils with ability in the former group being labelled as 'gifted' and those in the latter group 'talented'. It is not entirely clear why this choice of vocabulary was made. Nevertheless, there is a clear hierarchy, with schools having to ensure that at least two-thirds of the cohort is associated with 'gifted' subjects (DfES, 2002). Moreover, it is noteworthy that the National Academy of Gifted and Talented Youth, at the time of writing, has not set itself a remit to address the needs of 'talented' pupils, at all (Champness, 2003).

Excellence

Assessment of excellence should be defined within the context of each school, and specifically each year group (OFSTED, 1999). In other words, while it is entirely likely that one school may have, in a particular year, an unusually large number of very able pupils in a curriculum area, it is directed to identify approximately the same proportion of gifted and talented pupils each time. An obvious limitation arising from such a decision is that a pupil may be defined as gifted and talented and, therefore, eligible for special support and provision, in one school, but not in another.

> Discussion
> ■ What are the main causes of under-achievement in your school? How does under-achievement show itself?
> ■ Using Montgomery's model of under-achievement, can you recognise any children in your school who fulfil her description of an under-achiever?
> ■ Is there a 'typical' gifted and talented child? Are there any patterns in the pupils who are identified in your school, in terms of gender, parental background or ethnicity? What might this tell us about equality of opportunity and outcome?

Meeting the needs of gifted and talented pupils

As discussed earlier in this chapter, the education of gifted and talented pupils can best be considered as part of more general commitment towards ensuring appropriate educational opportunities for all children. There is certainly no expectation that provision for gifted and talented pupils should be at the expense of others in the school. Rather, meeting the needs of gifted and talented pupils is essentially about building on general good practice (Eyre, 2001). So, schools that meet the criteria for effective schools (such as offered by Sammons *et al.*, 1995) will also be effective in meeting the needs of gifted and talented pupils (see Table 9.1).

> Discussion
> Using Table 9.1 as a framework for discussion, consider the changes that might be brought about in schools that you know in order to maximise opportunity for gifted and talented pupils. You might begin this exercise by adding a further column to the right of Table 9.1, and draw out implications for the education of the gifted and talented.

HLTA
3.1.3

Table 9.1 Criteria for effective schools

Criteria	Implications
Professional leadership	Firm and purposeful A participative approach
Shared vision and goals	Unity of purpose Consistency of practices Collegiality and collaboration
A learning environment	An orderly atmosphere An attractive working environment
Concentration on learning and teaching	Maximisation of learning time Academic emphasis Focus on achievement
Purposeful teaching	Efficient organisation Clarity of purpose Structured lessons Adaptive practice
High expectations	High expectations all round Communicating expectations Providing intellectual challenge
Positive reinforcement	Clear and fair discipline Feedback
Monitoring progress	Monitoring pupil performance Evaluating school performance
Pupils' rights and responsibilities	Raising pupil self-esteem Positions of responsibility Control of work
Home-school partnership	Parental involvement
A learning organisation	School-based staff development

Source: Drawn from Eyre (2001) and Sammons *et al.* (1995)

The White Paper *Schools Achieving Success* (DfES, 2001b) sets out a policy statement for gifted and talented education. In doing so, it offers a useful summary of good practice. It is suggested that provision should do the following:

- Build on pupils' particular strengths and tackle any weaknesses, making sure they receive a broad and balanced education.
- Combine in-school learning with complementary opportunities out of school hours.
- Provide more opportunities for pupils to progress in line with ability rather than their age and, where possible, achieve mastery rather than superficial coverage of all subjects.

HLTA
1.1

■ Blend increased pace, breadth and depth in varying proportions according to pupils' ability and needs.

To help make such lists more concrete, reflect upon the following case studies. In each case, consider what you and your school might do to adequately meet each child's needs.

Case study 1

> Paul enjoys mathematics and finds learning its concepts relatively easy, compared to his peers. In fact, at only six years of age, he is carrying out GCSE coursework at home, because his parents cannot find a school that could meet his needs. He rarely plays with other children outside his home. At school, he is starting to become restless and bored, and his parents are concerned that he may soon begin to misbehave.

Discussion

■ What can schools do to meet the special needs of children like Paul?
■ Is there a specific role for teaching assistants, who may not have his level of ability in an area of the curriculum?

Case study 2

> Ahmed, 12, enjoys politics, and has told you that he would like to become a journalist. He reads his parents' broadsheet newspaper every day, and frequently engages you in discussions about current affairs. He has recently joined the school debating club, and has rapidly become one of its 'stars'. His spoken language is excellent, but his written work is less strong.

Discussion

Ahmed's parents ask you for advice with regard to meeting his educational needs, and keeping him motivated. What could you suggest to them?

Case study 3

> Sally is an excellent games player. In fact, according to her PE teacher, she is one of the best athletes she has seen. However, Sally's poorly developed social skills, her lack of understanding of others in her team, and her frequent outbursts of frustration during competitions means that she rarely makes school teams. Her teacher says that she has the potential to do very well, but at the moment, she is a long way from realising it.

Discussion

■ In what ways could a mentor contribute to Sally's development in PE?
■ What strategies could be employed to address her areas of weakness and build on her strengths?

Key issues

This chapter has reviewed the background to the emerging agenda for gifted and talented education, and has suggested that our most able pupils have educational needs that deserve recognition. However, there is no implication here that there is anything esoteric or highly specialist about gifted and talented education. It is simply good practice applied to a particular population within the school. The sorts of practices that effective teachers and teaching assistants employ in their general work will succeed in this context too.

Professional Standards for Higher Level Teaching Assistants (HLTA)

If you can demonstrate your understanding and professional use of the key issues illustrated in this chapter, it is hoped that you will be able to fulfil the following HLTA Standards:

1.1	3.1.2	3.1.3	3.3.2	3.3.3	3.3.7

References

Abbott, A., Collins, D., Martindale, R. and Sowerby, K. (2002) *Talent Identification and Development: An Academic Review*, Edinburgh: sportscotland.

Atkinson, J.W. (1978) 'Motivational determinants of intellective performance and cumulative achievement', in J.W. Atkinson and J.O. Rayner (eds), *Personality, Motivation and Achievement*, New York: Wiley, pp. 221–42.

Bailey, R.P. and Morley, D. (2002) 'Talent in physical education and sport: The Excellence in Cities Initiative', *Bulletin of Physical Education*, vol. 38, no. 2, pp. 111–17.

Bloom, B.S. (ed.) (1985) *Developing Talent in Young People*, New York: Ballantine Books.

Champness, F. (2003) 'National Academy for Gifted and Talented Youth', *Curriculum Briefing*, vol. 1, no. 2, p. 63.

DfEE (1997) *Excellence in Schools*, London: The Stationery Office.

DfEE (2000) *Excellence in Cities: Report March 1999–September 2000*, London: Department for Education and Employment.

DfES (2001a) *Excellence in Cities: Annual Report 2000–2001*, London: Department for Education and Employment.

DfES (2001b) *Schools Achieving Success*, London: Department for Education and Skills.

DfES (2002) Excellence in Cities Homepage, available on http://www.standards. dfes.gov.uk/excellence/ (accessed 10/05/02).

Dracup, T. (2003) 'Understanding the national approach to gifted and talented students', *Curriculum Briefing*, vol. 1, no. 2, pp. 7–12.

Education and Employment Committee (1999) *Government's Response to the Third Report from the Committee, Session 1998–1999: Highly Able Children*, London: HMSO.

Eyre, D. (2001) 'An effective primary school for the gifted and talented', in D. Eyre and L. McClure (eds), *Curriculum Provision in the Primary School*, London: NACE/Fulton.

Freeman, J. (2001) *Gifted Children Grown Up*, London: David Fulton.

Gardner, H. (1983) *Frames of Mind: The Theory of Multiple Intelligences*, New York: Basic Books.

Gardner, H. (1999) *Intelligence Reframed: Multiple Intelligences for the 21st Century*, New York: Basic Books.

Howe, M.J.A. (2001) *Genius Explained*, Cambridge: Cambridge University Press.

Kay, T.A. (2000) 'Sporting excellence: the impact on family life', *European Physical Education Review*, vol. 6, no. 2, pp. 151–70.

Koshy, V. (2002) *Teaching Gifted Children 4–7*, London: David Fulton.

Montgomery, D. (2003) *Gifted and Talented Children with Special Educational Needs: Double Exceptionality*, London: David Fulton.

OFSTED (2001) *Guidance to Inspectors. The Identification and Provision for Gifted and Talented Pupils*, London: Office for Standards in Education.

Perleth, C., Schatz, T. and Mönks, F.J. (2000) 'Early identification of high ability', in K.A. Heller, F.J. Mönks, R.J. Sternberg and R.F. Subotnik (eds), *International Handbook of Giftedness and Talent*, 2nd edn, Oxford: Elsevier.

Perkins, D. (1981) *The Mind's Best Work*, Cambridge, MA: Harvard University Press.

Renzulli, J. (1973) 'What makes giftedness? Reexamining a definition', *Phi Delta Kappan*, vol. 60, pp. 180–4.

Rowlands, P. (1974) *Gifted Children and their Problems*, London: Dent and Sons.

Sammons, P., Hillman, J. and Mortimore, P. (1995) *Key Characteristics of Effective Schools: A Review of School Effectiveness Research*, London: OFSTED.

Shermer, M. (2001) *The Borderlands of Science: Where Sense Meets Nonsense*, Oxford: Oxford University Press.

Tannenbaum, A. (1992) 'Early signs of giftedness: research and commentary', *Journal for the Education of the Gifted*, vol. 15, pp. 104–33.

White, J. (1998) *Do Howard Gardiner's Multiple Intelligences Add Up?* London: Institute of Education.

Winner, E. (1996) *Gifted Children: Myths and Realities*, New York: Basic Books.

Winner, E. (2000) 'Giftedness: current theory and research', *Current Directions in Psychological Science*, vol. 9, no. 5, pp. 153–6.

Ziegler, A. and Heller, K. (2000) 'Conceptions of giftedness from a meta-theoretical perspective', in K. Heller, F. Mönks, R. Sternberg, and R. Subotnik (eds), *International Handbook of Giftedness and Talent*, 2nd edn, Oxford: Elsevier.

Supporting the inclusion and achievement of learners with Autistic Spectrum Disorders (ASD)

10

Mike Blamires

Introduction

The inclusion of learners with Autistic Spectrum Disorders (ASD) has become a key issue for education in the past few years. This may be because there is increased awareness of ASD as its definition has become broader. Also the trend towards inclusion has made the needs of this group of learners more apparent. Perhaps, also, the pressures on schools in recent times have made schools less concerned with the emotional and social development of learners than their academic achievement needed for league tables. This in turn has meant that children with autism have had to been labelled in order to have their needs met.

Classically, autism was associated with a group of children described by Leo Kanner in the USA in the 1940s who appeared to be emotionally distant and reluctant to engage in social interaction. A study at the end of the Second World War by an Austrian clinician, Hans Asperger, was discovered in the 1970s by Uta Frith. This described older children than Kanner dealt with, who had poor social and communication skills, yet appeared to have elaborate language but with circumscribed interests. This eventually led to the concept of the Autistic Spectrum which encompassed a larger group who shared common areas of difficulty.

How does an ASD affect the individual?

The term Autistic Spectrum Disorder (ASD) is a relatively recent label used to recognise that there is a range of conditions or subgroups within autism that does not form a gradual continuum of disability or difficulty, but rather an uneven

HLTA
2.5

spectrum of conditions that are different but, at their heart, share a triad of impairments. This triad provides a focus for intervention.

The differences between the subgroups provide an ongoing focus for research by clinical and developmental psychologists but it is what each person with ASD has in common that can help us to understand their individuality, what they have in common with people without autism and promote their inclusion. All learners with ASD share the triad of impairments. This impacts on their ability *to understand and use non-verbal and verbal communication*. This ranges from a child without spoken communication who may need to be supported in communication through the use of objects, photos, pictures or symbols, to a child who appears to talk with ease using elaborate language beyond his or her years, but only on a small range of topics that interest him or her. The talk will often be a talk rather than a conversation because they find it difficult to take turns or understand the cues that govern conversation.

For example, a child who likes to talk about buses may be able to share his interest for a short while with his peers, but they may become bored eventually if the same information is shared again and again in minute detail without seeking the listener's experience or views on the topic. Therefore, the skills that every other child has and knows without knowing they know, have to be taught to the child with ASD. They can become very isolated because everyone else knows, more or less, the secret rules to the game of social interaction. This is the second part of the triad and it impacts on the ability of learners with ASDs *to understand social behaviour which affects their ability to interact with children and adults.* They find it difficult to understand the world at a social level. The fact that our behaviour is governed by needs, hopes and expectations that we attribute to others all the time in order to make sense of the world of people.

The last area of the triad of impairment is the ability of learners with ASD *to think and behave flexibly – which may be shown in restricted, obsessional or repetitive activities.* There is a reliance on routine and a dislike of change so that changes have to be signalled and warned of well in advance. People with ASD may have limited and unusual areas of interest. For example, they may talk endlessly about dinosaurs, Thomas the Tank Engine, a cartoon programme or bus routes. They may have to carry out tasks in certain prescribed ways because that is the way they first did it. This can constrain family life a good deal if parents have not been supported in developing structured management strategies to accommodate change and flexibility. In the classroom this 'love of routine' can be used to advantage as they are usually very structured places. However, it may still be that the implicit etiquette of school may need to be made visually explicit.

A word may have only one meaning for a learner with ASD so that humour, sarcasm and colloquialisms may be lost on the learner. Witness the look of fascination on the face of a child with ASD being told by his teacher who has just coughed, 'Sorry, I have a little frog in my throat.' Rather than avoid humour and sarcasm, we have to teach it so that the child learns about our world that is full of

HLTA
3.3.1

humour, gentle wind-ups and ribbing but also, and unfortunately, bullying. Taking things literally may cause problems in exam questions. I was once given a photocopy of a maths SAT paper of a boy with ASD. In the margin he had drawn a picture of a boy at a desk. This was because the instruction had said, 'Show your working.'

Once we know this triad of impairments, we know that what we do to help the learner will have to address these needs. We have to use this knowledge to understand that the learner may not understand the world in the same way that people without autism do. Garry Mesibov of the TEACCH centre at the University of North Carolina has suggested that this difference might be thought of as a cultural difference, in that culture is a set of understandings about the world that guide our interaction with the world. For example, if we are scared of sudden noises to the extent that we might find them physically painful, we might be motivated to avoid at all costs potential encounters with situations that might produce loud and sudden noises, something that might puzzle another person who did not understand that culture. One can attribute many of the problems that occur with teaching learners with ASD in schools to this culture clash.

In a busy classroom, in a school under pressure to achieve, there can be an emphasis on the normalisation of pupils by bringing them up to expected levels of performance using prescribed strategies. For the learner with ASD who likes explicit routine, such a standardisation may be supportive provided it is communicated in a way that he or she can understand. The assumption that all children generally think and are motivated in the same ways, however, does not hold when we are dealing with learners with ASD.

The recent OFSTED Report on the inclusion of learners with special educational needs into mainstream schools (2003: 6) looked at practice in settings that were regarded as providing good provision and they noted that:

> Attention to personal and social development was a high priority and paid dividends. Secondary schools found it more difficult to provide structured and consistent support for older pupils with SLD and, sometimes, ASD as their social skills and interests diverged increasingly from those of their peers.

Incidence

The incidence of ASD is estimated to be 60 within 10,000 or 6 in a thousand or 3 in five hundred so it can be assumed that every school will have at least one learner with ASD. ASD tends to affect more boys than girls. It has been estimated that there are four boys to every one girl with the condition (Public Health Institute of Scotland, 2001). This gender issue may not be as simple as the figures state because the recent Audit Commission report *Special Needs: A Mainstream Issue* noted that more boys than girls are identified with special educational needs generally. Specifically in respect of ASD, the condition may be different or 'lessened' in girls who tend to be more social than boys. However, this has not been proved.

Causation

The Medical Research Council (2001) has concluded that ASD is not caused by abnormal parenting but is a neurodevelopmental disorder that has a biological basis with a genetic component. The exact way that this develops or is caused is unclear but something clearly impedes the parts of the brain concerned with social and communication development. The exact impact of environmental factors is also unclear and the controversy over the role of the measles, mumps and rubella vaccine (MMR) has generated much interest with the science establishment taking great efforts to defend this cocktail of vaccines.

Diagnosis

Most children will be recognised as being within the Autistic Spectrum by the time they are five years old. A diagnosis may take longer as this involves a multiprofessional assessment taking into account a developmental history and the involvement of parents/carers is vital.

The good practice guide suggests example behaviours and experiences that would feature in a diagnosis. These are:

- delay or absence of spoken language (but not true for all children with ASD), including loss of early acquired language;
- unusual uses of language – pronoun reversal (for example, saying 'you' instead of 'I'); prolonged echolalia (that is, repeating others' words beyond the usual age); 'playing' with sounds;
- difficulties in playing with other children;
- inappropriate eye contact with others;
- unusual play activities and interests;
- communicating wants by taking an adult's hand and leading them to the desired object or activity;
- failure to point out objects/third parties with the index finger when sharing communication.

Some children with ASD may find it difficult to make eye contact. This can be exacerbated by making eye contact a target in Individual Education Plans (IEP) so that the child is 'trained up' to make artificial use of eye contact without understanding why eye contact might be useful, e.g. to check if someone is listening to you.

By taking the adult's hand, the child is using the adult as a tool to get what he or she wants without knowing that communication might be used to gain the same result. In this case an approach such as the Picture Exchange Communication System might be appropriate. For more information consult your SENCo and checkout the website (www.pecs.com).

Guidelines for the identification, assessment, diagnosis and provision for children with ASDs have been developed by the National Initiative for Autism: Screening and Assessment (NIASA, 2003). NIASA is an independent multi-disciplinary group of professionals supported by the National Autistic Society (NAS) and the Royal Colleges of Psychiatrists and of Paediatrics and Child Health, with the backing of the All Party Parliamentary Group on Autism. Therefore if you suspect a child you support may have ASD, you need to consult your SENCO to seek appropriate professional advice. It is so easy to have a little experience of ASD and then begin to see it in many children. There is a need to gather evidence if we have concerns and explore them with colleagues. Teaching assistants better than the teacher may notice difficulties in lessons or during unstructured times where a child may be having difficulties.

> **Discussion**
>
> Do you know how many learners within your school setting have a diagnosis of Autistic Spectrum Disorder; this includes Autism or Asperger Syndrome?

Having a diagnosis of ASD should be the starting point to ensure that the child is understood and educated appropriately. The DfES good practice guidance on autism (Autism Working Group, 2002) is a readable and practical resource that contains briefings, advice and pointers to appropriate provision. This should be a first point of reference as its states that all staff in contact with the learner with ASD need to have relevant knowledge and strategies to engage with the learner. This could be in the form of an IEP circulated to staff detailing what the child's strengths are and what strategies may be useful. Do not make the mistake of thinking all learners with ASD are the same. They have the characteristics of ASD that is the triad of impairments but these may not be in equal measure and they interact with their personality, strengths and weaknesses, family characteristics and the environment they are in. The ASD may also occur alongside other conditions such as epilepsy, dyslexia and dyspraxia.

HLTA
1.1

Mental health issues

As learners with ASD move into their teenage years, they may become more aware of their difference from others and their isolation. Consideration must be given to the quality of life that the learner has and what opportunities in the school and broader community may be exploited to improve this. Being part of a group and having something enjoyable to look forward to can keep morale high and prevent depression. (See the guidance at the end of this chapter.)

Interventions

Poor co-ordination

Dyspraxia is a motor co-ordination difficulty that used to be called clumsiness and is often associated with learners with Asperger Syndrome. It is related to a difficulty in motor planning in that new movement and actions that have to be concentrated on will be difficult. In collaboration with the PE specialist in the school and with advice from an occupational therapist, activities and games might be employed to develop ball and co-ordination skills. As would be expected, they may find PE difficult and team games perplexing. They are likely to have difficulty in getting changed before and after PE. Support systems such as visual prompts and social stories may be useful here.

Handwriting may be difficult and the learners with ASD tend to have good ICT skills so consider how the learner will have access to a word processor to overcome this barrier to writing. Having legible handwriting may be a noble aim but that should not cause extra frustration when the task in hand is to present ideas and when the majority of the world uses computers or mobile phones to communicate. Support for structuring their work can also be put in place by the use of headings and subheadings or writing frames which contain key questions alongside key words and concepts. Clicker by Crick Soft is a frequently used supportive word processor.

Visual learning

Learners with ASD tend to be highly visual learners and like structure. Classroom organisation can support pupils to work more independently. Figures 10.1–10.3 show visual supports produced to support the inclusion and dependent working of pupils with autistic spectrum disorders who may have difficulty understanding verbal instructions, especially when they are long and refer to routines they have not been taught explicitly, e.g. getting ready for PE. These supports can be just text if the pupil can read but they are often supported by symbols from the Rebus or Mayer Johnson sets and can be produced using word processing, desktop publishing or dedicated software such as Writing With Symbols from www.widgit.co.uk

Figure 10.1 is visual support showing the days of the week for a learner. This might be a resource for the whole class, which then has a display of what happens on a particular day. In a secondary school context this information may

Figure 10.1   Visual support showing days of the week

well be part of the learner's planner with the teaching assistant role being to ensure at the beginning of the day that the learner knows what day it is, where they need to be and what equipment they need. At the end of the day, the TA may want to check that the learner is clear about what homework is needed.

Figure 10.2 shows symbol-supported timetables that indicate what is happening during different parts of the day. These may be the instructions for carrying out an activity in class.

Figure 10.3 is an equipment prompt that has removable symbols according to the equipment requirements of a task. For older learners, the use of diagrams, charts, worksheets with pictures, spider diagrams and mind maps, videos, over-head transparencies and videos can help to make abstract concepts more concrete. As learners with ASD tend to focus on the detail rather than the big picture, it is helpful if you do have a big picture that shows the concepts being taught. Further guidance of visual strategies to improve communication can be found in Linda Hodgon's (1996) well regarded book.

Visual supports can also include written words and sentences. The key point is that instructions that are spoken are transitory. They are here one moment and gone the next. When verbal instructions are given, try to give them in a simple form and speak slowly, allowing time for the child to process the information.

Structure

The TEACCH approach harnesses the strength of learners with ASD which is their like of routine and structure and this is linked with their preference for things visual. The key principle is to show the learner with ASD what the task is,

HLTA
3.1.1

Figure 10.2 Symbol-supported timetables

Figure 10.3 An equipment prompt

how much there is to do, how do I know when I've finished and what do I do next? The final question can sometimes be the reward for doing the task.

> **Discussion**
>
> Make a note of the visual prompts that you encounter when you next go into town. These will include menus, signs, notices, sequences of instructions, labels and displays. What are they telling you and what implicit routines of the school are supported by such prompts?

Motivation

What motivates a person with ASD may not be social rewards such as verbal praise and encouragement. These should not be ignored but rather augmented by other rewards. These may be time spent on their area of interest or playing with a particular toy. For one child it was time to work with a Teaching Assistant who had sparkling ear-rings that the child had taken to.

Fairness and equity

The classic response to treating learners differently by giving them additional encouragement is that 'It is not fair to treat children differently. You are rewarding one child for something that another child does every day with no reward.' Well, children are not all the same, responding to difference in ways that enable achievement is central to the craft of the classroom. We are in fact not rewarding the performance of a skill in itself but the effort that has gone into learning that skill. That's what makes it fair.

Parental partnership

The involvement of the parents or carers is vital. Beyond the rhetoric within the guidance, there are many practical reasons for the involvement of parents and carers. They will have extensive knowledge of the learner and what he or she likes or dislikes and is able to do. Sometimes, the learner will be able to do something at home that they do not appear to know at school and they will often learn something at school that they will not apply at home because they do not generalise their learning so readily. A parent may provide an insight into a behaviour that is puzzling at school.

As a teaching assistant, you may have more access to parents if they see you at the beginning or end of the day, and they may communicate more readily with you than other members of staff in the school, so that you are a useful channel of communication between the home and the school. This needs to be undertaken sensitively with the advice of your line manager.

Developing social skills and understanding

These go together because social skills cannot be applied unless an individual knows when, where and how to apply them. This is the core area of difficulty for learners with ASD. Teaching social skills without understanding will result in mere training so that the skill may not be applied beyond a few rigid settings. Speech and language therapists may have a role in training and demonstrating to staff ways of developing social skills within the school.

Learners with ASD will find it difficult to take turns in conversation or play or consider the needs of others, and thus may appear selfish but we must not make the mistake of believing that this is their intention. It is not. They will need to be taught social skills to cope with the playground and other social demands such as working in groups. Social skills can be taught using games in small groups that include children who can model the appropriate behaviours. These might take the format of circle time and be based on the Social Use of Language Programme by Wendy Rinaldi (1992) or Alex Kelly's (1994) Talkabout which is aimed at older learners. It is, however, important that social skills should be taught alongside social understanding so that the skills are not learned in isolation.

Social stories

A social story introduces appropriate social knowledge in the form of a story that provides a visual support for the pupil. It explains the hows and whys of a social situation. The different types of sentences within a social story give the pupil information about a situation and provide clear guidance on possible ways to respond.

The stories are written by professionals or parents, to describe social situations that the child with autism is finding difficult, or to describe a successful outcome. According to Attwood (1997), it would appear that this technique is proving to be very effective, in enabling individuals with autism to understand cues for specific social situations.

Social stories are usually written in the first person, as though the pupil is describing the event, and Gray (1994) suggests that they should contain three types of sentence:

- *Descriptive sentences* that describe what happens, where the situation occurs, who is involved and what they are doing and why.

- *Perspective sentences* that describe the reactions and responses of others in the target situation and sometimes the reasons for those responses. They may also describe the feelings of others.

- *Directive sentences* that describe the possible responses to the social situation.

Gray recommends a ratio of between two to five descriptive sentences to every directive sentence.

Discussion

Why do you think this ratio is recommended?

The answer is that we are not writing a script to be followed in a rote fashion but are trying to enable the learner's understanding.

The following is a social story helping a learner with ASD to understand what is involved in getting ready for PE.

How to get ready for PE

When my teacher tells me that I am going to be doing PE, some children from my class will go and get the PE bags.

They give them out to each table.

I will try to get changed quickly and quietly.

Sometimes we will go to the hall. Sometimes we will go into the playground or into the field.

I like to play the different games and activities.

I can join in with the other children.

When PE has finished, I will go back to my class quietly with the other children.

I will try to get changed as quickly and quietly as possible.

I take off my shorts and T-shirt and put them into my PE bag.

I then hang up my bag on my peg.

I will try to sit quietly until everyone is ready.

The story is composed in consultation with the learner and is read to the learner before the activity. Once the learner understands and has developed a way of managing the situation, the story can be used less often.

Learner participation

Much recent legislation has emphasised the importance of the learner's voice in making provision. Within the area of ASD, this can be difficult because the

Figure 10.4 Comic strip conversation

learner cannot readily reflect upon their experiences, especially if they are anxious after they have been involved in an incident and you are enquiring about what happened and why. As well as observation and discussion with the teacher and parents about the possible reasons for a behaviour, a technique Carol Gray called comic strip conversations has been widely used. This involves the use of coloured felt tip pens, the drawing of stick men with cartoon speech and thought bubbles to denote what was said and what people may have thought (Figure 10.4). This can be used to discover what happened leading up to an incident, so the child has an external and literal representation of what was said and meant. The coloured pens are used to code the emotion of what was said. For example:

RED: Bad ideas, teasing anger, unfriendly

BLACK: Facts, things we know

GREEN: Good ideas, happy, friendly

HLTA
1.6

Discussion

In Figure 10.4, what do you think the teacher is thinking and trying to communicate. What is the child likely to say?

With older learners, a conversation might be carried out using a word processor so that the learner with ASD can focus upon the questions and their answers. Sometimes this can be just with the adult typing.

Peer support

Buddy systems and 'Circle of Friends' interventions are very important to support the inclusion of learners with ASD. A learner with ASD will be vulnerable because he or she may be told the rules of the school by staff but it is the children who know how things really operate. Both of these approaches involve peers in supporting a learner with ASD during unstructured times, with some support from staff. Essex LEA and Lucky Duck have produced packs with videos on Circle of Friends that enable peers to become a resource rather than another barrier, as they provide a format for peers to understand the difficulties of learners with ASD.

So what is the implicit or explicit role of the teaching assistant in relation to learners with ASD?

The role of the teaching assistant is a linchpin in enabling the inclusion of learners with ASD. This role may take a number of forms depending on the ways that TAs are employed in different classrooms across the school or during the day. These roles may at times increase or reduce the inclusion of the learner with ASD.

A filter to select or block out experiences

The teaching assistant may direct the learner towards or away from certain activities because of his or her prior experience with the learner. For example, taking the learner away from group activities, because the learner has failed previously at them. Equally, the TA might direct the learner to use the computer for a writing task because the learner finds it difficult to write by hand.

An interpreter: explaining to the child what is happening and perhaps explaining the behaviour of the child to peers

This is a useful role but can result in the learner not listening to the classroom teacher because he/she knows the teaching assistant will 'always show me what to do'. It can move the responsibility of the teacher for the learner with ASD away from the main position and on to the TA so that the learner becomes more isolated from the activities of the class. As the OFSTED report on the inclusion of learners with SEN (2003: 15) noted: 'The expectations of teaching assistants by a few teachers, mainly in secondary schools, were unrealistic. One example was the expectation that teaching assistants undertake all the necessary differentiation of tasks.' The teacher's knowledge of a subject is central and all the learners in the class must have access to it.

The teaching assistant can be in a position to explain to other children why the learner with ASD is behaving differently, provided that this is done sensitively and positively based upon a sound knowledge of the child. We have to be careful of labels at this point, because we can fall into excuse mode which at its extreme does nobody any good, for example, 'He does that because he has autism/ Asperger syndrome.' Empathy, however, is part of the broad curriculum aims of schools and this may be a means of teaching it, provided we are not patronising and belittling people with a disability.

An advocate and enabler to ensure the child is included and not excluded

The teaching assistant operates within an important sphere of influence enabling the learner with ASD to understand the social demands within the classroom and beyond, encouraging peer acceptance and helping the learner to understand what the lesson involves and how he or she can participate in the lesson.

> 37. The pupils' perception of the teaching assistant's role was intrinsic to the relationship.
> (OFSTED, 2003: 15)

There is also a danger that the learner who has ASD will become reliant upon the teaching assistants as a peer group because his or her age-appropriate peers are not as accommodating as adults who are being paid to listen.

A minder: protecting the child from the rest of the class or the rest of the class from the child

The behaviour always tends to have a purpose. If a child with ASD is non-compliant or badly behaved, it is likely that the child does not understand what is required or knows what is about to happen and wants to avoid it. As an extreme example, spitting, scratching or biting are a successful way of making people move away from you, but it is not a long-term strategy that will build friendships. Alternative behaviours need to be taught that are more socially acceptable and appropriate. Observations considering the antecedents, the actual behaviour and the consequences of the behaviour carried out with staff with expertise in behaviour analysis and an understanding of ASD will be needed.

If a physical intervention has to be used, make sure that this conforms to the national and local guidance (see the end of the chapter). It should not become the first form of intervention because it removes choice and control from the individual. Other proactive strategies of prevention should be employed whenever possible. Make sure you know them.

Sometimes a quiet area is needed as a secure base to prepare for a lesson or social event or to relax after the challenge of a social event. However, one needs to be aware of the degree of exclusion that may be occurring because of this.

A cultural attaché from our culture to the culture of autism: providing explanations and understandings

As noted above, it can be useful to think of autism as a culture, a way of engaging with the world. This means that the TA should be aware of these two cultures and be sensitive to when these cultures can complement each other but should also be aware of potential culture clashes.

Catherine Leigh of the West Kent Attendance and Behaviour Service noted a difficulty arising from the literal misunderstanding of a child with ASD as reported by his parents. One child was impossible to bath because he constantly jumped up and down in the water. It was later observed that prior to bath-time, his parents would indicate it was bath-time by saying it was time to 'jump in the bath'. Once his parents used a different more literal expression of what was expected, the problem stopped.

We can learn a couple of things from this vignette. First, we can learn something about ourselves and about people with ASD who are non-compliant with our expectations. We communicate with each other using short-hand phrases, which often do not mean what we literally say and this is called implicature.

A lack of familiarity with implicature can get a school child with ASD into trouble quite quickly, if there is no knowledge among staff about autistic thinking. For example, a child with ASD is talking to other children on his table about his enthusiasm for a particular brand of trading cards, rather than doing the work that has just been outlined by the teacher. The teacher waits for the child to stop talking but he doesn't, so she asks the boy, 'Rajik, would you like to stop talking and get on with your work?' To which Rajik replies, in all sincerity, 'No, Miss.' This is an implicature double whammy because Rajik, not only does not understand what the intention of the teacher is; she is not asking a question here, this is an instruction to get on with the work, but he also answers the question in a way that implies non-compliance and cheekiness. With the wrong teacher at the end of a stressful and demanding week, the outcome for Rajik may be unfortunate.

The second thing we can learn from the bath vignette is that non-compliance often arises from not understanding what the task exactly is or involves. If we can make the implicit demands of the situation explicit in a form that the learner can understand, he or she will stand a better chance of doing what is required.

So a person with autism may find it difficult to understand the culture of people who do not have autism. This is a vital point to understand. A culture consists of values, concepts and ways of doing things. Most children learn the culture from reciprocal interaction with their carers, significant others and peers. They can do this because they automatically think about the meanings and intentions of others from about the age of three when the theory of mind begins to start work, but before this they will interact with carers to build shared attention that creates common meaning. For example, a young child will follow the direction of gaze of its mother, or may recognise the expression in the face of an adult that denotes a preference or a dislike. Infants with ASD may not have access to such interactions so that they do not develop cultural understandings.

Key issues

This chapter has provided a range of starting points to develop appropriate responses that will enable the inclusion of learners with ASD. Building on the knowledge and experience of the school and beyond, much can be done. The follow-up readings and websites provide an extensive resource to develop your understanding of the challenging and perplexing condition. While there is as yet no cure for ASD, there is a vast amount that can be achieved by thinking and acting positively as part of a team that includes outside agencies, parents, the school and the child.

Professional Standards for Higher Level Teaching Assistants (HLTA)

If you can demonstrate your understanding and professional use of the key issues illustrated within this chapter, it is hoped that you will be able to fulfil the following HLTA Standards:

1.1	1.3	1.4	1.5	1.6
2.4	2.5	2.9	3.1.1	3.3.1

In addition to the further reading and websites, you might want to take a training course on ASD, often run by Special Schools, LEAs or local colleges.

Further reading and websites

Autism Working Group (2002) *Autistic Spectrum Disorders: Good Practice Guidance*, Part 1, DfES/DoH. Available on: www.teachernet.gov.uk/management/sen

Autism Working Group (2002) *Autistic Spectrum Disorders: Good Practice Guidance*, Part 2, DfES/DoH. Available on: www.teachernet.gov.uk/management/sen

ACCAC, Qualifications, Curriculum and Assessment Authority for Wales, (2000) *A Structure for Success: Guidance on the National Curriculum and Autistic Spectrum Disorder*. Available from ACCAC Publications, PO Box 2129, Erdington, Birmingham B24 0RD, Ref. AC/GM/0091. Website www.accac.org.uk

National Autistic Society, provides a wide range of information and advice in relation to ASD. http://www.nas.org.uk

Assessment

Ann Le Couteur, Chair, Core Working Group, National Initiative for Autism: Screening and Assessment (NIASA) (2003) *National Autism Plan for Children (NAPC): Plan for the*

Identification, Assessment, Diagnosis and Access to Early Interventions for Pre-School and Primary School Aged Children with Autism Spectrum Disorders, (ASD), London: The National Autistic Society. The report is available from Barnardo's Despatch Services Tel: 01268 522872 and on a number of websites including: http://www.nas.org.uk/profess.niasa.html and www.bacch.org.uk/niasa

Circle of friends

Essex Advisory Service for ASD Circle of Friends technique for Autism, Essex County Council.

Maines, B. and Robinson, G. (1997) *All for Alex: A Circle of Friends*, Lucky Duck Publishing.

Curriculum

DfES (2001) *The Daily Mathematics Lesson: Guidance to Support Pupils with Autistic Spectrum Disorders*. Available on: www.standards.dfes.gov.uk/numeracy/publications or from the DfES Publications Centre. Tel: 0845 6022260. Ref. 0511/2001.

Mental health guidance

DfES (2001) *Promoting Children's Mental Health within Early Years and School Settings*, DfES Publications, Tel: 0845 6022260. Ref. 0112/2001 (contains information on ASD).

Physical intervention

British Institute of Learning Disabilities (BILD) (2001) *BILD Code of Practice for Trainers in the Use of Physical Interventions: Learning Disability, Autism, Pupils with Special Educational Needs*. Available on Tel: 01562 850 251.

DfES/DH (2002) *Guidance on the Use of Restrictive Physical Interventions for Staff Working with Children and Adults who Display Extreme Behaviour in Association with Learning Disability and/or Autistic Spectrum Disorders*. Available from DfES Publications Tel: 0845 6022260, Ref. LEA/0242/2002, and on www.doh.gov.uk/learningdisabilities/publications.htm.

Social skills

Kelly, A. (1994) *Talkabout*, New York: Winslow Press.

Rinaldi, W. (1992) *The Social Use of Language Programme*, Windsor: NFER

Social stories

Available from: http://www.thegraycenter.org/

Software

Crick Soft source of Clicker Software, available from: www.cricksoft.com

Structured teaching and visual supports

University of North Carolina's Treatment and Education of Autistic and Related Communication Handicapped Children (TEACCH) centre. A briefing on structured approaches to teaching. Available on: http//education.cant.ac.uk/xplanatory/assets/presentations/teacch.htm

Joan Ratcliffe, Advisory Teacher for ASD in Bexley, http://education.cant.ac.uk/xplanatory/assets/presentations/teacch.htm

The Foundation for People with Learning Disabilities (2001) *All About Autistic Spectrum Disorders: A Booklet for Parents and Carers.* Available from The Mental Health Foundation, Tel: 020 7802 0302 and www.learningdisabilities.org.uk

References

Adams, J.I. (1997) *Autism – P.D.D.: More Creative Ideas from Age Eight to Early Adulthood*, Ontario: Adams Publications (available from Winslow in the UK).

Attwood, A. (1997) *Asperger Syndrome: A Guide for Parents and Educators*, London: Jessica Kingsley.

DfES (2001) *Inclusive Schooling: Children with Special Educational Needs*, DfES Publications. Tel: 0845 6022260. Ref DfES/0774/2001.

Frith, U. (ed.) (1991) *Autism and Asperger Syndrome*, Cambridge: Cambridge University Press.

Frith, U. (2004) *Autism: Explaining the Enigma* (revised edition), Oxford: Blackwell.

Grandin, T. (1995) *Thinking in Pictures*, New York: Doubleday.

Gray, C. (1994) *The Social Story Book*, Jenison MI: Jenison Schools.

Happé, F. (1994) *Autism: An Introduction to Psychological Theory*, London: UCL.

Hodgon, L. (1996) *Visual Strategies to Improve Communication*, Delaware: Quark Roberts Press.

Jordan, R., Jones, G. and Murray, D. (1998) *Educational Interventions for Children with Autism: A Literature Review of Recent and Current Research*, DfEE Publications Research Report RR 77.

Jordan, R. and Powell, S. (1996) *Understanding and Teaching Children with Autism*, London: Wiley.

Medical Research Council (2001) *MRC Review of Autism Research: Epidemiology and Causes*, available via www.mrc.ac.uk

Mesibov, G.B. and Shea, V. (1996) *The Culture of Autism: From Theoretical Understanding to Educational Practice*, New York: Plenum Press.

OfSTED (2003) *Special Educational Needs in the Mainstream*, HMI 511, London: OFSTED.

Public Health Institute of Scotland (2001) *Autistic Spectrum Disorders: Needs Assessment Report*, Published by PHIS, Clifton House, Clifton Place, Glasgow G3 7LS, Tel: 0141 300 1010, www.show.scot.nhs.uk/PHIS

Sacks, O. (1998) *An Anthropologist on Mars*, London: Picador.

Meeting motor developmental needs

Sue Soan

Movement can be recognised as a fundamental activity of life. It is perceived in liveliness of thinking, in the fluctuations of feeling and human interaction and most obviously in the physical body.

(Nash-Wortham and Hunt, 1994)

Introduction

This chapter will explore the social, academic and emotional difficulties that learners can experience if they have motor control development (movement) problems. It will provide the reader with a theoretical understanding of the difficulties encountered and their effects on the whole child. However, unlike the rest of the chapters in this book, case studies and the author's personal experiences will form the main body of information to which other sources will be linked. The effects of the changes in society and the educational system on learners with this type of additional difficulty will also be discussed. Awareness of what to look out for in learners as well as interventions that are easily included within a normal mainstream setting will also be discussed.

What do motor problems have to do with learning?

This is an area of learning that is all too frequently overlooked, because the focus and measure of success of a child and a school's ability to educate that child have tended to be based on academic achievement since the 1970s. However, when educators begin to look at children's lifelong needs of social acceptance and emotional stability as well as educational achievement, the need to develop the physical capabilities of a child become all too obvious and essential. This understanding is not new; indeed the Plowden Report (1967) emphasised the need for teachers to take account of a child's intellectual, emotional and physical 'developmental age'.

Recognising motor difficulties

Working for the first time in a unit for learners with Moderate Learning Difficulties (MLD) twelve years ago, I struggled to understand why they could not make good progress with their reading and writing, despite small group and individual working and a large amount of resources. I could not accept that these lively and frequently well-motivated learners could neither learn nor be taught. At the age of seven they still desperately wanted to learn and be successful, but every time they felt they 'failed', a little more of their self-esteem and self-confidence was eroded away, leaving opportunities for behaviour difficulties and lack of effort to gain footholds. This refusal to be professionally beaten started a search for answers that is still continuing to this day.

While observing these pupils with learning difficulties, it became very clear that many of them also had a motor difficulty. It was almost as if the physical problems were actually 'blocking' the development of their cognitive knowledge and skills, their social interaction skills and their emotional maturity. As an educator I began to recognise that sitting these learners down at a desk all day writing and reading was not actually what they needed to help them learn. As Russell (1993: 13) says:

> If you have a locked door in your house and the key to that door has been lost, the greater the variety of keys you can collect to try to unlock the door, the more chance there is of finding one which will work.

During PE lessons I saw that these children did not have the ability to carry out many early gross motor physical skills, such as the ability to stand on one foot, to skip, to hop, to walk backwards (or even forwards!) in a straight line, to be able to catch a large ball and even to be able to move their heads without the arms moving with them. Hence the search for literature and programmes to solve these difficulties commenced. However, it was the children's progress once programmes were put into action that really reinforced the need for this type of learning to be included in their curriculum.

Case study 1

Dan was a Year 3 pupil attending a MLD Unit attached to a mainstream school. He had immense expressive language difficulties and fine (small movement skills such as pencil skills) and gross (larger physical skills like hopping and skipping) motor difficulties and was emotionally immature. His academic progress was very limited, although he was always willing to 'have a go'.

During a planned motor skills lesson where there were a number of activities set up around the hall, Dan tried to walk, heel to toe, backwards on a rope placed on the floor. Even with arms outstretched to aid his balance he could not manage to place one foot behind the other without falling over and within seconds was in a heap on the floor, in floods of tears.

As the teacher I began to unpick what this movement involved and then began giving Dan the skills, piece by piece to be able to achieve this motor and balance skill. Within a month of regular practice, support and encouragement, Dan could walk backwards on the rope without wobbling and without tears!

How did this impact on his learning?

As a classroom practitioner (not under research conditions), I began to notice that Dan's ability to concentrate, to write (fine motor skills) and to relate to others improved. For the first time he was also able to express his feelings openly, shocking everyone once by crying to a piece of music and telling everyone how it made him feel.

It became very clear, therefore, that there was a link between the learners' learning and movement. As Hannaford (1995: 11) says: 'Thinking and learning are not all in our head.' Normally the brain is thought of as separate from our bodies. However, research by Hannaford (1995) and Jenson (2000) clearly suggests that the body and the brain effectively act as one (Doherty and Bailey, 2003: 51). Doherty and Bailey (2003: 51–2) state: 'Movement is integral and essential to all learning. Through it we can express learning, our understanding and ourselves. The body is the medium for learning and movement is the choreography of our brain's systems.'

What are the physical skills children need to be able to learn?

When children first attend school, it is considered good practice for educators to give them many pieces of work that contain essential elements of what is required for the actual skills of reading and writing. These include:

- listening and talking
- vocabulary
- auditory and sequential memory
- visual discrimination perception
- gross motor control

- fine motor control
- balance
- body awareness
- spatial awareness
- coordination
- the ability to distinguish between left and right
- visual tracking
- rhythm.

(Russell, 1993: 10)

It is clear that the vast majority of the items on the list are of a physical nature. Attempting and gaining mastery of them through physical movement should afford the learner considerable help in the learning processes which can take place as the skills are acquired. However, are the children given enough practice with these skills or are many left to struggle to gain academic skills without these basic movements fully learnt?

Case study 2

While working with Joe, a very able Year 6 pupil in a mainstream school who had specific learning difficulties (dyslexia), I soon realised that he still had:

- gross motor control difficulties
- fine motor control difficulties
- balance problems
- body awareness problems
- spatial awareness problems
- visual tracking problems.

I immediately set up a programme of work that incorporated ten minutes of traditional individual desk learning, but also had a motor time each lesson. This included *eurhythmy* exercises, a programme practised in Steiner schools (see list of useful addresses and book), and motor activities adapted from Russell (1994) and Nash-Wortham and Hunt (1993), specifically aimed to help the problems identified above. Within a couple of months, Joe went from a boy who could not aim a bean bag accurately or follow a passage in a book from left to right without losing his place, to a boy who could throw a bean bag accurately to a person behind him and whose spelling and reading skills improved drastically so that instead of being two years behind his chronological age was actually three years above! Staggering results. Consequently Joe made the transition to the local secondary school confidently and successfully.

For some reason Joe had not managed to really learn these early motor skills, but once they were achieved, his cognitive abilities were also able to develop without hindrance.

Goddard (2002: xvi) says:

> reading depends largely on oculo-motor skill involving precise eye movements and writing involves hand–eye coordination with the support of the postural system. Most academic learning depends on basic skills becoming automatic at the physical level. If a child fails to develop automatic control over balance and motor skills, many other aspects of learning can be affected negatively, even though the child has average or above average intelligence.

Goddard continues:

> Control of the body also lays the foundation of self-control. Immaturity in the functioning of the nervous system is often accompanied by signs of emotional immaturity such as poor impulse control, difficulty in reading the body language of others (social cues) and unsatisfactory peer relationships.

Case study 3

Following inset at a small country school, the teachers wanted to think of a way they could identify the motor needs of the pupils and also facilitate intervention in groups rather than individually. They decided to start the day prior to assembly with a movement session – everyone together using exercises, first, concentrating on stimulating the coordination of the upper and lower limbs to enhance the children's awareness of the many diagonal positions of the limbs on opposite sides of the body. Rhythm and spatial awareness were also focused on. With the Deputy Head at the front of the hall leading the session, the other teachers were able to watch their classes. The children who had difficulties completing the exercises were all identified as having a learning difficulty of some kind. Not surprisingly, this encouraged the school to proceed with this intervention, particularly focusing on the movements that caused most problems.

Obviously this type of intervention is only possible in a small school, but individual educators can undoubtedly carry out similar assessments and the necessary interventions during PE or games lessons.

Discussion Do you know which children you work with have motor difficulties? If so, what are the school and educators doing to support this area of development? Choose one child with a motor difficulty to observe for a day. Does their difficulty, do you think, affect their learning and/or social interaction?

Are more children in this generation experiencing motor difficulties? If so, why?

Modern society generally does not help children to actually master the skills they need that lead to whole brain integration. A variety of reasons have influenced the way children exercise and spend their free time. Computers, game boys and television have meant that after school, instead of playing outside with friends, many children go straight home and sit for the rest of the evening, frequently in very poor seating positions in front of screens. Hand-written letters are now most often replaced with word-processed, attractive alternatives and colouring, drawing and making models appear to be less favourable activities.

Safety is also another factor that has meant children do not go into play areas to climb, balance and run about as much as they did a few decades ago and certainly not without an adult. Even the very young do not escape this eagerness to protect and provide for, by preventing babies and toddlers moving around, and thus preventing vital motor and visual skills from developing. Baby cradles and other such equipment help parents entertain and occupy their young, but by using this type of equipment too much, babies do not get the opportunities to learn to crawl, develop hand–eye coordination skills and strengthen their neck and spine, all vital for many learning skills. Children do not even walk, let alone run as much as they did a few decades ago.

The school curriculum during the past thirty years has also greatly ignored the importance of supporting motor development. When first introduced in the late 1980s the National Curriculum squeezed the Art subjects so tightly that PE and Games lessons could only be fitted in once or perhaps twice a week. Hence, whether at home or in school, children's motor skills were and are still not being practised as much or for as long as many require them to be. Flat school tables and seats, often unsuitable for the size of the child, plus poor classroom organisation, also play a part in causing major problems for many learners who have motor and/or ocular difficulties. Motor skills occur sequentially, but 'the rate of development and the extent is determined individually and influenced by the task itself and factors in the environment. Basic motor skills do not simply unfold as part of a "master plan", rather they are learned' (Doherty and Bailey, 2003: 46).

Understanding motor learning

Children, even prior to birth, are constantly learning new skills and different patterns of movement. Motor skill acquisition, as mentioned earlier, is sequential and is progressive, from generic movements to complex, specific actions. Gallahue and Ozmun (1995) proposed that there are five stages that children go through when they are learning a new movement skill. Figure 11.1 is an adapted version of this.

Hence, as skills are practised and refined, children learn to have more control and develop greater fluency in their physical movements. The range of factors associated with physical development include biological, motor, perceptual and social skills and therefore it is not surprising that in the past many different perspectives have contributed to understanding motor learning and development.

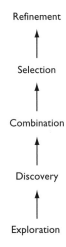

Refinement

↑

Selection

↑

Combination

↑

Discovery

↑

Exploration

Figure 11.1 Five stages of development of movement skill
Source: Doherty and Bailey (2003)

When teaching children and young people with extremely severe social, emotional and behavioural difficulties, many of the programmes I had previously used for similar learning problems failed to have any positive effect on them. Following observations and discussions with colleagues, I began to recognise that the exercises given were not actually reaching far enough back in the children's development.

Neuro-developmental approaches

Further research led me to find out more about the neuro-developmental approach to supporting learning. This approach aims therapy at the lowest level of identified dysfunction, and 'attempts to build links from lower to higher centers, through the use of specific stimulation techniques' (Goddard, 2002: xv). I visited the Institute of Neuro-Physiological Psychology, run by Peter Blythe and Sally Goddard for further training. The programme I learnt cannot be described in the pages below, because it needs to be taught by qualified trainers. However, it is hoped that the following case studies and examples will whet your appetite enough to make you want to find out more!

Reflexes

When a baby is born, he uses a set of *primitive reflexes*, which emerged in utero, to help him survive for the first few months of life. These primitive reflexes are 'automatic, stereotyped movements, directed from the brain stem and executed without cortical involvement' (Goddard, 2002: 1) and provide training for many later skills. However, these reflexes should not remain active beyond the first 6–12 months of life, because within this time frame higher centres of the brain should have controlled them, enabling more complex neural structures to develop. If this does not happen, the child cannot move on to a stage where he can control voluntary response. Any retained primitive reflexes beyond the first year of life are evidence that there is an 'immaturity within the central nervous system (CNS)' (ibid.).

So, what may happen if primitive reflexes are still active after the first 6–12 months of life?

- The *postural reflexes*, which develop after primitive reflex activity, may be blocked, preventing the child's effective interaction with the world around him.
- This can mean that immature behaviour remains prevalent.
- They can affect the functioning of gross and fine motor coordination skills.
- Sensory, perceptual and cognitive skills can also be affected.

In fact, as mentioned above, retained reflexes can act like a tied rope, not allowing later learning skills to develop to a state when they occur automatically. For those children with just a slightly abnormal reflex profile, normal teaching strategies will probably be sufficient to help. When there are moderate difficulties, educators will also need to improve balance and coordination. However, as I discovered, when there are a number, or cluster, of remaining active primitive reflexes, then it is most likely that a reflex stimulation/inhibition programme will be needed as a neuro-developmental delay exists.

So how can educators identify retained primitive reflexes?

Importantly, it is not the aim of this chapter to show how to assess if primitive reflexes remain active within the children you teach, but to help you identify those children who may well have these underlying motor problems, so that further assistance and assessment can be sought.

Case study 4

Jenna, a Year 6 pupil, always looked as if she was going to fall asleep at her desk. She would slump over her work with her elbow on the desk and her hand under her chin holding her head up. Jenna found it extremely difficult to copy correctly from the board to her piece of paper, always losing her place. She would get disheartened quickly and begin to chat and disturb others.

Primitive Reflex: Symmetrical Tonic.

How to help: Provide a sloping board to write on. Many older children will quite happily use an arch file for this purpose. In PE lessons practise creeping and crawling on hands and knees.

By giving Jenna a sloping board, she had to change her seating position and she also could not put her elbow so easily on the desk, preventing her holding her head up with her hand. This encouraged her to strengthen her neck muscles. Being able to keep her head up also helped her hand–eye coordination and thus her copying and writing skills.

Case study 5

Cassey was a great cause of concern for her teacher as she would always turn her paper to an angle of about 180 degrees to write. She also had really poor handwriting and found it extremely hard to follow anything without using a finger or marker to track the words. Many hours of handwriting practice, reading trying not to use a marker to follow and correcting the positioning of paper and books proved fruitless.

Primitive Reflex: Asymmetrical Tonic Neck Reflex.

How to help: It became very clear that Cassey could not cross her midline; that is, she could not write using her right hand when the paper was in front of the left side of her body. In very young children this reflex is seen when they move an object or toy to the middle of their bodies holding it in their right hand. When the toy crosses over the midline, the left hand will be used to move the toy. Exercises helping develop these skills can be slowly introduced to help develop this skill. Poor eye tracking can be developed by using tracking book exercises or games, as well as some specific movement work. Forcing a child to practise handwriting without dealing with the real problems just causes frustration and loss of self-confidence.

Discussion

Following these two case studies, can you identify individual children in your educational setting who may well have these motor difficulties? Identify what their difficulties are and discuss with a colleague whether motor problems may be the cause.

Case study 6

Steven was always falling over and was frequently teased by his peers for his funny running. He found it very hard to organise himself and his work and he also had a very poor sense of time and rhythm. His artwork identified visual and perceptual difficulties and reading was also a problem, because he constantly missed out words or even whole lines.

Primitive Reflex: Tonic Labyrinthine.

How to help: With specifically selected exercises involving rolling, rocking and turning round, Steven's balance improved, as did his perceptual and visual difficulties.

The most stunning example I have seen of the need for a stimulation/inhibition programme was a small, ten-year-old boy. He was labelled with Attention Deficit Hyperactive Disorder (ADHD), as well as SEBD and the Autistic Spectrum. As his SENCO at the time I was not convinced that either the labels ADHD or Autistic Spectrum were either helpful or correct. I asked for permission to carry out a neuro-developmental assessment and discovered that he was so sensory bound that he could not even tell when someone was touching his hand unless he was looking at the hand.

Case study 7

Jason lay on the PE mat totally relaxed (which was very unusual) and listened to the instructions. I told Jason that one of the two adults present would touch either his hand or foot very gently with the flat end of a pencil and asked if that was all right with him. Both adults were well known to Jason in the school. Jason closed his eyes and I then touched his right palm with the pencil. There was no response and after a few seconds I asked if he had felt anything. He asked me to have another go. My colleague touched the bottom of one of his feet with a pencil and again there was no response. He then very calmly asked if he could sit up and look at where we were touching so that he could give us an answer. I was totally stunned and realised what a frightening place the world must be for him if he could not tell where he was unless he touched and looked at everything at the same time. No wonder he would run round a room touching the walls and furniture when entering it – without this he could not get a sense of where he was and if he was safe.

Fortunately after a carefully worked out programme within a few weeks, Jason could feel all touch accurately. Surprisingly he also physically grew, emotionally began to mature and started to access learning more successfully. Jason was also receiving other therapy simultaneously and thus it must be accepted that other input may also have had positive effects, but without a doubt his enjoyment of the sessions and the improvements seen, provided much evidence of the need for this type of intervention.

Primitive Reflex: Moro

How to help: In this case a specific training programme was necessary.

Other children who may have retained primitive reflexes may include those who do the following:

- constantly wriggle in their seats;
- moving their tongue around their mouth when writing;
- dribble a lot;
- continue to use an immature pencil grip;
- cannot kick a football accurately or throw and catch a ball;
- cannot ride a bike without help.

This indeed is only one approach to developing motor skills, but it is one that I have found helps children with these problems develop a link between their inner world and the outer world. With the changing curriculum in the past thirty years, combined with the changes in society, the need to support the physical development of children appears to be vital. If this is not acknowledged, not only will their physical, emotional and social skills be impaired, but their learning potential will also remain unfulfilled. Russell (1992: 7) supports this view, identifying some negative outcomes that could arise if motor learning problems are not correctly managed: 'motor learning problems have been shown to be a persistent characteristic associated with educational failure, social isolation, anxiety, withdrawal and depression persisting into adolescence *and beyond*' (my emphasis).

I now cannot imagine just giving desk-type exercises to children with motor difficulties and just looking at their cognitive achievements, and all too frequently their failures, for guidance. All educators, I believe, need to consider the whole child when trying to construct an intervention programme. Without this level of inquiry many children will continue to be learners who cannot retain knowledge and new concepts, not because they are not concentrating or trying, but because they do not have secure foundations. The Bible story that uses the image of a house built upon sand being knocked down by the sea, and a house built on rocks remaining firm and steady, clearly illustrates the point that, without the foundations, the later additions can be built on top but will not be retained.

This chapter is only a brief visit to an area of need utilised to develop educational skills, but as Goddard (2002: xv) says, although learning takes place in the brain; 'it is the body that acts as receptor for information and then becomes the vehicle through which knowledge is expressed'. In fact 'movement lies at the heart of learning' (ibid.: xvi).

Key issues

It is anticipated that you will now:

- have a good understanding of how motor development problems can affect children's social, academic and emotional growth;
- have an understanding of how motor difficulties can affect children in a classroom situation;
- have an awareness that children may have motor difficulties as well as a learning problem;
- see the need for children to be able to practise motor skills, especially nowadays;
- have an understanding that children's physical development is sequential;
- know that movement is important for learning to take place.

Professional Standards for Higher Level Teaching Assistants (HLTA)

If you can demonstrate your understanding and professional use of the key issues illustrated within this chapter, it is hoped that you will be able to fulfil the following HLTA Standards:

2.5	3.2.2	3.2.3

These Standards have not been identified in the text of this chapter due to the specific nature of this subject matter. It cannot therefore be said that the information within this chapter can fully demonstrate the Standards illustrated above.

Useful information and contacts

Brain Gym
Dennison, P. and Dennison, G. (1989) *Brain Gym: Teacher's Edition*. Ventura CA: Edu-Kinesthetics, Inc.
Edu-Kinesthetics Website: www.braingym.com

The Institute for Neuro-Physiological Psychology (INPP)
Chester, England.
Email: inpp@virtual-chester.net
Website: www.inpp.org.uk

Steiner Schools
List of Waldorf (Steiner) Schools can be obtained from:
Steiner Schools Fellowship
Kidbrooke Park
Forest Row
Sussex, England.
Website: www.steinerwaldorf.org.uk/

WriteDance
Ragnhild Oussoren Voors, graphologist and originator of WriteDance.
Suppliers of WriteDance: www.luckyduck.co.uk

References

Doherty, J. and Bailey, R. (2003) *Supporting Physical Development and Physical Education in the Early Years*, Buckingham: Open University Press.

Gallahue, D.L. and Ozmun, J.C. (1995) *Understanding Motor Development*, Madison: WCB Brown and Benchmark.

Goddard, S. (2002) *Reflexes, Learning and Behavior*, Eugene: Fern Ridge Press.

Hannaford, C. (1995) *Smart Moves: Why Learning Is not All in Your Head*, Arlington: Great Ocean Publishers.

Jensen, E. (2000) *Learning with the Body in Mind*, San Diego: The Brain Store.

Nash-Wortham, M. and Hunt, J. (1994) *Take Time*, Stourbridge: The Robinswood Press.

Plowden Committee (1967) *Children and their Primary Schools* (The Plowden Report), London: HMSO.

Russell, J. (1993) *Graded Activities for Children with Motor Difficulties*, Cambridge: Cambridge University Press.

Speech, language and communication needs (SLCN)

12

Janet Tod and Sue Soan

Introduction

> Language is central to learning. It provides the main tool for teaching and learning and, by experiencing language for these purposes, children's language develops further. Through active participation and through interaction with people and with their environment, children learn to make sense of their world. Learning and in particular, learning through the use of language is an intellectual, emotional and social activity.
>
> (Martin and Miller, 1999)

This chapter seeks to provide an increased understanding of the process, pace and purpose of normal language development for those who support learners with speech language and communication needs (SLCN). This will be used as a basis, for providing a framework for assessing SLCN within educational contexts and identifying appropriate support strategies. Most children have not only 'learned to talk' but are also able to 'talk to learn' prior to school entry. For children who do not experience difficulties with speech, language and communication, their ability to use language to communicate, reflect and reason, and plan and monitor their own behaviour appears to happen with comparative ease. However, for those who teach pupils with SLCN, progress is often frustratingly slow. Although 'early identification' has been enshrined within Special Educational Needs (SEN) policy for at least a decade (DfE, 1994; DfES, 2004) and is an important component of educational practice, there is little doubt that language difficulties have a long-term pervasive effect on educational attainment.

It is crucial that the development of the use of language is regarded as a whole-school responsibility with all staff having an awareness of how to support and enhance language development through their interaction with pupils.

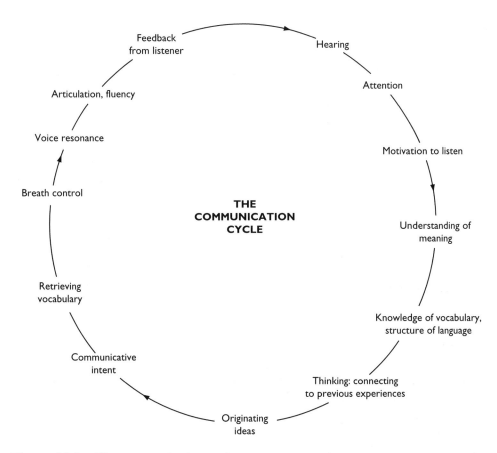

Figure 12.1 The communication cycle

In thinking about the development and use of language, it is clear that there is a contrast between the complexity of the communication process (see Figure 12.1) and the apparent ease with which the majority of infants learn to understand and use language. The next section is concerned with the contexts and condition that underpin this normal language development.

Figure 12.1 describes the processes involved in communication. The right of the diagram is concerned with 'input', i.e. listening and understanding that we refer to as 'receptive language' and the left-hand side is concerned with the output of speech and language that we refer to as 'expressive language'. In normal language development, receptive language (i.e. understanding) precedes expressive language development. Parents and caretakers continue to talk to their babies, even though they may get limited response, in order to promote understanding of language. It is important that those who support learners with SLCN ensure that the development of receptive language is not limited by the learner's restricted use of language. Talking, commenting on what the pupil does, reading stories, etc. are important activities for those who support learners with SLCN.

Normal language development

There is a consensus of opinion that humans are born with the capacity to make use of symbols and code events, i.e. humans have a 'language instinct' (Pinker, 1995) that parents/caretakers activate and fuel during their child's early years. The language instinct is powerful and appears to have an optimum time for activation, that is, from birth to around three years of age during which the infant develops from being a recipient of undifferentiated stimuli to becoming a social being who has mastered the attentional styles, language, and reciprocity inherent in effective social communication. For children who have impaired language functioning, the power and flexibility that characterise the development of the language instinct are much less evident and progress is considerably slower.

The prime purpose of language

The prime purpose of language development at this stage is social. In pursuit of this aim, the adult seeks primarily to establish joint attention, and this is achieved by closely monitoring the child's gaze and commenting on what he or she is doing. When the infant's gaze wanders to another focus, the adult follows the infant's line of gaze and continues to comment. This is an important process as it ensures the following:

- joint attention is secured and increased;
- language and gesture are repeatedly received by the infant and associated with an activity or event that was initiated by the child;
- the infant experiences that he or she is very important to the adult and that the adult enjoys being with the child – this contributes positively to the development of the child's *self-esteem*;
- The purpose of language during this stage is social – the adult wants to relate to the infant and with time (6–9 months) the infant responds by wanting to communicate with the adult ('communicative intent'). During this period of development the adult uses strategies which follow the sequence: gain child's attention – modify input to ensure that it is relevant and understandable – extend and clarify using close monitoring of child's response and utterances to inform next sequence of language input.

Examples of strategies used in this process are:

- gaining the child's attention by:
  - speaking in a higher than normal tone;
  - using exaggerated intonation or rhythm;
  - making use of child's name, or nickname, to start a sentence;

- using eye-level contact, gesturing and pointing;
- using visual cues (e.g. hiding objects, then 'finding' them, etc.).

- reducing the complexity of language input by:
  - using shorter sentences;
  - avoiding complex sentences;
  - selecting vocabulary which is meaningful to the child often using visual cues.

- extending and clarifying language by:
  - monitoring that child is understanding, if not, speech is adjusted with key words being emphasised and repeated;
  - speaking clearly and slower than in normal conversation, pausing between topics;
  - providing a commentary on the child's play, direct questioning is avoided;
  - using 'here and now' familiar topic of conversation. If the child makes an error, the adult does not correct but responds with the correct format: (Child: 'Sheeps'. Adult: 'Yes, you are right, there are sheep in the field, you are so clever!')

So, while it is important for those who support pupils with SLCN to have knowledge of the stages of 'normal' language, it is probably even more helpful to reflect upon the 'how' of normal language development. Although home contexts differ from school contexts, in that the child has more individual attention, more effective monitoring and subsequent adjustment of language input, and more opportunities for repetition via commentary on basic care-taking routine activity (eating, dressing washing, etc.), there are aspects of 'home' language development that can be successfully transferred to classroom contexts. These include:

- *Social contexts for learning*: the basic impetus for language is a social one and contexts make a difference. It follows that if those who support pupils with SLCN can 'set up' communicative contexts, which encourage social communication, then the pupil is more likely to be motivated, if required to answer a question (to which the adult probably knows the answer). Arranging for the response to the curriculum to be framed in a 'communicative context' requires considered planning with emphasis on peer–peer, small group, and collaborative groupings. Useful support material includes Social Use of Language Programme (SULP) (Rinaldi, 1992) and Circle Time activities (Mosley, 1996).

- *Securing and enhancing the underlying skills for language development*: these include motivation, attention, listening, and memory. Useful strategies include commentary on child's activities, allowing time for child to respond, securing joint attention, encouraging selective attention by the use of visual cues, etc., and giving opportunities for language to meet a personal and social developmental function as well as being the medium for academic learning.

- *Monitoring pupil response* and making subsequent adjustments to curricular delivery, task requirements, and/or social contexts.

Once children have 'learned to talk', parents and caretakers skilfully change their communication style in order to prepare their child to use language 'to learn' in the school setting. Instead of merely communicating socially, the adult adopts a more 'teaching' style approach and asks the child questions to which the adult knows the answer ('What colour are your shoes?). They also encourage the child to allow their attention to be directed by an adult – 'Why don't you draw me a lovely picture of the Tellytubbies?' Parents/caretakers also try to get the child to sit down, listen, and engage in directed 'school' activities – reading, drawing, countings, etc. Parents can often offer the one-to-one attention needed for the initial development of this 'on task' behaviour. They encourage their child to make choices and to direct his or her own attention. Strategies are also applied to enable the child to develop social skills needed for school. Their child is encouraged to play with same age peers and social behaviours such as listening, turn taking, sharing, etc. are made explicit and rewarded, 'Here are some sweets, give one to Jenny and one to Peter. Good boy for sharing.' These behaviours are developed in a supportive safe setting for the child so that the chances of success are maximised. The important point to note is that these behaviours are explicitly taught and learned during the years prior to school entry. If a child does not have these experiences, and arrives in school without the appropriate 'learning behaviours', then he or she will find it difficult to self-direct attention, share attention with peers, and use language for learning. It is important to be aware that children with language difficulties are at increased risk of developing behavioural problems (Stevenson *et al.*, 1985, in Ripley *et al.*, 2001), and that strategies to improve language and communication can have a beneficial effect on behaviour.

Discussion

- How might knowledge of the way parents and/or caretakers support 'normal' language development help you to foster listening, attention and understanding for a pupil with SLCN?
- How might placement in a nursery or other early years setting impact upon the language development of a young child with SLCN?
- What changes, if any, could be made in your own setting to enhance the development of language for pupils with SLCN?

Although parents/caretakers use the relatively few key strategies described above with their infants, the effect is impressive with most children arriving at school with sufficient competence and confidence in language to be able to learn in group settings and mix socially with peers and staff. The use of a few core strategies by all school staff consistently can also be effective in supporting pupils with SLCN. These include:

- Encourage *active* language processing, i.e. use discussion, review, appropriate questioning style, problem solving, reflection, etc.

- Use *visual* strategies – cue cards, visual timetables, etc. to support understanding and memory.

- Make the *implicit explicit* – reinforce if possible with visual cues; this strategy is particularly important for the development of routines and rules needed in classroom settings.

- Give the learner *time* to respond; if necessary, ask questions in advance in order to give pupils time to plan their response.

- Record and build on what the learner *can do*.

- Try to keep the pupil *motivated* by creating activities and groupings that use the *social* and *communicative* function of language.

- To monitor listening and understanding, use *recognition* activities before *recall*, i.e. use choice or multi-choice tasks before asking the pupil to generate their own responses. If the pupil is unable to recognise the correct response, it is unlikely that he or she will be able to recall or generate his or her own response.

- Comment on what the pupil is doing to encourage the development of *concentration* and *attention*.

Assessment of speech and language difficulties

Obviously speech and language are complex processes and assessment often will be a collaborative activity between a range of professionals, e.g. speech and language therapist, educational psychologist, teacher, and of course parent/caretaker and the pupil. Contexts make a difference to communication and language performance and a reasonable aim of assessment is to establish consistencies and inconsistencies in the individual's communication profile across a range of contexts. If, for example, the pupil can function better in an ICT lesson than, say, in the playground, this provides useful information about how the context influences the pupil's ability to understand and communicate. Using this information the educator can modify the environment in order to maximise performance, i.e. by the use of visual support (possibly in some cases via the use of sign language); teaching and practising the conventions of social communication in a one-to-one or small group setting, etc.; use of a peer support 'buddy' in the playground; explaining the rules of games that are played in the playground; use of TA support as a facilitator of playground interaction, etc. Observation in a range of contexts is thus an important assessment strategy for pupils with SLCN. Parents/caretakers are also crucial in informing schools as how to best to communicate with their child and can supply information about activities, siblings, other relatives, interests, likes/dislikes, etc. that will enable staff to establish and sustain conversations.

Different professionals have developed different approaches to assessment and it is important that there is some shared understanding between professionals if coherent planning is to be achieved.

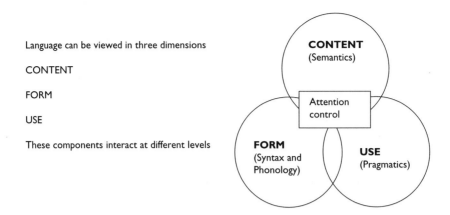

Language can be viewed in three dimensions

CONTENT

FORM

USE

These components interact at different levels

CONTENT	FORM	USE
Semantics: the *meaning* of words and how they relate to each other Consists of *Vocabulary*: 'coat' *Concept*: e.g. colour *Categories*: food *Meaning*: 'I've spilt my food on my blue coat.'	How sounds are combined to form words (*Phonology*) and words are combined to form sentences (*Syntax* and *Morphology*) – both according to systematic rules. *Sounds*: 'p', 't', 'k' (phonetics) 'mat', 'hat' (phonology); *Words*: adjectives, verbs, -ing and -ed endings, plurals, etc. *Syntax*: phrases and sentences	Pragmatics: the reason why we use language to interact and the way in which we do it. *Why?* intention *How* did we go about conveying our message – did we monitor reaction of the listener and adjust accordingly?

Figure 12.2   Framework for describing language

Speech and language therapists have traditionally used the linguistic model described in Figure 12.2 (Bloom and Lahey, 1978). Assessments based on this model seek to describe language in term of these functions and identify where to focus therapy and or the 'extra or different provision' that might be needed in educational contexts via Individual Education Plans (IEPs) (DfES, 2001a). For many children with SLCN their difficulties seldom fall into 'neat' categories of content, form and use due to the interdependence of these areas of language and communication.

Psycholinguistic and cognitive approaches

These approaches are often adopted by professionals within educational settings and are based upon how language is processed. Using this model assessment involves looking at how language is received, interpreted and used in a range of social and subject contexts in order to identify:

- the individual's particular speech and language processing problem;
- the implications for learning in group settings;

- how curriculum delivery and assessment might be modified;

- the social, emotional and behavioural implications of the language impairment;

- action that needs to be taken within the framework of the Code of Practice, i.e. School Action and School Action Plus, including the 'different or otherwise extra provision' delivered via Individual Education Plans;

- roles and responsibilities within the school, including peers, for implementing enhanced provision;

- pupil and parental expectations for success and their contribution in achieving these success criteria.

Assessment in educational settings is currently influenced by national and global policies for inclusion. In essence, inclusion is concerned with securing 'access', 'engagement' and 'participation' (Tod, 2000) for all learners in order to reduce barriers to achievement learning and social participation. Such a model fits well with educational assessment frameworks that seek to identify how the individual's speech and language difficulty affects his or her confidence and competence to access the curriculum; to process the range of inputs; and to respond academically and socially.

Assessment in educational contexts is very much concerned with how pupils use language. As learners progress through the education system, it is this language use that determines their progress. During the early years an individual's use of language at home is linked to their personal needs, e.g. to ask for help, to seek information, to secure attention, to interact, etc. However, once in school the purpose of language changes. 'Pupils' talking and writing provides evidence of their abilities to understand, imagine, explore, analyse, make explicit, evaluate, elaborate, interpret, hypothesise, and reflect' (SCAA '97). We expect pupils to develop their language use as shown in Figure 12.3, a progression from simple to complex answers, etc.

It is therefore very useful for those who support pupils with SLCN to assess 'how the child/young person is using language'. Once this has been established, the aim of teaching can be to consolidate the uses already evident and to increase the range. Anne Locke (Teaching Talking, 1992) provides a comprehensive assessment

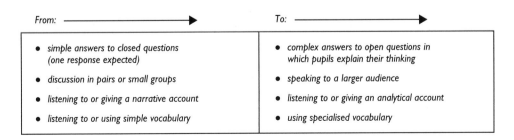

Figure 12.3 Language development

and teaching package. Examples from this include a useful 'Purpose of Talk' for infant and junior age pupils against which pupil progress can be assessed.

Use of language

Obviously use of language is influenced by the social context. A child may well use language differently in a one-to-one structured setting in which the adult can give time and support to social communication. Figure 12.4 illustrates different contexts that may influence language use in the primary classroom.

This framework for social communication states that important variables include:

- number of people involved in the communication;
- amount of adult intervention;
- type of activity: structured vs unstructured;
- amount of social interaction required;
- degree of autonomy needed.

It is important that staff work together when assessing the educational and social needs of pupils with SLCN. Keeping brief notes about the pupil's response to support is crucial to effective monitoring and evaluation. Schools, quite appropriately, embed the assessment of SLCN within the whole-school framework for assessment. Assessment of progress in some curricular areas is particularly relevant in identifying the needs of pupils with SLCN. These include National Curriculum English 'Speaking and Listening' and the different levels that make up the framework of the National Literacy Strategy:

- *word level*: phonics, spelling and vocabulary;
- *sentence level*: grammar and punctuation;
- *text level*: comprehension and composition.

Dependent ———————————————————→ **Independent**

Structured	CA sits next to child and reads a book to him while he's playing in the sand	Child looks at book with adult	Child reads book to adult – told when to start and finish	Child reads silently in class when directed	Child selects a book from school library because he needs it for information to do homework	Child chooses a book and reads it for pleasure
Unstructured	Child plays with adult next to him	Child plays in playground with adult supervising	Child plays alone or watches TV unsupervised in house or classroom	Child plays next to other children with adult supervision	Child plays in small group without direct adult supervision	Child plays cooperatively with other children without direct supervision

Figure 12.4   Different contexts can influence language use

Discussion

■ What do you consider the main purposes of assessment for learners with SLCN in your own setting?
■ How do you contribute to the assessment process in your own setting?
■ What effect does your assessment of pupil response to your support have on your own behaviour?
■ How might you bring about improvements in using collaborative approaches to assessment to improve provision for learners with SCLN in your own setting?
■ To what extent do you involve the pupil in assessment of his/her learning?

Strategies to support learners with SLCN

Given the complexity of language development and use in educational settings, it is not surprising that there are many resources to support learners with SLCN. It is useful to be familiar with the resources available in your school setting. The strategies used must be linked to the assessment of pupil need, as described in Figure 12.5.

In addition to specific strategies, there remains a need to be skilled in using strategies that support 'generic' aspects of learning for pupils with SLCN. Such pupils are likely to have a residual need across all contexts for support that does the following:

■ builds *confidence* and *independence*;

■ enhances and monitors *attention* and *listening skills*;

■ encourages the *development of memory* for learning;

■ enables the learning of *'new' vocabulary*, e.g. subject specific;

■ provides guidance on how to respond to different *question forms*;

■ fosters the development of *written language skills*;

■ provides contexts and conditions that foster *social participation*.

Attention and listening

A pupil is more likely to attend and listen if the following conditions are met:

■ He or she has some familiarity with the content and purpose of the lesson. TAs can fulfil a valuable role in 'briefing' the pupil before the lesson about vocabulary that will be used, etc. Homework set may be 'in preparation' for the next lesson so that the pupil has had time to familiarise her or himself with the content.

■ Distractions and noise are kept to a minimum.

■ He or she is 'cued' to listen either by the instruction 'Listen, *Jamie*' or by a cue card (containing the class symbol for listening).

Name.......................... Class............................... Date............................ Teacher...............................

Highlight relevant BEHAVIOURS and add any others observed. Highlight the appropriate LANGUAGE COMPONENT. Use the suggested STRATEGIES and highlight those found to be particularly effective. Add any others found to be successful.

LANGUAGE COMPONENT	OBSERVED BEHAVIOURS	SUGGESTED STRATEGIES
Phonetics The articulation of units of speech	Inability to enunciate some speech sounds Confusion between similarly produced speech sounds. e.g. voiced and voiceless 't/d', 'k/g'	• Model correct usage by extending what has been said in the correct form. • Seek advice from speech therapist on best approach i.e. use of cued articulation to show production of sound, etc.
Phonology/phonological awareness The awareness of sounds within words	Difficulty in generating rhyme Difficulty breaking down words into syllables (segmenting words into phonemes) Difficulty in identifying phonemes in speech and writing Difficulty with blending phonemes into words	• Music-based activities which encourage listening, recognition and generating: high/low; short/long; loud/soft • Auditory discrimination games e.g. sound lotto • Listening to rhymes, picking out non rhyming word. • Clapping out patterns, i.e. 3 claps for elephant • Use multisensory techniques, listen to word, look at visual pattern, trace in sand, say out loud, etc. • Supported generation of rhyme (cued?) hat, cat, mat, etc.
Morphology The combination of sound into basic units of meaning (e.g. one morpheme 'house', two morphemes: house/s, three, house/keep/ing	Word endings not used or inappropriately used (in relation to chronological age) Tenses not used or incorrect	• Model language, e.g. if the child says 'I rided my bike yesterday' the response could be 'So you *rode* your bike yesterday – where did you go?' • Don't correct; • Use visual cues to correct word endings, e.g. colour code or use puzzle shapes so that the pupil can recognise and fit the correct ending
Syntax The grammatical relationships between words, phrases, and clauses	Use of immature sentences (i.e. two word 'gone pen' etc; inappropriate use of word order Lack of or limited use of grammatical function words, e.g. articles, connectives, etc. Misuse or omission of pronouns Difficulty in predicting words when reading that make sense	• Aim to improve language through: commentary on child's activities; use of cued short requests which convey grammatically correct order and use • Use of stories or familiar incidents (e.g. video of football game for who? what? when? where? questions and answers) • Sorting of written words into the correct order, e.g. boy, the, head, on, his, put, hat, his • Object hunt with clues, *on the shelf; under* the bin • Use written format to stress grammatical format e.g. question marks, commas, link to oral speech pauses, intonation, etc.

Semantics The meaning of individual words and of word relationships	Difficulty in understanding language Difficulty with expressive language Word finding difficulties Inappropriate responses to questions Difficulty with classification i.e. use of concept words – 'fruit' Literal understanding Difficulty with concepts of time, space, comparison etc. Need time to process and respond to information Often exhibits sequencing and short-term memory difficulties	• Use visual language strategies • Use short clear sentences • Make implicit instructions explicit – makes sure that the pupil knows what is expected of him/her • Use practical materials to support input • Use objects and pictures to reinforce key word • Make use of multimedia software for language and reading development • Build on the language the child already has
PRAGMATICS Language for communication 'social use of language' How language functions in varying contexts	Talks 'at' rather than 'to' the listener Difficulty in 'reading' social situation – does not heed social conventions of classroom e.g. may talk at same time as teacher, interrupt, not take turns, etc. Literal response e.g. 'have you finished talking? Answer: 'No, not yet.' May seek to reduce stimulation by avoidance e.g. limited or absent eye contact, attention directed away from social activities towards solitary repetitive activity May talk about a topic over and over again even though listener has heard about it previously May have limited attention span at times, rigidity of attention at other times	• Make implicit social conventions of the classroom explicit ('when we are in class, we usually sit down', via use of social stories, etc). • Try to understand why the pupil is responding as he does, if social stimulation is frightening, then ensure pupil has his own space for working free from distractions; seek guidance from teacher/SENCO before making the pupil make eye contact when talking as this may confuse the pupil if he has difficulty 'reading' facial expression • Use visual timetables and explore the use of TEACCH strategies • Teach turn taking and other social behaviour in a structured safe setting initially, – e.g. circle time • Use written instructions, visual prompts • Make use of 'impersonal' ICT to teach new skills before transfer to social setting • If changes to routine have to be made, try to explain beforehand, emphasising the full sequence of events, e.g. 'Today we are going to the swimming pool. When we have finished swimming we will come back to school'.

Figure 12.5   Classroom analysis of speech, language and communication difficulties

■ Verbal or written instruction is supported by pictorial cues and use of gesture.

■ The content of the lesson is meaningful to the pupil and linked to familiar vocabulary.

■ Instructions are brief and explicit.

■ He or she is clear about what he or she has to listen for, e.g. not a whole story, but the names of animals in the story.

■ Intersperse short bouts of listening with doing – not both at once.

■ He or she is motivated but not overly anxious.

Pupils remember best when the following conditions are met:

- The things that need to be remembered are of interest and value to them.
- There is opportunity for re-processing the material in different formats: i.e. making flow diagrams; mind maps, mnenonics, re-telling the main points to a peer; making a poster of key points, etc.
- Learning involves practical activities and social experiences.
- There are opportunities for practice and regular use.
- Explicit links are made to the individual's existing knowledge and understanding.

Learning new vocabulary

Try to ensure that new vocabulary is topic based and can be linked to or grouped with other words, e.g. living things; plants/animals, types, etc. Start with the big picture first so that the pupil can place the new word within a conceptual framework:

- Get the class to 'brainstorm' links and meanings of the new vocabulary.
- Link to real-life 'active' situations so that the word has meaning for the pupil.
- Use multi-sensory approaches: colour, shape, feel of materials.
- Encourage the pupil to be aware of the word's sound structure 'ha/bi/tat' and how it looks in written and pictorial formats.
- Provide opportunities for reinforcement of key words, regular revisiting to test that the pupil has remembered the new words, providing opportunities to use vocabulary in a range of contexts and/or curriculum activities.

Use of question forms

Teach by giving the pupil a cue list of the type of response required:

- 'What' refers to things
- 'Who' refers to a person;
- 'When' refers to time:
- 'Where' refers to place;
- 'How' refers to method or procedure;
- 'How many' refers to number;
- 'Why' refers to a reason.

Stressing the key cue words in a question will allow the pupil to select a 'type' of response – if correct, this can be made more precise. Games and activities can be used to reinforce the use of questions and answers.

This section of the chapter has been concerned with identifying effective ways to support learners with SLCN. Some general strategies to support learning and social participation have been identified by looking at the pace, process and personal relationships involved in 'normal language development'. Obviously learners with SLCN have different profiles of development and many may need individualised support. There are, however, some key principles and strategies that can be used inclusively to support all learners. The important skill to develop when supporting learners with SLCN is that of monitoring their response to teaching so that adjustments can be made. The key characteristic of human language is that it is flexible and responsive – it is important that those who support learners with SLCN share these characteristics.

> **Discussion**
>
> ■ How do you decide what strategies to use when supporting a pupil with SLCN?
> ■ What strategies have you found to be useful in supporting both an individual pupil with SLCN and the whole class/small groups?
> ■ What do you consider are the barriers to inclusion for a learner with SLCN?
> ■ What strategies have been effectively used in your setting to promote the inclusion of pupils with SLCN?
> ■ How might you develop confidence and independence in a learner with SLCN?

Augmentative and alternative communication (AAC)

> Socio-linguistic research indicates that AAC systems need to be seen as living, developing languages within whole school communities, and not just as tagged-on extras for peripheral individuals.
>
> (Chinner et al. 2001: 10)

There are increasing numbers of learners requiring Augmentative and Alternative Communication (AAC) systems in mainstream as well as in special educational settings at the present time. If these learners are to be successfully included, it is essential that a supportive communication environment is provided. This will undoubtedly require all the involved professionals, parents/carers, and learners themselves in planning, and implementing the necessary programmes together. For this to be achieved, training, assessment and resources are vital to ensure the most appropriate system is provided for the learner at the relevant time by educators who understand and support their needs.

Recent documentation and funding

Since 1995 the National Curriculum has acknowledged the importance of AAC. The National Curriculum 2000 went much further, requiring teachers to use 'ICT, other technological aids and taped materials' and 'alternative and augmentative communication, including signs and symbols' (NC online, downloaded 14.05.2002). The National Literacy Strategy, the National Numeracy Strategy and the National Curriculum for IT all acknowledge the usefulness of AAC systems.

In 2001 the Department for Education and Skills (DfES) published the Statutory document *Inclusive Schooling* (2001a) and also the *Special Educational Needs Code of Practice* (2001b). Both these documents reaffirmed the government's commitment to providing for learners' communication needs. Following on from *Every Child Matters* (HMSO, 2003), *Removing Barriers to Achievement: The Government's Strategy for SEN* (DfES, 2004: 31, 2.5) also acknowledges the need for greater attention to communication support: 'Overcoming speech, language and communication difficulties is crucial to enabling children to access the whole curriculum.' Using a case study from the Communication Aids Project (CAP) this document also encourages the use of ICT to support learning (DfES, 2004: 30, 2.4).

The government has, since 2002, financially supported the provision of voice-output communication aids (VOCAs) for children in England through the Communication Aids Project (CAP) and also the Integrated Community Equipment Services Initiative. This funding is to provide hardware and training for the provision of AACs (Chan, 2003). A VOCA or Communication aid, is a piece of computer hardware (PC or Laptop) with special communication software. They may also have either a synthesised or digitised voice.

What does the term AAC mean?

Augmentative and Alternative Communication is defined thus:

> [AAC] refers to any means by which an individual can *supplement* or *replace* spoken communication. Communication may range from any movement or behaviour that is observed and interpreted by another person as meaningful, to the use of a code agreed upon between people where items have specific meanings, ie. a language.

This definition continues:

> AAC is both a means of accessing an educational curriculum and language in its own right. It is appropriate for individuals who have difficulty with receptive and expressive language due to physical, sensory or learning disability. It provides an opportunity to attain economical, social, educational and vocational goals.
>
> (Chinner *et al.*, 2001: 3)

To enable AAC to be considered in a manageable and understandable manner for school planning and policies, it can be subdivided into *unaided* and *aided* communication (Glennen and DeCoste, in Chinner *et al.*, 2001). However, it is important to state at this point that individuals will probably require the use of both unaided and aided communication equipment so that total communication is achieved.

- *Unaided communication*: These methods of communication only use the learner's body and do not require any type of equipment.
- *Aided communication*: These methods of communication involve additional equipment. They may be 'low-tech' (an item that does not require a battery) or

'high tech' (an item that requires a battery at least to operate) (Communication Matters, 2001).

> **Discussion**
>
> Following the definitions above, try to place the types of communication systems listed in italic below, into a table using the headings 'unaided' or 'aided'. (If you do not know what a particular type of system is, use the information at the end of this section of the chapter to help you.)
>
> *Boardmaker, photographs, Picture Communication Symbols, British Sign Language, Makaton vocabulary, Voice Output Communication Aids (VOCAs), finger spelling, Rebus, objects, Signalong, use of a trackerball or joystick, a switch, cued articulation, light pointer, keyboard.*

One thing AAC systems definitely do not do is replace or minimise the role of any professional, such as speech and language therapists. In fact, it is most frequently their expertise and knowledge that will guide the selection of AAC systems. AAC systems do not prevent or hinder a learner from speaking, but can sometimes actually help to improve it.

What is known about the effectiveness of AACs?

Advantages of AAC systems are:

- They do not interfere with speech development and may encourage it.
- They may involve modality, specific styles and strategies.
- They can provide:
  - a means of communication for people at an early stage of development.
  - a means of communication and language for those whose speech is unintelligible.
  - a bridge to spoken language.
- They require interdisciplinary assessment, coordination and monitoring.
- Teachers, teaching assistants and therapists, schools and families can make a difference.

> **Discussion**
>
> - Make a list of advantages you have noticed in a classroom or other learning environment, where a learner with a speech and language difficulty has been given either an aided or unaided means of communication.
> - Then discuss with a colleague how the educators managed to implement this specific strategy for the learner.
> - Who else was involved before it could be initiated? Was training required?

Disadvantages of AAC systems are:

- If learners have to use their AAC system away from the rest of their school peers, the system user can feel isolated.

■ If learners cannot use their AAC system freely, but are tied to subject timetables or school terms for availability, they become less useful and less productive.

■ Limited speech and language therapy input and training.

■ Negative attitudes towards the use of AAC systems.

■ Lack of training for professionals may drastically restrict the use or effectiveness of AAC systems.

(Chinner *et al.*, 2001: 6)

> **Discussion**
>
> **If you know of an incident when a learner's AAC system has unsuccessfully been introduced into the learning environment, identify the reasons why you feel this was not successful.**

Working with others

Throughout this chapter the need for close collaboration between professionals, parents/carers and the learners themselves has been identified as an essential factor in the successful planning and implementation of a programme of support involving an AAC system. The most recent government documents continue to emphasise the role of parents (DfES, 2004) and for the need for partnership working, to enable effective working practices to develop and support learners. However, it has also been clear that, in addition to joint working, there are other factors that are of particular importance if ACC system programmes are going to be successfully implemented as well as planned.

These include:

■ adequate and regular training on the AAC system for everyone involved with the learner (teacher, teaching assistant, parent, peers, siblings, speech and language therapist, extended family, SENCO);

■ the provision of an inclusive learning environment that supports the use of the AAC system all of the time (if required);

■ regular opportunities for joint meetings to take place in a planned manner;

■ early identification and provision of the AAC system;

■ local means of repair (if aided communication system).

Further information

It has not been possible to give details about the ever-expanding range of VOCAs within this chapter. However, it is hoped that a flavour of the range of AAC systems now available has been offered. A list of suppliers and of types of equipment is given at the end of the chapter for further research purposes.

Key issues

It is anticipated that you will now:

- have an understanding of 'normal' language development;
- recognise the importance of language in all aspects of the curriculum and social life of an educational environment;
- encourage the use of effective strategies, assessments and interventions;
- have an understanding of what Augmentative and Alternative Communication (AAC) needs are;
- understand what AAC systems are and how they can support a learner with speech and language needs;
- recognise the importance of collaborative working with particular regard to the implementation of programmes for the use of an AAC system.

Professional Standards for Higher Level Teaching Assistants (HLTA)

It has been difficult to identify individual standards that could be specifically met within this chapter. However, it is recognised that with the knowledge and understanding gained from actually planning, training and implementing programmes for AAC systems and Speech, Language and Communication Programmes, a teaching assistant would indeed be able to demonstrate understanding and professional use of a number of the Standards.

Useful addresses and websites

Access to Communication and Technology
Selly Oak
Birmingham B29 6JA
www.wmrc.nhs.uk/act

The CALL Centre
Edinburgh
www.callcentrescotland.org.uk

Communication Aids Centre (ALAC)
Llandaff
Cardiff CF5 2YN
Tel: 02920313956

Communication Matters
The Ace Centre
Oxford
www.communicationmatters.org.uk

Crick Computing
www.cricksoft.com

FIND A VOICE
Ashford
Kent TN23 5NU
www.findavoice.org.uk

I-CAN Helps Children Communicate
www.ican.org.uk

Inclusive Technology
www.inclusive.co.uk/infosite/spandl.shml

Makaton Signs
www.makaton.org.uk

1Voice Communicating Together
Halifax HX1 2XL
www.1voice.info

Widgit Software
www.widgit.com.index.htm

References

Bloom, L. and Lacey, M. (1998) *Language Development and Language Disorders*, London: Wiley.

Chan, S. (2003) 'Barriers to AAC implementation', *Communication Matters*, vol. 18, no. 1, pp. 11–13.

Chinner, S., Hazell, G., Skinner, P. Thomas, P. and Williams, G. (eds) (2001) *Developing Augmentative and Alternative Communication Policies in Schools: Information and Guidelines*, Oxford: ACE Centre Advisory Trust.

Communication Matters (2001) *What is AAC?* Oxford: Communication Matters (ISAAC UK).

DEE (1994) 'The Code of Practice on the Identification and Assessment of Special Educational Needs.

DfES (2001a) *Inclusive Schooling*, Annesley: DfES.

DfES (2001b) *Special Educational Needs Code of Practice*, Annesley: DfES.

DfES (2004) *Removing Barriers to Achievement: The Government's Strategy for SEN*, Annesley: DfES.

HMSO (2003) *Every Child Matters*, Norwich: The Stationery Office.

Locke, A. and Beech, M. (1992) *Teaching Talking*, Windsor: NFER Nelson.

Martin, D. and Miller, C. (1996) *Speech and Language Difficulties in the Classroom*, London: David Fulton.

Mosley, J. (1996) *Quality Circle Time in the Primary School*, Wisbech: LDA.

NC online *Inclusion: Providing Effective Learning Opportunities for all Pupils* (downloaded on 14.05.2002) www.nc.uk.net/inclusion.html

Pinker, S. (1995) *The Language Instinct*, London: Penguin.

Rinaldi, W. (1992) *The Social Use of Language Programme*, Windsor: NFER Nelson.

Royal College of Speech and Language Therapists (1996) *Communicating Quality*, London: RCSLT.

SCAA (1997) *Use of Language: A Common Approach*, ref: Com/97/640. Hyes SCAA.

Tod, J. (2000) '20/20 Inclusive learning and teaching in the 21st Century .... perspectives for individual learners'. BERA symposium.

Tod, J. and Blamires, M. (2000) *Speech and Language: Individual Education Plans*, London: David Fulton.

Wright, J. and Kersner, M. (1998) *Supporting Children with Communication Problems: Sharing the Workload*, London: David Fulton.

Specific Learning Difficulties (SpLD)/dyslexia

Janet Tod and Sue Soan

Introduction

This chapter seeks to provide a working understanding of dyslexia that is linked to provision for learners who experience Specific Learning Difficulties (SpLD)/ dyslexia. The use of both terms, i.e. SpLD and dyslexia, in the title reflects the fact that at times some practitioners and policy-makers use the terms synonymously. However, for some professionals in the field the use of two terms reflects a difference in definition and conception. For the purpose of this chapter, 'dyslexia' will be the term used and will be considered to be an example of a 'specific learning difficulty'. This is consistent with the view expressed by the government in the Special Educational Needs (SEN) Code of Practice: 'Children who demonstrate features of moderate, severe or profound learning difficulties or specific learning difficulties, such as dyslexia or dyspraxia, require specific programmes to aid progress in cognition and learning' (DfES, 2001b: 7:55, 7:58).

Policy context

Given that the dominant philosophy influencing current educational practice is that of inclusion (DfES, 2001a), it is expected that most dyslexics will have their learning needs met within mainstream educational settings with 'different or otherwise extra' provision being delivered within the framework of the 2001 Code of Practice (DfES, 2001b).

For learners who experience dyslexia, *Removing Barriers to Achievement: The Government's Strategy for SEN* (DfES, 2004) is important as it outlines a programme of sustained action and review to support early years settings, schools and local authorities in improving provision for children with SEN in four key areas. These are: Early interventions, Removing Barriers to Learning, Raising Expectations and Achievement and Delivering improvements in Partnership.

What is dyslexia? controversy and consensus

The question 'What is dyslexia?' has resulted in considerable debate since the condition was described by W.R. Gowers in 1893 as 'a cerebral symptom ... a peculiar intermitting difficulty in reading'. There are now a number of definitions available in the literature including:

> Dyslexia is one of several distinct learning disabilities. It is a specific language-based disorder of constitutional origin characterised by difficulties in single word decoding, usually reflecting insufficient phonological processing. These difficulties in single word decoding are often unexpected in relation to age and other cognitive and academic abilities; they are not the result of generalised developmental disability or sensory impairment. Dyslexia is manifest by variable difficulty with different forms of language, often including, in addition to problems with reading, a conspicuous problem with acquiring proficiency in writing and spelling.
>
> (The Orton Dyslexia Society Research Committee, April 1994)

This can be contrasted to the following definition:

> Dyslexia is best described as a combination of abilities and difficulties, which affect the learning process in one or more of reading, spelling, writing and sometimes numeracy. Accompanying weaknesses may be identified in areas of speed of processing, short-term memory, sequencing, auditory and/or visual perception, spoken language and motor skills. Some children have outstanding creative skills, others have strong oral skills, yet others have no outstanding talents; they all have strengths.
>
> Dyslexia occurs despite normal intellectual ability and conventional teaching; it is independent of socio-economic or language background.
>
> (Peer, 2000)

A working party from the Division of Educational and Child Psychology of the British Psychological Society (BPS) produced this definition:

> Dyslexia is evident when accurate and fluent word reading and/or spelling develops very incompletely or with great difficulty. This focuses on literacy learning at the 'word level' and implies that the problem is severe and persistent despite appropriate learning opportunities.
>
> (BPS, 1999:18)

Discussion

- How do these definitions compare with your own understanding of dyslexia?
- To what extent do the definitions agree about the 'cause' and 'symptoms' of dyslexia?
- Do these definitions help you to support learners with dyslexia in your educational setting?

Level of representation	What does it mean?	Implications for assessment and learning support
BEHAVIOURAL Teachers are most likely to describe dyslexia at this level	This is what we observe. In educational settings this may include: • Difficulty in learning to read in contrast to rate of progress in non-written work • Listening comprehension (being read to) better than reading comprehension • Difficulty with syllabification, blending, segmentation and rhyme • May exhibit letter reversal, left/right confusion • May be hesitant or slow when generating oral language • May exhibit specific difficulties with number work • Difficulty generating written language, slow speed, spelling errors, often irregular layout – work may look 'messy' • Difficulty with sequencing, days of week, etc.	Tends to be curriculum-based assessment, looking at pupil's rate of progress, overall profile that may reveal within-subject discrepancies; response to teaching and additional support The National Literacy Strategy (DfES1998) provides a useful framework for classroom-based assessment via analysis of pupil response to word level, sentence level and text level work. It is important to embed support within curriculum and use additional support materials provided within the NLS
COGNITIVE This level of description of dyslexia is usually included in reports from educational psychologists and 'specialist' teachers/advisors	This level of representation is concerned with how the learner processes information (i.e. thinking, memory, etc.). Typically dyslexics would be predicted to have: • slow speed of processing written or symbolic material in contrast to the speed at which they are able to process non-written material, e.g. oral language and stories that are read to them. They may spend a long time on their written work but produce very little – it appears laboured and requires considerable effort • Difficulty with phonological processing (see main text) • Problems with sequencing and organisation and 'bringing together' information. Errors they make are often inconsistent • Difficulty with 'working memory', i.e. handling amounts of information within short time frame (e.g. listening, writing and spelling at the same time)	We have no way of 'observing' how the pupil is processing material and so we 'infer' this from their response to teaching. Looking at correct /expected responses and 'errors' (e.g. miscue analysis) can give a clue as to how we think they are handling the information they are given. Traditionally cognitive differences have been assessed by educational psychologists using psychometric assessments and standardised tests that seek to assess aspects of cognitive processing, e.g. speed, visual and auditory memory, motor skills etc. Classroom-based assessments are available (e.g. Aston Index, Phonological Assessment Battery, Cognitive Profiling Systems (COPS)) that assess aspects of cognitive processing thought to be relevant to the identification of dyslexia
BIOLOGICAL LEVEL This level of interest is often of concern to medical professionals and the focus for multi-disciplinary research activity	This is how dyslexia is thought to be represented at the level of brain functioning. There is considerable evidence that dyslexia is constitutional in origin with differences in brain	Genetic: Dyslexia tends to run in families so family history is very relevant to the assessment process. This is important as some parents may have difficulty with written communication

	structure and function being increasingly identified as medical technology develops	between school and home and in giving their child literacy support. Dyslexia is more common in males. Given the evidence that supports a view that dyslexics exhibit differences in form and function of left and right brain hemispheres some programmes of intervention seek specifically to address these differences. It is important to note that in developmental dyslexia that early intervention using a combination of holistic activities (for synthesising brain activity) and specific interventions (e.g. to promote phonological awareness, competence, and automaticity) is increasingly likely to be evident in educational contexts
EMOTIONAL This level is of primary concern to the pupil, his or her parent/caretakers and to all those designing and delivering support programmes	This is the level at which the learner 'experiences' dyslexia. This naturally varies between learners and is not normally included in 'representations' of dyslexia. However, dyslexics are conscripts to an educational system that naturally places considerable emphasis on written language skills – this is the main form of formal national assessment. It is not surprising that many dyslexics experience low self-esteem and anxiety as they progress through the educational system	Strategies available include: • Making sure that the dyslexics' relative strengths are acknowledged, valued and used when planning support and pupil groupings within the NLS • Working with parents/caretakers/peers to encourage engagement in other activities that are not concerned with written language so that the pupil can experience 'achievement', e.g. Art, ICT, sailing, debating, drama, video making, etc. • Encouraging pupil involvement in planning and monitoring of educational support so that they feel involved and in control in dealing with a condition that may be puzzling to them • Ensuring that pupil receives appropriate concessions for exams and alternative means of evidencing achievement in class other than through written work undertaken within a time frame. • Ensuring that all staff are aware of the dyslexics' difference and difficulties and do not attribute poor written work simply to laziness or lack of ability • Access to study support and work on developing study skills throughout school life is important for dyslexics

Figure 13.1   Levels of representation

As can be seen from the exemplar definitions, there are some elements of consensus about dyslexia that may help those new to the field to understand learners who experience dyslexia. It is important to understand that dyslexic learners are individuals and although they may share some common features of dyslexia, there are wide individual differences. It may be that one learner only exhibits mild difficulties and can have their learning needs met within the context of the mainstream environment, while another learner with dyslexia may require an Individual Education Plan (IEP) in order to secure provision that is 'additional to or different from' that provided for their peers (DfES, 2001b: Section 6:59). In looking at the definitions of dyslexia, it can be seen that dyslexia is represented at different levels. These are consistent with the schema described by Morton and Frith in 1993 and 1995. In order to understand dyslexia, it may be helpful to consider 'levels' of representation and how they impact upon assessment and learning support for dyslexic learners (Figure 13.1).

Clearly, dyslexia is not 'experienced' at all these separate levels but the level at which dyslexia is represented often influences the choice of support programme/intervention, e.g. a parent may choose to build his/her child's confidence or may see that he/she needs to 'protect her child from failure' by seeking a special school placement whereas a teacher may concentrate on delivering additional support for word level work. The next section examines in more detail the two levels of representation of dyslexia, *biological* and *cognitive*, that impact upon the behavioural level of dyslexia.

Biological level

There is considerable evidence to support the view that dyslexia is a condition with a genetic origin and a biological basis in the brain. Dyslexia is more common in males and tends to run in families (Hermann, 1959). There is also evidence of physiological brain differences between dyslexics and non-dyslexics while they are reading or doing reading-related tasks (e.g. Brunswick *et al.*, 1999; Paulesu *et al.*, 2001). There has been considerable research that links dyslexia to differences in the form and function of the right and left hemispheres of the brain. It has been found that 75 per cent of human brains are asymmetrical but that the brains of dyslexics are more likely to be symmetrical. It had initially been believed that language, both spoken and written, is mediated by the left cerebral hemisphere and visuo-spatial perception by the right cerebral hemisphere. This had led to a 'balance model of reading' that describes reading as the developmental integration of two processes:

1 The *perceptual* analysis of text features. This is needed in order to establish how letter shapes make up text e.g. letters may be reversed and have different meaning (e.g. 'b' and 'd'), but different shapes could be the same letter ('b' and 'B'). The development of this early reading skill involves considerable right hemisphere processing and reading fluency involves automatisation of this skill.

2   The *linguistic* analysis of text. As the child 'automates' the perceptual aspect
    of reading, he/she becomes more acquainted with the syntactic rules and
    his/her vocabulary grows as reading progresses. As a consequence, the child
    does not read letter-by-letter or syllable-by-syllable but by processes. The
    balance model of reading holds that fluent reading that is developed by use of
    syntactical rules and linguistic experience is predominantly guided by the left
    cerebral hemisphere.

In 'normal' development it is proposed that the right hemisphere guides early
reading initially and then the left hemisphere predominates. There is evidence to
support the view that 'right' and 'left' hemisphere differences provide a useful
explanatory basis for some of the differences observed in the development of
reading fluency between dyslexic and non-dyslexic individuals. However,
this explanation is not as clear-cut as originally conceived due to findings that
question the clear and stable delineation of right and left hemisphere functions
into 'perceptual' and 'language' respectively (Fagaloni *et al.*, 1969). In addition
to exhibiting differences in the development of reading, particularly in the development of 'automaticity', differences in form and function of the brain and
hemispheric activity are thought to contribute to the fact that dyslexics often
exhibit difficulties with sequencing, synthesising information and with overall
organisation. The biological basis of dyslexia remains a fertile area of research and
neuropsychological intervention (Robertson and Bakker, 2002) and is increasingly
likely to be seen as a useful addition to the repertoire of specialist teaching
approaches available for dyslexic pupils. In essence, approaches that stimulate
'weaker' areas of processing, and improve synthesis between right and left brain
activities (i.e. perceptual and language processing) are likely to be useful. Other
implications arising from 'biological' representation of dyslexia are:

- Early identification via use of family history, possible use of technologies (e.g.
  positron emission tomography (PET) and magnetic resonance imaging, (MRI)).

- Understanding that dyslexia is 'lifelong' and cannot be 'cured' but barriers to
  achievement can be identified and reduced.

- Some specialist programmes based on 'biological' explanations of dyslexia
  that seek to reduce development differences and delays and enhance overall
  synthesis of brain functions, i.e. movement, memory, language and perception
  etc. (Hemisphere Specific Stimulation Programmes (HEMSTIM) (Bakker and
  Vinke, 1985), Brain Gym (Dennison and Hargrove, 1986), Mind mapping
  (Buzan, 1993)).

- The achievement of increased 'fluency' in written language is the aim of many
  specialist programmes for dyslexics. This requires attention to the development
  of automaticity of the perceptual analysis of text. Hence specialist programmes
  are usually phonic-based and seek to use multi-sensory techniques, structured
  approaches, and opportunities for over-learning (e.g. Hickey Multi-sensory

Language Programme (Augur and Briggs, 1992). The National Literacy Strategy (DfES, 1998) and linked support materials seek to achieve 'automatic' perceptual analysis of text through structured 'word level work'.

- The need to be sensitive to the grouping of pupils with dyslexia to ensure that even if they have difficulties with 'perceptual analysis' of text (word level work) that the opportunity to develop their vocabulary and syntactic knowledge is made available to them. Ensuring that dyslexics have access to written language commensurate with their comprehension level is important by reading to them (peers/parents) or listening to story tapes, etc.

- The importance of monitoring pupil response to teaching in order to identify differences or difficulties that he/she may have with synthesising perceptual and linguistic features of text, e.g. miscue analysis.

Cognitive level

Typically dyslexics exhibit difficulty with: phonological awareness, (Goulandris *et al.*, 2000), working memory automatisation and slow processing speed. So what is 'phonological processing', its role in the development of literacy skills, and its link to working memory? During language acquisition children normally develop knowledge about the sound system of their language as well as learning to understand the language that is used around them. When they arrive at school and are expected to learn to read, most children have a knowledge of nursery rhymes, can make up rhymes, are aware that whole words (e.g. elephant) are made up of three syllables and some children can blend sounds (d/o/g/) to make up a word. Learners with dyslexia arrive at school with a good understanding of language and its meaning but experience difficulty when they are required to break down this meaningful language into 'meaningless' sound components in order to read and spell. As a consequence, this core skill needed for reading, writing and spelling takes longer to develop in dyslexic pupils and places heavy demands on their 'working memory' which is needed for both word recognition and comprehension. An analogy might be that of learning to drive. Initially new drivers have to concentrate on many skills – gear changes, looking in the mirror, predicting traffic movements, reading signals, etc. and this takes up all their available attentional space. Once these skills become 'automated' through practice and experience, the driver has much more 'capacity' to do other things, i.e. listen to radio, think, talk, etc. This specific problem with phonological awareness and processing results in dyslexics taking longer to acquire literacy skills than would be expected, given their overall level of ability in other areas of their work. Typically dyslexics might transpose sounds when writing, (i.e. 'saw' for 'was' because they remembered the sounds but not their order. Sometimes they spell, based on what the word 'sounded' like, e.g. 'cumfert' for 'comfort' and sometimes they use a combination of what the word sounded like and looked like. While not all dyslexics exhibit difficulties in learning to read, the majority do exhibit a residual difficulty with spelling and often with the 'multi-tasking' that is required within written language activities i.e., reading, memorising, comprehending, analysing and generating original written text. While not all theorists subscribe to the 'phonological deficit hypothesis' as a single causal explanation for dyslexia, it is supported by empirical findings (Snowling, 2000) and is increasingly used to plan teaching programmes. The implications of cognitive explanations of dyslexia include:

- It is important to remember that reading and writing places considerable attention demands on learners with dyslexia. It is important not to 'overload' them and ask them, for example, to listen, comprehend and write at the same time. When planning, it is advisable to break tasks down into component parts so that thinking, planning, writing and correcting are not done simultaneously as might be the case for more fluent writers. Specialist programmes for learners with dyslexia are very structured to avoid 'overload'. They also tend to be 'multi-sensory', using visual, auditory and kinaesthetic channels so that the learner has more chance of remembering the information given to them for processing. Dyslexics need additional time to become familiar with sound patterns and need time to generate their own 'words' from language sounds components. These may involve nonsense words or rhymes to give the learner practice in making up, and writing words from their sound components. Activities that support this include:
  - *Rhyming activities*: the learner is asked to discriminate between rhyming and non-rhyming pairs of words using a variety of game formats, e.g. cards, highlighting, etc.
  - *Onset and rime activities*: asking the learner to generate words with the same rime unit i.e. it, nit, pit, lit, etc. and then splitting words into onset and rimes and making links with the written word.
  - *Syllable awareness and manipulation*: breaking words down into component parts i.e. powerful = pow-er-ful; looking for words within words e.g. handbag = 'hand' and 'bag'. More difficult is the task of segmenting words into separate sounds e.g. land = l/a/n/d and rebuilding them.

- Memory: learners with dyslexia tend to have relative strength in reasoning and comprehension, i.e. the meaningful aspect of language. They have difficulty with the sound system of language because it is not meaningful and is difficult to place in long-term memory storage. It often helps to let the individual learner give his/her own meaning to the phonic sound they are learning. Some specialist programmes have cards with the sound written on one side and the trigger word that the learner has identified as a cue, e.g. the sound 'i' might be triggered by a child saying 'iglosaurus' – not an easy word but meaningful to the child. Memory is also supported by the learner saying out loud (or to themselves if preferred) when they are writing – this helps prevent then from forgetting and transposing letter sounds.

HLTA
2.1
2.3
2.5

Programmes used in schools

Programmes used in schools to support phonological awareness include NLS materials, Jolly Phonics (Wernham and Lloyd), and Sound Linkage (Hatcher, 2000).

In addition to programmes that specifically support literacy development, programmes that are used to enhance cognitive functioning in particular areas are frequently used to support dyslexic students. These include:

Thinking Skills (Blagg *et al.*, 1988)

Mind Mapping (1993)

Instrumental Enrichment (Feuerstein, 1980)

Philosophy for children (Lipman, 1984)

Learning styles (Given and Reid, 2001; Coffield *et al.*, 2004)

Study Skills (Ostler, 2001)

ICT (Johnson, 2002).

> ■ Think about some of the support strategies programmes you use with dyslexic pupils. Why do you use these particular methods?
> ■ How might the methods you use for individual support differ from those you use with small groups and/or the whole class?
> ■ When you are working with an individual with dyslexia, how would you record his/her response to teaching to help you improve your support and collaboration with the class/subject teacher and parent?

Strategies to support learning

There are a considerable number of strategies and programmes available to support dyslexic pupils. Given that it would not be possible to cover all the programmes that are available in schools, this section will identify some key strategies that can be used both at individual and whole-class level to support learning (Figure 13.2). These have been adapted from Tod (2000b).

These strategies are not 'special' and underpin good practice for all learners. It is in the understanding of 'why' they are used, the consistency with which they are applied, and the monitoring of their effect on learner progress that they become powerful to those who support learners with dyslexia.

> ■ How might you support learners with dyslexia in your own setting?
> ■ In what way do you encourage pupils to be independent when you are delivering individual support?
> ■ In your experience, how has pupil grouping affected their learning behaviour? How might you use this experience?

You should now have developed your understanding as to why you use certain programmes and approaches to support learners with dyslexia in your own setting.

WHAT?	WHY?	HOW?
MULTI-SENSORY	Dyslexic pupils often exhibit particular difficulty with processing material that requires sound or symbol processing at speed, e.g. in order to spell 'animal' the pupil has to sound out the word in his/her head and then change the sounds into their written code at speed and produce them in the right order. Using vision and touch to support learning helps the dyslexic to compensate for his/her relatively weak 'sound' processing and working memory skills	Using visual, auditory and kinaesthetic inputs either sequentially or simultaneously depending on the task and learner need. One of the most commonly used strategies used is 'look, cover, say, write, check' to support spelling. Sound input fades quickly whereas visual and kinaesthetic input can be revisited and remains stable over time. Specialist 'dyslexic' programmes are underpinned by multi-sensory approaches.
MEANINGFULNESS	Aspects of learning to read and generate written language involves breaking down meaningful language into sound components that are 'meaningless' i.e. from 'dog' to d-o-g. Dyslexics are particularly weak at remembering meaningless phonic components of language but normally have relative strengths with comprehension reasoning, etc. It makes sense to try and use approaches that encourage the learner to make meaningless material meaningful to them.	Encourage the learner to become actively involved in their learning. What does 'ch' sound make you think of, etc.? This meaningful cue word can then be used to help recall and 'locate' the meaningless sound component. Encourage class groups to build mind maps of words to support writing. Make sure 'meaning' of written word is maintained and extended through reading to the pupil.
MEMORY	Memory is cited to be more important in GCSE results than IQ! (Wilding et al., 1999). Dyslexics have difficulty with their working memory that can be seen by the written language errors they make.	Try to reduce 'overload' by making sure that the task given is manageable for the pupil in terms of what has to be 'held in his/her head'. Encourage active and repeated processing of essential word level work, i.e. getting pupils to generate their own 'words' from sounds given, drawing mind maps, etc. Use multi-sensory approaches. Try to achieve 'automaticity' of some phonic skills by daily practice and repetition. Once 'automatic', skills do not place demand on memory capacity. Parents can use vegetable racks labelled as days of week to support the pupil in remembering what day it is and what he/she has to take to school.
METACOGNITION	Metacognition stresses the importance of the learner 'being aware of his own learning'. Effective learners are clear about task demands, how they responded and how they need to improve their performance. Dyslexics often are confused by their own learning and cannot understand why they are not able to tackle literacy when other pupils do so with ease.	Involve the pupil in planning and evaluation of his/her educational support; Encourage active 'reflection': 'I started writing without thinking then I forgot what I had to do; next time I will try and change that'. Study skills integrated throughout the curriculum and developed from start of school. Self- and peer marking against given criteria
MANAGEABILITY	Most dyslexics suffer from overload particularly as they progress to secondary school.	Make sure that dyslexics are not given too many things to do in too short a time.

Figure 13.2 Strategies to support learning (*continued overleaf*)

	As many of them have not 'automated' reading and writing, they cannot cope with having to 'think', plan, synthesise written material in order to write projects, essays, etc.	They are traditionally slow workers and often fall behind with coursework and/or underestimate the time needed for completion. Work on structuring the task into 'do-able' components and monitor each stage using visual monitoring sheet so that the pupil can plot his/her progress. Make use of ICT for planning and organising work. Use discussion, videos, etc. to support understanding of written texts. Encourage the use of coloured folders, etc. to support organisation of work.
MOTIVATION	Motivation is an important precurser for learning and is a complex construct requiring action at a range of levels. Dyslexics are prone to loss of motivation in education where speed and competence in written language underpin the majority of assessed work.	Curriculum: try to identify what interests the pupil has and how he can apply/use the work he is doing. Ensure reading materials have interest value. Involve pupil in target setting and monitoring. Use multi-sensory approaches and 'short' periods of activity as dyslexics become very fatigued by the processing demands of literacy. Give opportunities to work collaboratively with peers using pupil strengths, i.e. imagination, understanding, reasoning, etc. Plan for the pupil to succeed! Social setting/groupings: Be sensitive to groups according to reading level. Work on building a good relationship with the student. Encourage staff to understand the pupil's experience of barriers to achievement. Have high expectations. Monitor, re-visit and celebrate progress.

Figure 13.2 *continued*

Scotopic Sensitivity Syndrome

What is Scotopic Sensitivity Sydrome (SSS)?

First, when describing this particular syndrome 'Scotopic' does not mean 'night vision'. Also SSS is not a vision problem that involves difficulties with the functioning of the eye, but rather is a *perceptual dysfunction*. The brain of a person with SSS appears to have difficulty managing *full spectral light*, causing many different types of print distortions or background interference. It is suspected that this sensitivity to full spectrum light could be linked to a structural brain deficit involving the central nervous system (Irlen, 1991: 57). If this is the case, and it is still only a theory, then the signals sent to the brain would not be processed in the normal way, thus causing perceptual problems. It is not a separate learning difficulty, but is 'a complex and variable condition often found to exist as a component of dyslexia, dyscalculia, attention deficit hyperactivity disorder (ADHD), Autistic Spectrum Disorders (ASD) and many other learning problems' (Irlen, 1991: 31).

Who can have Scotopic Sensitivity Syndrome (SSS)?

As SSS is not an actual vision problem, people who have perfect vision as well as those who have to wear glasses for particular visual difficulties may have it. Opticians, optometrists and other vision specialists probably will not identify this problem, because it is not a visual system weakness and testing is not readily available in all educational settings. It affects both sexes equally and there does appear to be a hereditary factor.

How can Scotopic Sensitivity Syndrome (SSS) affect learners?

Learners with SSS may have:

- a variety of reading problems including tracking difficulties;
- a lack of motivation and actually try to avoid reading;
- poor energy and work production;
- a poor attention span;
- handwriting problems – poor punctuation, an inability to write on lines, letters bunched together or spread too far apart;
- poor gross motor skills;
- problems with depth perception;
- a preference to read in dim light.

Due to this list of difficulties it is easy to understand that SSS can affect not only learners' academic success, but also their sporting, driving and musical ability. Coordination skills are frequently affected as are learners' self-confidence and self-esteem.

There are five components of SSS and a learner may experience only one of these, some of them or all five. The five components of SSS are:

1 *Light sensitivity*: A learner with a light sensitivity problem may not like glare, or bright lights from fluorescent lighting, for example, or other light conditions such as haze or overcast lighting. Learners may experience, dizziness, restlessness, fatigue, headaches or even migraines and may become agitated if they are expected to read in a room where the lighting conditions are problematic for them. If a learner is sensitive to glare, then he/she may have to battle to focus clearly on a white page or on a whiteboard and may find it difficult to read across a line effectively.

2   *Restricted span of recognition*: A learner with this problem, also sometimes called tunnel reading, will find it very difficult to read a group of words or symbols at the same time. Learners may have difficulties copying, moving from one line to another, proofreading, skimming or speed reading.

3   *Poor attention span*: This is frequently the result of a learner having to concentrate very hard on each word to enable them to keep them readable. Due to the immense effort it takes for a learner with this problem to read each word, he/she will become tired very quickly and will therefore need a lot of breaks. To educators in a classroom such a learner can often appear to be lazy or lack good concentration skills. Learners with this difficulty may exhibit reading fatigue, causing eye problems. As a result of this, they may become inefficient readers, skipping words or lines and needing to use a marker or finger to keep their place while reading.

4   *Inadequate background accommodation*: This difficulty arises for learners when there is not enough contrast between the colour, the writing or symbols are written in and the background. For learners with SSS, black letters with a white background can frequently cause a problem. This is because the white background competes for attention with the black letters, making the letters more difficult to read. Learners with this problem may have to frequently re-read the same material, because the words or the background move about irregularly, making it very hard to read.

5   *Poor print resolution*: This is when the print, whether letters or any other type of symbols, change constantly. The letters may turn around, vibrate, jiggle, dance or fade in and out and even drop off the edges of a book. This does also seem to depend on the size of the print, spacing and the actual amount of print on each page. Learners with poor print resolution will read very disjointedly and may rub their eyes or look away before having another go at reading a word.

How can learners be helped?

Coloured filters

Coloured filters, like those used with the Irlen Method, actually change the spectral content of the light, perhaps even reducing troublesome wavelengths of light. If this is achieved, then the colours that are causing the distortions are reduced, enabling the brain to more effectively process information. The coloured filters do appear to stabilise the printed page, helping the learner to read and process the information more efficiently. Some surveys of coloured filters have proved very positive with 82 to 93 per cent of users reporting that reading, handwriting, spelling, eye strain, school performance and self-image had improved (Irlen and Robinson, 1996).

Case study 1

Andrew was causing great concern because, despite a massive amount of individual and small group learning support and a high level of motivation on his part, he was unable to improve his reading ability. The SEN teacher asked Andrew what he could see when he read a page of writing. He described the letters as constantly moving up and down, making it very hard for him to see a complete word at any one time. At the time the only coloured filters available (and it is not suggested that these are used at all) were theatre light filters, but out of interest the SEN teacher asked Andrew to read using the various coloured filters as overlays. The discovery was wonderful to witness. When a green filter was placed on top of a page in Andrew's reading book, he smiled and then cheered and refused to let the filter go. The letters remained still and he could read whole words without the struggle of having to read the letters as they moved. With supportive parents and a local optometrist, a pair of coloured filter glasses were made for Andrew and within three months his reading had improved by three years. The immense pleasure and growth in his self-confidence was amazing to see – the effect the coloured filter had achieved was undeniable. Andrew's academic achievement, including his handwriting skills and gross motor skills improved steadily and he progressed so well in secondary school that it was felt unnecessary to retain his Statement of Special Educational Needs.

Learners with SSS often do not realise that letters should be still and clear and so it is only when educators ask appropriate questions about what it is like when they try to read that probable reasons for some of their learning difficulties can be identified.

HLTA
3.3.2

Discussion

Do you think you have any learners who may be experiencing SSS? If so, who will you need to speak to about this and what steps could you, with the other educators in your team, immediately take to enhance the learning of the pupil with SSS?

Classroom adaptations

Educators can help learners with SSS in the following ways:

- Use beige, green, grey or recycled paper instead of white.
- Computer screens can also be used with different coloured backgrounds.
- Think about the lighting – encourage the use of natural light and try to avoid using fluorescent lights.
- Use sloping boards to reduce the glare of light from the page. Caps can also be used in a similar way, but this may well not fit in with general school rules.
- Do not expect learners with SSS to share reading material.
- When working on a board or overhead, use coloured chalk or highlighters.

HLTA
3.1.3
3.2.3

It is clear to all educators that there is a whole range of connections within this section on SSS with other difficulties for classroom identification. However, as the case study shows, it is another link that an educator can use to make that complete chain of learning skills and experiences for learners.

Key issues

It is anticipated that you will now:

- have an understanding of what dyslexia is;
- have begun to understand why certain programmes are used to support learners with dyslexia;
- be able to understand the types of difficulties learners with dyslexia may experience and thus prepare appropriate materials and interventions;
- be aware of visual perceptual difficulties such as Scotopic Sensitivity Syndrome (SSS);
- be able to recognise factors that may indicate a learner has SSS;
- be able to adapt a classroom environment to enable a learner with SSS to access the curriculum more efficiently;
- understand the different areas of learning that SSS can affect.

Professional Standards for Higher Level Teaching Assistants (HLTA)

If you can demonstrate your understanding and professional use of the key issues illustrated within this chapter, it is hoped you will be able to fulfil the following HLTA Standards:

2.1	2.3	2.5	2.9	3.1.3
3.2.1	3.2.2	3.2.3	3.3.1	3.3.2
3.3.3	3.3.5			

Useful websites

www.autism.org (useful information on Autism).

www.irlen.org.uk (lists all research on the Irlen Method).

www.latitudes.org (articles on ADHD, Autism, Irlen Syndrome and Tourette Syndrome).

References

Bloom, L. and Lahey, M. (1978) *Language Development and Language Disorders*, New York: Wiley.

British Psychological Society (1999) *Dyslexia, Literacy and Psychological Assessment*, R. Reason, N. Frederickson, M. Hefferenan, C. Martin, and K. Woods (eds) draft report, Leicester: British Psychological Society.

Brunswick, N., McCrory, E., Price, C., Frith, C.D. and Frith, U. (1999) 'Explicit and implicit processing of words and pseudowords by adult developmental dyslexics: a search for Wernicke's Wortschatz?', *Brain*, vol. 122, pp. 1901–17.

Buzan, T. (1993) *The Mind Map Book: Radiant Thinking*, London: BBC Books.

Coffield, F., Moseley, D., Hall, E. and Ecclestone, K. (2004) *Should We Be Using Learning Styles?* Available on: www.lsrc.ac.uk

DfE (1994) *Code of Practice on the Identification and Assessment of Special Educational Needs*, London: HMSO.

DfEE (1998) *The National Literacy Strategy: Framework for Teaching*, London: HMSO.

DfES (2001a) *Inclusive Schooling*, Annesley: DfES.

DfES (2001b) *The Special Educational Needs Code of Practice*, Annesley, Department for Education and Skills.

DfES (2004) *Removing Barriers to Achievement: The Government's Strategy for SEN*, Annesley: Department for Education and Skills.

Fagaloni, P., Scotti, G. and Spinnler, H. (1969) 'Impaired recognition of written letters following unilateral hemispheric damage', *Cortex*, vol. 5, pp. 120–33.

Given B. and Reid G. (2001) 'Assessing learning styles', In Smythe, I. (ed.) *The Dyslexia Handbook 2001*, Reading: The British Dyslexia Association, pp. 135–45.

Goulandris, N., Snowling, M.J. and Walker, I. (2000) 'Is dyslexia a form of specific language impairment? A comparison of dyslexic and language impaired children as adolescents', *Annals of Dyslexia*, vol. 50, pp. 103–20.

Hermann, K. (1959) *Reading Disability: A Medical Study of Word Blindness and Related Handicaps*, Copenhagen: Munksgaard.

Irlen, H. (1991) *Reading by the Colors*, New York: Avery Publishing Group Inc.

Irlen, H. and Robinson, G.L. (1996) 'The effect of Irlen coloured filters on adult perception of workplace performance: a preliminary survey', *Australian Journal of Psychology*, vol. 88, pp. 531–48.

Locke, A. (1995) *Living Language*, Windsor: NFER Nelson.

Locke, A. and Beech, M. (1992) *Teaching Talking*, Windsor: NFER Nelson.

Martin, D. and Miller, C. (1996) *Speech and Language Difficulties in the Classroom*, London: David Fulton.

Morton, J. and Frith, U. (1993) 'What lessons for dyslexia from Down's Syndrome? Comments on Cossu, Rossini and Marshall', *Cognition* vol. 48, pp. 289–96.

Morton, J. and Frith, U. (1995) 'Causal modelling: a structural approach to developmental psychopathology', in Cicchetti, D. and Cohen, D.J. (eds) *Manual of Developmental Psychopathology*, New York: Wiley, pp. 357–90.

Mosley, J. (1997) *Quality Circle Time*, Wisbech: UK LDA.

Paulesu, E., Demonet, J.-F., Fazio, F., McCrory, E., Chanoine, V., Brunswick, N., Cappa, S.F. Cossu, G., Habib, M., Frith, C.D. and Frith U. (2001) 'Dyslexia – cultural diversity and biological unity', *Science*, vol. 291, pp. 2165–7.

Peer, L. (2001) 'What is dyslexia?', in Smythe I. (ed.) *The Dyslexia Handbook 2001*, Reading: British Dyslexia Association, p. 67.

Pinker, S. (1994) *The Language Instinct*, London: Penguin.

Pumfrey, P. and Reason, R. (1991) *Specific Learning Difficulties (Dyslexia): Challenges and Responses*, London: Routledge.

Rinaldi, W. (1992) *Social Use of Language Programme*, Windsor: NFER Nelson.

Robertson, J. and Bakker, D.J. (2002) 'The balance model of reading and dyslexia', in G. Reid, and J. Wearmouth, (eds) *Dyslexia and Literacy*, Chichester: Wiley, pp. 99–114.

Singleton, C. (2002) 'Cognitive factors and implications for literacy', in G. Reid and J. Wearmouth (eds) *Dyslexia and Literacy* Chichester: Wiley.

Snowling, M.J. (2000) *Dyslexia*, 2nd edn, Oxford: Blackwell.

The Orton Dyslexia Society Research Committee (1994) Baltimore, MD, Orton: Dyslexia Society.

Stevenson, J. *et al.* (1985) 'Behaviour problems and language abilities at three years and behavioural deviance at eight years', *Journal of Child Psychology and Psychiatry and Allied Disciplines*, vol. 26, no. 2, pp. 215–30.

Tod, J. (2000a) *Individual Education Plans*, London: David Fulton.

Tod, J. (2000b) *Inclusive Learning and Teaching in the 21st Century: Perspectives for Individual Learners*, available on: http://www.isec2000.org.uk/abstracts/papers_t/tod_1.htm

Tod, J. and Blamires, M. (2000) *Individual Education Plans: Speech and Language Difficulties*, London: David Fulton.

Wilding, J., Valentine, E., Marshall, P. and Cook, S. (1999) 'Individual differences in memory ability and GCSE performance', *Educational Psychology*, vol. 19, pp. 117–31.

Assessment and teaching programmes

Augur, J. and Briggs, S. (1992) *The Hickey Multisensory Language Course*, London: Whurr.

Bakker, D.J. and Vinke, J. (1985) 'Effects of hemispheric specific stimulation of brain activity and reading in dyslexics', *Journal of Clinical and Experimental Neuropsychology*, vol. 7, pp. 505–25.

Blagg, N., Ballinger, M., Gardner, R., Petty, M. and Williams, M. (1988) 'Thinking skills', in *Somerset Thinking Skills Course*, Oxford: Blackwell/Somerset County Council.

Dennison, P.E. and Hargrove, G. (1986) *Personalised Whole Brain Integration*, Glendale, CA: Educ. Kinaesthetics.

Frederikson, N. and Reason, R. (1995) 'Phonological assessment of specific learning difficulties: the development of the Phonological Assessment Battery (PhAB)', *Journal of Educational and Child Psychology*, vol. 12, no. 1, pp. 53–69.

Feuerstein, R. (1980) *Instrumental Enrichment: An Intervention Programme for Cognitive Modifiability*, Baltimore, MD: University Park Press.

Hatcher, P.I. (2000) *Sound Linkage*, 2nd edn, London: Whurr.

Lipman, M. (1984) 'The cultivation of reasoning through philosophy', *Educational Leadership*, vol. 42, no. 2, pp. 51–6.

Newton, M. and Thompson, M. (1982) *The Aston Index*, Cambridge: LDA.

Ostler, C. (2001) 'Study skills: using strengths and weaknesses', in I. Smythe (ed.) *The Dyslexia Handbook 2001*, Reading: The British Dyslexia Association, pp. 268–73.

Singleton, C.H., Thomas, K.V. and Leedale, R.C. (1997) *CoPS Cognitive Profiling System* (Windows Version) Beverley, Easy Yorkshire UK: Lucid Research Limited.

Wernham, S. and Lloyd, S. (1993) *Jolly Phonics*, Chigwell: Jolly Learning.

Young people with physical and sensory disabilities

14

John Cornwall

Introduction

It is hoped that reading this chapter will contribute to the development of a rational and broad view of the way in which you support pupils and students experiencing physical or sensory disabilities. All of us have our own view of disability, and work done with over 200 teachers and teaching assistants has elicited a tremendous variety of responses (Cornwall, 1995) to the question 'What is the difference between the words *impairment*, *disability* and *handicap*?' The answer depends upon your own definition of disability or your understanding of the current definitions. Often people's perceptions of these differences are reflected in their use of language to describe the phenomena of disability intertwined with descriptions of individuals. They become one and the same and hence reflect many unclear views about disability and ambiguous feelings about disabled people. This is quite surprising and does not mean that they are uncaring or ignorant. It simply reflects the hidden nature of the concepts and ideas surrounding disability. The best definition is the one that comes from people who are, themselves, disabled. It is important that no matter what the origins and consequences of a young person's disability, they are not treated as if they have the group characteristics. Each pupil should be treated as an individual, not as an illness or a condition.

Definition of terms

There are many definitions of those three key words used in relation to disability and they all point quite clearly to the relationship between an individual and his or her social and physical environment.

United Nations and World Health Organisation definition:

Impairment   is a physical deviation from what is considered usual in terms of structure, functional, physical organisation or development. It is objective and measurable (e.g. sickle cell anaemia, loss of tissue or sensation from parts of the body).

Disability   is the functional limitation experienced by the individual because of an impairment. It refers to what the individual cannot do in the usual or expected way. Measurable to some extent but dependent upon a number of variables such as age, occupation, culture, wealth and how they, themselves, regard the disability.

Handicap   is the disadvantage imposed by an impairment or disability. The social and environmental consequences to the individual. It is not measurable, but experienced and includes the actions and reactions of others as well as the reaction of the person with the disability which dictates the degree of disadvantage.

Disabled Persons International (DPI) definition:

Disability   is the functional limitation within the individual caused by physical, mental or sensory impairment.

Handicap   is the loss or limitation of opportunities to take part in the normal life of the community on an equal level with others due to physical or social barriers. (Driedger, 1989: 92)

British Council of Organisations of Disabled People (originating from the Union of Physically Impaired Against Segregation (UPIAS)) definition:

Impairment   lacking part or all, or having a defective limb, organ or mechanism of the body.

Disability   the disadvantage or restriction of activity caused by a contemporary social organisation which takes little or no account of people who have physical impairments and thus excludes them from participation in the mainstream of social activities – physical disability is therefore a particular form of social oppression.

A brief look at the history of the care and education of children and young people with physical and/or sensory disabilities will show the reader very quickly that it is peppered with, at best, misunderstanding and, at worst, downright cruelty. Listening to the stories of people who were the subject of care and education in the 1940s and 1950s, it becomes clear that it was not so much the physical separation of children from their families that caused grief but the insensitive and cruel treatment of children and young people who were disabled by the people who worked in and ran those institutions. Even into the 1960s young people with disabilities were contained in medical and institutional 'care' settings where their potential as human beings was largely ignored. Eventually in the 1960s, the setting up of Junior and Senior Training Centres within the Health Service at least recognised that young people with disabilities were 'trainable'. The setting up of the Spastics Society (now SCOPE) in the 1960s was a response by a small number (that grew to a large number) of parents whose children's educative potential was being largely ignored by the health and educational services of the day. In the early 1970s legislation came into being that transferred responsibility for disabled youngsters from health to education, though it was still to be a while before children and young people with disabilities were felt to be 'educable' in the fullest sense of the word.

Why is all this important and what does it have to do with current provision and inclusion of disabled children and young people into society and education?

It is interesting to note that the 'inclusive' policies of the late Victorian and early modern era were to put disabled children into these institutions so they could be properly 'cared for'. The alternative for some was a miserable life on the street, begging or worse. For others, their families would care for them, whatever their means. Current 'inclusive' wisdom says that it is better for a child to be educated in a mainstream school in their local community. Rather like the Victorians, we could accept the current social dogma of the day and not question that this is the case. There are many arguments for diversity in education, as in life. What you, the reader, should consider in your professional capacity is not how severe or what the nature of a disability is, although this will inevitably be apparent, but whether the environment that the child or young person is attempting to learn in (and live in) goes some, if not all, of the way to meeting their needs.

This is an expression of what is called the 'social model' of education in which we all have a responsibility and the ability to adjust the physical, social and educational environment to enable a young person to achieve in the broadest sense. It is in direct contrast to the 'medical model' where all the problems are seen as 'within the young person' and their ability to achieve anything lies solely within the domain of so-called 'experts'. There is absolutely no doubt that this view, spread abroad by the language of medical and psychological 'experts' (as in comparative studies of psychology and biology) has contributed greatly to a societal view of disabled people as 'abnormal'. Other influences have been religion (it is God's punishment), eugenics (breeding of the perfect human, prevalent in Europe and America in the 1920s and 1930s), and more recently media and advertising that promotes unreal stereotypes for us all to aspire to.

All these historical and ethical perspectives have an impact on what happens in classrooms every day. The deeper social and psychological influences that pervade professional practices cannot be ignored.

So what is the situation more recently?

The following statements and statistics are taken from a DfES Disability Briefing in February 1999. Here are some key facts and figures taken from a Labour Force Survey (LFS) (1998):

■ Disabled people account for nearly a fifth of the working-age population (men 16–64, women 16–59) in Great Britain. There are over 6.2 million people with a current long-term disability or health problems.

■ Estimated number of people covered by the Disability Discrimination Act (DDA) in Great Britain: of all ages: current disability: 8.5 million; current or past disability: 9.7 million.

■ Disabled people have fewer qualifications than their non-disabled counterparts. They are more than twice as likely to have no formal qualifications.

■ Disabled people are only half as likely as non-disabled people to be in employment.

■ Employment rates vary greatly between types of disability.

■ There is little difference between disabled and non-disabled people with regards to whether their job is permanent.

■ The average hourly pay of disabled employees is around 10 per cent lower than that of non-disabled employees.

■ The unemployment rate for long-term disabled people is nearly twice as high as that for non-disabled people, 10.7 per cent compared with 5.7 per cent. Their likelihood of being one of the long-term unemployed is also higher.

So the picture is one of gradual improvements in the quality of life for disabled people over a very long period of time. In our current social climate, however, there are still barriers reducing the potential for disabled people to function successfully both in education and in the workplace.

> **Discussion**
>
> How has the history of treatment of disabled people affected our current thinking? Are disabled pupils really emancipated in our current education system?

What is equality of opportunity?

Figure 14.1 illustrates how disability is one area of equality of opportunity. The reader may well be wondering at this point what all this has to do with teaching, learning and school activity. It is important to remember that children with disabilities are now only in schools at all because of attitude changes, militant parents and

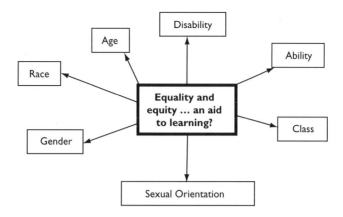

Figure 14.1 How disability is one area of equality of opportunity

eventually the political will to develop equitable and socially constructive policies. Nevertheless, working alongside disabled children in school is still a political act to some extent simply because of institutionalising practices and prejudices that emphasise so-called normality, difference and disability. These are still daily and institutionally reinforced by the use of social and physical space, and through both mainstream and segregated schooling (Corker *et al.* 1999). The same study found that children themselves are less prone to make judgements of others based on labels that come from professional classifications. In a sense, for children the quality of the relationship and experience is more important than the label. A good educator can learn from children and be aware of the needs of children in their care, without treating them as if they *were the label*.

> **Discussion**
>
> How does the term 'equality of opportunity' apply to the school and classrooms you work in? Do processes and procedures provide barriers to disabled students' learning in your school?

Understanding the needs of children with physical and sensory disabilities

What are the practical areas that need attention when it comes to ensuring that children with physical or sensory disabilities have 'access to learning' (Cornwall, 1996)? These are summarised in the list below:

1. *Assumptions, attitudes, behaviour and expectations.* Educators' attitudes and expectations are shaped by their own history and experience. Often people working with disabled people have a disabled person in the family. They have experience of the barriers encountered by disabled people. An example of this

occurred not long ago in a school I was visiting where a teacher pointed to a child in a wheelchair and two others (presumably with less visible disabilities) and said, 'That's our inclusion table …' I leave you to think about that.

2. *Procedures and customary practices.* The most obvious example of this is the school timetable. Particularly in secondary and tertiary education, the rush from one classroom and activity to another militates against equal participation by a disabled youngster. However, this involves a radical change of customary practice by government (as OFSTED) as well as by schools themselves.

3. *Ethos of the institution.* This important area is the most potent influential factor in making a difference to the learning opportunities experienced by a disabled youngster. The education system in the UK is faced now with a choice that has faced other systems in Canada and in the USA. Forest and Pearpoint (1991) describe 'the road to inclusion' as one of building intentional educational community in our schools. It demands hard work and commitment to the new ABCs. These new ABCs are:

*A*CCEPTANCE of natural diversity and talent.
*B*ELONGING through genuine partnerships.
*C*OMMUNITY that assumes collective responsibility.

> **Discussion**
>
> This may seem a very simple mantra but educational institutions are part of a highly competitive system, for example, SATs and league tables. Have a good look around your school. What kinds of attitudes and expectations make up the school ethos? Does it have an ethos? Or is it simply an institution dependent upon the whims of government and the drive for academic success? Is natural talent outside academic limitations (e.g. numeracy and literacy) recognised and celebrated?

The reader might ask what has happened to physical access, and the author would like to emphasise that this is important but that the above areas are actually *more important*. Physical and educational barriers can all be overcome, if there is the will to do so.

> Choice and opportunity for disabled pupils and students can be achieved in such a way that it is part of the general evolution of our education system. Quality education for the minority of diverse learners will mean sharpening and improving the skills of teachers [and teaching assistants] and the organisation of school or colleges, to the benefit of all.
>
> (Cornwall, 1995: 112)

Also focusing specifically on physical barriers is often disempowering for educators in schools, because they may not have much influence on potential changes. However, focusing on the above issues is empowering because every member of staff has both responsibility and the ability to make changes and encourage development. It leads to asking some more pertinent questions about the support that should be given.

HLTA
2.1

Support for whom? Is the support really what the individual pupils or student needs or has it got more to do with the following?

■ existing customs and practice;

■ making the adults feel useful;

■ what resources are available.

What criteria? How do you decide when to give support or when it is not needed? *What support?* Support for learning takes many forms from interventions by teaching assistants through to the provision of materials and physical adaptations. It is important that the adults concerned with the child make careful decisions about the nature of the support.

Who decides? Later in this chapter you will see how important it is that the pupil or student themselves is empowered to make decisions for themselves and to have control of the situation as far as possible. Choice is a key factor in this process.

Changing attitudes and beliefs through education

There will always be *tensions* between what is expected as curriculum contents and the *decisions* a teacher must make about priorities, whether on an individual or a group basis. Choices have to be made both by the teacher and the learner, and *priorities* will emerge for both. Any subject-defined curriculum will have its limitations but it is perfectly possible to interpret any activity in a number of ways. The most important factor is that the learner is motivated, exercising their analysis and judgement, picking up useful chunks of knowledge and is involving themselves in the subject. Special Educational Needs, for example, is still perceived by many as having to do with identifying the problem within the pupil or student. In fact, this is not the case. Knowing that a certain syndrome or illness has particular symptoms is necessary for health professionals because they hope to be able to treat the symptoms (i.e. find a cure for the problem or manage the difficulties). A person is described by a set of group characteristics and is then treated according to those group characteristics. One definition of discrimination has to do with judging an individual on the basis of some ill-defined, or inappropriately defined, set of group characteristics and then treating them in this way, regardless of their individual humanity, their rights or their unique characteristics.

The restrictions imposed on the use of language and the narrowing of concepts inherent in the process of diagnosing and labelling have only a limited use from an educational or social viewpoint. Teachers, teaching assistants, lecturers, psychologists and researchers (in education) are interested in the learning process and in ascertaining what learning has taken place. This can only be observed or measured by watching an individual's reactions, responses and performance. In other words, it is concerned with the interaction between the individual and his/her environment. This would either be in specifically constructed circumstances or in the course of tackling problems and activities in real life. In other words, we should be looking at the interaction of the individual who is disabled and his/her (learning) environment, not at obscure descriptions or definitions of the seat of impairment or illnesses. When these physical or medical characteristics or statements about physical characteristics are overtly emphasised, they can radically change and even dictate a general perception of that person's whole functioning or personality. It would be farcical to invent a special needs category of people who are over 7 feet tall, or children who have small feet or children who have freckles, or blue eyes. It is important to be clear about whatever purpose is involved in any kind of categorisation based on physical or medical characteristics. Educators should concentrate on each pupil's individual capabilities and capacities in order to support the development of meaningful learning strategies and plans.

Deficit teaching (or 'symptomatic' focus for planning) for example, which is the result of clumsy or simplistic labelling, can be very damaging to an individual. Not only can it 'label' an individual negatively but it can also make them jump through unnecessary hoops to limited ends. It can have more to do with the needs of the adult, teacher or trainer to be seen to be positively or professionally active, than any particularly effective teaching or learning strategies.

Case study 1

For example, a child has the labels of 'perceptual motor problem' (and cerebral palsy which simply means brain damage) and cannot draw shapes (circle, rectangle, triangle) successfully. The 'deficit' approach would be to focus on this and give more practice at holding and manipulating the pencil ('pencil exercises'), backed up by drawing the offending shapes … pages and pages of further practice. This is not to say that practice does not have its place but not more and more of the same in a soul-sapping diet. This applies to reading, mathematics and many other subjects or forms of teaching across the curriculum and through the phases of schooling.

A more 'empowering' approach to this pupil would be to structure the environment to 'scaffold' or support the learner's attempts in this area. The learner needs to have opportunities to show what he or she knows, understands and can do (Moore and Morrison, 1989). Using the example above, it is more acceptable to the learner and more effective in learning terms to point out these shapes occurring in the normal environment, to discover related activities that the pupil/student is motivated to achieve or complete, to find related activities (e.g. cutting, pasting, art, design, craft, PE) where these skills and concepts can be explored in different ways. An alternative with this pupil might be to forget using a pencil at all and invest in a small tape recorder or a computer keyboard, although even the keyboard may need some adaptation.

The language of self-image and self-concept

We live in a society where plastic surgery is available for cosmetic reasons. Who could deny any individual the possibility of improving their physical appearance when it means so much to them? Images of almost impossible physical perfection (or at least the appearance of it) are constantly promoted in the popular media. There is a profound effect on a person's image of themselves by linking physical 'perfection' with acceptance, success, sexuality and power which can lead to the following:

■ striving for the illusion of physical perfection;

■ real fear of those who appear different, or are made to feel inadequate, that they will be socially isolated and marginalised because of some physical or mental characteristics;

■ influence on professional practice and research to pursue strategies and lines of enquiry that will normalise rather than recognise uniqueness, creative individuality and diversity;

■ a common assumption or message that the problem for a child or young person lies entirely within that individual and not in the way the social environment around them is organised.

This context has a profound effect on the way in which we build up (and feel about) our physical image of ourselves and it is vital to understand the impact of this culture on disabled people generally and on the pupils and students who require learning support. It is important to understand that the way a child feels about themselves will be a result of others' behaviour and language.

An important part of our understanding of ourselves as individuals arises from the way in which others see us and this continues from the moment we are born until we die. According to Maslow (1962), there are five sources of self-concept development:

1. *Body image*, in realising and understanding the physical self as a distinct object.
2. *Language*, through the ability to conceptualise and verbalise about self and others.
3. *Academic*, in terms of success and failure in the education system.
4. *Feedback* from the environment, particularly from significant others, gives a person information on how the individual stands as regards his or her feelings, opinions and values.
5. *Child-rearing* practices also have a long-lasting impact on developing self-confidence, self-direction and general attitudes towards oneself.

A constructed measure of this is called self-esteem. Self-esteem is understood as a measure of the feeling we have about ourself and the platform from which we launch ourselves at life. It is a crucial factor in our functioning as a social animal and in enabling us to make the most of the living and learning experiences that life has to offer. Sadly, there are many parts of our culture which undermine an individual's self-esteem and these are not limited to an accepted view of disabled or non-disabled. We still accept the most outrageous and apparently perfect physical and sexual stereotypes paraded day after day in our media (television, magazines, newspapers) and in advertising. It changes our appreciation of ourselves and of each other as real, though imperfect, human beings and has an impact on the way in which disabled students see themselves.

Partnership with parents

It is clear that the school experience for children with disabilities is inherently different and the experience of parents of children is also radically different. This is an important starting point for all adults within a school community, because it implies that partnership with parents involves listening to, and understanding, their experience. Parents are often experts in their own particular area even though they may feel 'at sea' with it or even incapable in the face of professional expertise. They have an in-depth knowledge, through experience, not only of the condition itself, but of the consequences (social, emotional and cultural) of that particular condition. Their knowledge and understanding are very often part of the solution when it is unlocked by effective and sensitive partnership.

Case study 2

A parent of a young disabled child talks about their experience of professionals (Cornwall, 1996).

> My experience of dealing with professionals from education, social services, health and the voluntary sector over the last eight years continues to astound me. The range of emotions my family and I have had to cope with: from frustration to anger and disillusionment, makes me wonder whether having a child with cerebral palsy has made me a stronger or weaker person … We encountered a range of problems when dealing with professionals from various services. My biggest bone of contention is those bright sparks who pass judgement on their clients without having full knowledge of the facts.

Discussion

Does your school have an effective partnership with parents? Is their 'expertise' fully recognised?

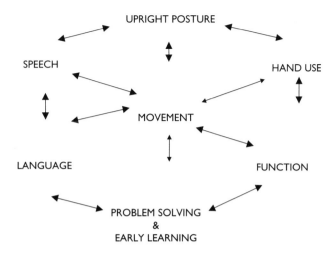

Figure 14.2 Interconnectivity of skills

Children's early development is usually integrated from a young age. This means that movement, hand use and function, speech, language and problem solving (and other early learning) develop together. The consequence is that a young child quite naturally builds on his or her interdependent skills in these four areas of learning. It is important to realise that the difficulties a child may encounter may not be because of any so-called deficiency in their cognitive functioning (thinking) but more to do with their different experience. Being able to gain an upright posture is very important for the very young child to be able to build further skills and explore the environment (Figure 14.2).

Parents often understand the way that a pupil has developed (or not) in one of these areas, and more importantly, the ways in which they might have compensated or solved some of the problems thrown up by their disability or condition. This knowledge can be very important in helping to build meaningful strategies to encourage learning and progress.

Quality of life is a somewhat vague term but it is used here to describe the growth of love, security, positive relationships and self-esteem. Parents are the vital central point for a child as he or she grows and children spend more time at home, from birth to ten years, than at school. Parents, not having professional status in meetings about a child, are sometimes not listened to sufficiently. Yet, it is they who are the key to providing the foundations for learning, for independence, motivation and the ability of the pupil to take risks and actively pursue their goals. It is likely that a pupil with disabilities will have experienced, by proxy, different, but no less caring, experiences within a family as a consequence of the public nature of disability and professional intervention.

Professional interventions, particularly for pupils born with a disability or condition, usually start at a young age. Even when the condition is diagnosed in older children, say, at nine or ten years old, the pupil can suddenly be subject to a 'confusing soup' of professional interventions and encounters (Figure 14.3).

HLTA
3.3.6

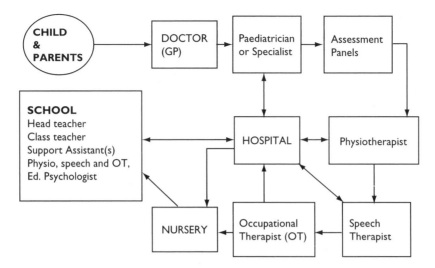

Figure 14.3 A confusing soup for a young child?
Source: Cornwall (1997)

A young pupil may have missed many early childhood experiences. Instead, they will have been subject to a more adult, professional culture. The tendency for the child to become a passive recipient is ever present and parents are under pressure 'to do the best' for their child. Looking at the equation from the parents' perspective can shed a different light on matters. From the parents' viewpoint professional collaboration is a double-edged sword sometimes involving *frustration and bewilderment* when dealing with the SEN bureaucracy, with professionals in different locations, paperwork, appointments galore and sometimes ignorance or misapprehension about the problems they face; yet at other times; *relief and encouragement* when professionals are able to do the following:

- understand the nature of their problem;
- recognise the capabilities of their child;
- show a positive, empathetic approach to difficulties encountered;
- accurately assess the situation and give clear responses to their situation (not vague professional proclamations).

Strategies for teaching and learning

Much research into disabled childhood has been preoccupied with impairment, vulnerability and service use; this has compounded a view of disabled children as passive and dependent. The voices of disabled children themselves have frequently been excluded as research has focused on the perspectives of parents, professionals and other adults. A more recent project (Corker *et al.*, 1999) aimed to explore the perspectives of disabled children themselves, their own roles in negotiating their daily lives, and to investigate the relationships, environments and structures that shaped their experiences:

> The transition from living a life as others want (dependence) to living it as the adolescent wants to live (independence) is extraordinarily difficult for most teenagers and their families. The difficulty is compounded in the case of adolescents with disabilities … [the] key to independence which is CHOICE: choosing to complete physical tasks without assistance or choosing to complete physical tasks with assistance whilst being in control of how and when that assistance is offered.
>
> (Fenton and Hughes, 1989)

It is important that helpers of younger students with disabilities (i.e. 7th to 9th Year) encourage them to make decisions about whether they want help or not, and which part of the task they want help with and which part they can manage on their own. Equally for younger students it may be important to encourage them to try things themselves as much as possible. Older students (e.g. by the 10th and 11th Year) should be encouraged to CHOOSE if they need help or not with a particular task, on a particular day – depending on how they feel. They need to be able then to negotiate with the helper, efficiently and politely. This is an important skill for a young person and should be part of their skill development planning.

According to Fenton and Hughes (1989) helpers:

- should *not* assume what help is wanted.
- should *not* insist on everything being done independently by the older student with a disability. Students may feel, for example, that for some work that is to be displayed, they would rather ask the helper to do the cutting out, and they will direct how the display is to be arranged – this is their choice.

When working with a student with a disability on any task, it is necessary to explore together the possible ways of helping. The student can then choose for this task, with this helper, on this day, in this context, at this time how much help he/she wants. It is necessary to be aware that some students may ask for more help than they really need (Webber, 1991).

- WAIT – The student may not need help or may organise you to help.
- A CHOICE OF 2 OPTIONS – e.g. 'Would you like me to cut this out for you, or shall I help you to do it?'
- NO HELP NEEDED – Move away. You could say, e.g. 'If there is anything you need later, could you ask me, please?'
- ADVICE OR EQUIPMENT HELP – e.g. 'Should we ask someone about other ways of doing this, or equipment that might help? We could ask another helper, occupational therapist or a teacher.'
- STUDENT DIRECTS HELP – Prompt, e.g. 'How do you want me to help with this, today?', 'Can you tell me the best way of doing this, please?' (e.g. helping with a coat).

- FUTURE OCCASIONS – When you have worked out together a way of helping for a particular task, it is not necessary to keep on asking.

If you have already negotiated with a learner how he/she wishes to be helped – then you only need to check that he/she wants the same help as last time. *Do not assume what kind of help the student wants, as this will take away his/her control and force him/her into a passive role.*

> **Discussion**
> - Does your school recognise that how pupils feel about themselves and that how they take responsibility for their learning is a crucial factor in making progress?
> - How much chance do pupils with special needs have to express their own individuality or are they seen simply as a 'problem'?

HLTA
3.1.1
3.1.2
3.1.3
3.1.4

The teacher is responsible for creating an environment in which all students can learn to the best of their ability and the teaching assistants are vital components in making this happen. Without the work of support staff, teachers in mainstream provision would find it extremely difficult to create such a social and learning environment. Students need to be encouraged to take increasing responsibility for their own learning and this is a vital role for support staff. In this context it is important that the teaching assistant understands the best way to assist the student's learning and does not leave this to the teacher to decide. This is particularly important in secondary schools where the teaching assistant may even advise the teacher about these matters.

Here are some suggestions for ways in which staff could develop a more inclusive setting for students with disabilities:

- While for some children associating with their own impairment group is an active choice, for example, for communication reasons, for others they can often become separated even within mainstream schools. Where peer relationships with non-disabled children are developed, they are sometimes dominated by the assumption of need and care (Corker *et al.*, 1999). Most children also highlighted a common experience of being picked on, even if they were sometimes able to resist the process. Arrange for other students to accompany, or assist a student in a wheelchair to lessons, at break or into lunch. Emphasise the social aspects, NOT the helping aspect.

- Encourage students with disabilities to sit with other students and encourage other students to sit with disabled students. This may mean overriding students' own choices of where to sit, on occasions. Again, emphasise the social and learning aspects of this request, not making the non-disabled child into a 'helper' of the other child. This may happen naturally.

- When providing learning support, make yourself available to help other students in the class, not just the student with a disability; also to encourage the student to negotiate with you and teacher how much help he/she wants.

- Consider whether another student, if asked, could take books out of a bag or set up a computer or other equipment for a student with a disability. Try to develop cooperation with other students and the skills that the pupil will need to be clear about the kind of help needed and to negotiate this with others.

- Ask the teacher to provide worksheets in advance or alternative methods of recording (e.g. tape recorders) what goes on in the classroom or ask other students or pupils to make written copies of notes for the student with a disability.

- Give advice about the kind of resources needed for effective learning support for specific pupils. For example, the way the seating is arranged or adapting furniture to make it the correct height and size – so that the student with a disability can sit at the table with a friend.

- Enlist the help of other pupils and students for other activities such as clubs, wheelchair sports and holidays.

Learning support for effective differentiation, teaching and learning

It is clear from experience that the relationship between educators and pupil is absolutely crucial as a mediator in the learning and in the social interactions that take place. The educator can have great influence on the learning experience of the pupil both as a skilled professional, but also as an advocate for a young person with a disability.

Here are some suggestions:

- Keep up a positive attitude and encourage peer support and interaction between the pupil who is disabled and other pupils in the classroom.

- By knowing students' interests and their own needs and strengths, the teaching assistant is a vital mediator and advocate in the classroom.

- In order to choose relevant materials, the teacher will need advice from the teaching assistant who will be able to ask significant questions and make any assessments more relevant to the young person with a disability.

- Communication at various levels is vital in the job. Educators need to gain rapport with the pupils because a positive personal relationship will facilitate learning. He or she also needs to have great clarity and purpose when talking to colleagues in acting as an advocate and explaining the pupils' responses to the learning environment and learning needs.

- Educators working with children should be aware of the powerful impact of focused praise and encouragement. This applies to all children, not just disabled pupils.

Teaching assistants will be integrally involved in the following:

- *planning* – giving advice about mode of presentation
- *groups* – deciding on which activities and resources are appropriate
- *content and outcome* – understanding and contributing to the content and recording the outcomes of activities

How will you know when good learning has taken place?

It is important for educators to be aware of what constitutes effective learning and teaching and to be sensitive to the responses of the learner. This applies to disabled learners as much as any other.

HLTA
3.3.5

Discussion

The following list of questions exemplifies points to be aware of when assessing teaching and learning in the classroom.

- How much new learning is taking place?
- Does the pupil want to learn and come back for more?
- Is the activity coherent with and building on previous learning?
- Is the pupil internalising the skill or knowledge? Do they own the skill or knowledge and are they able to use it outside the structured setting (are they 'fluent)?
- Does the student see the relevance and the point of any given activity?
- Can the student see the longer-term benefits and is he or she able to enjoy the short-term benefits?
- Does the pupil contribute to lessons/activities?
- Does the pupil interact with other pupils and with the teacher?
- Is the pupil able to challenge and ask questions?
- Does the pupil have the confidence and means to show his or her ability?
- Does the pupil retain information and how is he/she helped to do this?
- What new information and skill does the pupil need to gain?
- Is the pupil consistently engaged, involved and taking responsibility for his/her own learning?
- Does the teacher involve the student, for example by asking questions appropriately?

Case study 3

A maths teacher was at a loss as to how to involve her pupil who was a wheelchair user in the more active explorative aspects of the maths curriculum where pupils were out collecting data and observing. She wanted to organise activities where pupils could explore the environment and use it to develop certain mathematical and geometrical principles. While talking about and showing triangles on the board, the pupil put his hand up and said 'That looks like the ramps I use to get up steps – from the side, Miss.' This then led to the discussion about ramps, doorway widths and turning circles for the wheelchair, which in turn led to a whole range of mathematical activities based on exploring the accessibility of the school for a wheelchair. Dead ends where the chair could not turn around, doorways that were too narrow, ramps where the angle was too steep, and so on.

Teaching assistants in particular will be responsible for taking advantage of any opportunities for developing and applying skills across the curriculum. They are in a unique position to be with the pupil or student across a wide variety of circumstances and subject areas. This gives a very specific perception of the pupil's learning. In this case it is important to consider which skills are important in a cross-curricular sense. All staff are responsible for helping pupils to develop these skills from the Early Years to the end of Key Stage 4 and beyond so that pupils are prepared for the opportunities, responsibilities and experiences of adult and working life. Pupils need to encounter a range of opportunities to practise, consolidate and refine these skills in real contexts and for real purposes. Indeed, pupils who find themselves in need of a particular skill – perhaps a mathematical skill within a geography lesson – may well be more motivated to develop that skill now that they have found it to have real relevance and purpose.

Important skills areas that pupils develop and can apply across the curriculum and in contexts outside school are:

- *communication skills*: their skills of speaking, listening, reading, writing and expressing ideas through a variety of media;
- *mathematical skills*: their knowledge and skills of number, shape, space, measures and handling data;
- *information technology skills*: their IT skills to obtain, prepare, process and present information and to communicate ideas with increasing independence;
- *problem-solving skills*: their skills of asking appropriate questions, making predictions and coming to informed decisions;
- *creative skills*: their creative skills, in particular the development and expression of ideas and imagination;
- *personal and social education*: the attitudes, values, skills, knowledge and understanding relating to personal and social education.

The language of positive relationships and inclusive classrooms

This chapter has outlined some of the important aspects of working alongside and supporting the learning of pupils with disabilities. Teaching assistants are a vital component in the inclusive activities of mainstream and special schools.

They are the vital link between the pupil or student and his or her learning opportunities. If these are to be equitable (may not be 'equal'), then the learning support person is the vital factor in that equalisation process. To sum up, it is important to realise that the process of inclusion requires cooperation and collaboration to solve problems. It involves understanding and needs actively working on over a period of time and then reviewing and re-visiting constantly. It is a process, not an end point. The road to inclusion is also a choice. People choosing inclusion, look at whole systems and only label partnerships at many levels. Inclusive educators, paramedic professionals and teaching assistants know through experience that they can solve virtually any student problem by getting together with the student and brainstorming on the problem. The people know the person involved intimately, and they care. The first label is citizen, then neighbour, relative or friend (some of whom may be psychologists and doctors). Inclusion proponents believe in technology and science which serves people and is not used to make profit or war at the expense of human beings (Forest and Pearpoint, 1991). To summarise:

- We are unique in value; however, each has unique capacity.
- All people can learn. Social development, (academic) achievement, movement skills, therapeutic outcomes and successful partnerships are all part of a LEARNING PROCESS.
- All people have contributions to make towards 'entitlement' and 'access' and support is all about enabling disabled youngsters to make their contribution to the learning process.
- We all have a responsibility and an opportunity to give every person the chance to make a contribution.

Approximately one in twenty children are considered disabled. Social policy research has revealed that families with disabled children experience a range of social and economic difficulties. However, most research into disabled childhood has been preoccupied with impairment, vulnerability and service usage, and has compounded a view of disabled children as passive and dependent. Moreover, the voices of disabled children themselves have frequently been excluded, as research has focused on the perspectives of parents, professionals and other adults. This has often had the effect of objectifying and silencing disabled children. As a consequence, research has often concealed the roles of disabled children as social actors, negotiating complex identities and social relationships within a disabling environment, and as agents of change who can adapt to, challenge and inform the individuals, cultures and institutions which they encounter during their childhoods. In such an environment, all children will feel better about themselves and learn more efficiently. We know that, when children feel these ABCs. They will also learn the famous educational three R's (Forest and Pearpoint, 1991):

READING

'RITING

RELATIONSHIPS

Relationships, seen in their broadest sense, are the building blocks of effective and good quality partnership. Partnerships between pupil or student and teaching assistant or teacher facilitate learning, and partnerships between teachers or teaching assistant in a school or college make for a pleasant and productive learning and working environment. The data from the study undertaken by Corker *et al.* (1999) challenges a universal concept of 'a disabled child' and instead identifies the range of ways in which accepted meanings and values are contested or reinforced in daily interactions and institutional practices. In reality, the mixing up of categories and dynamics of daily experience all suggest that listening to children's voices leads to a more nuanced understanding of their lives. If this process, which demands that adults reflect on their practices, were part of policy and practice, then the structures that promote a disabling environment could begin to be dismantled.

Key issues

It is anticipated that you will now:

- have an understanding of the history of the treatment of disabled people;
- understand what is meant by the term 'equality of opportunity';
- understand how school processes and procedures may provide barriers to disabled students' learning in your workplace setting;
- understand how important it is to encourage independence for all learners;
- recognise how important it is to have effective partnerships with parents of disabled children;
- understand how important it is that disabled learners take responsibility for their learning.

Professional Standards for Higher Level Teaching Assistants (HLTA)

If you can demonstrate your understanding and professional use of the key issues illustrated within this chapter, it is hoped that you will be able to fulfil the following HLTA Standards:

1.1	1.2	1.5	2.1
2.8	3.1.1	3.1.2	3.1.3
3.1.4	3.2.1	3.2.2	3.2.3
3.2.4	3.3.1	3.3.2	3.3.3
3.3.5	3.3.6	3.3.7	

Useful websites

www.daras.co.uk
www.disinhe.ac.uk
www.equipservices.hefce.ac.uk
www.skill.org.uk

References

Corker, M., Davis, J. and Priestley, M. (1999) *Life as a Disabled Child: A Qualitative Study of Young People's Experiences and Perspectives*, ESRC Research Programme, *Children 5–16: Growing into the Twenty-First Century*. Disability Research Unit, University of Leeds, LEEDS, LS2 9JT, England.

Cornwall, J. (1995) 'Choice, Opportunity and Learning: Educating Children and Young People who are Physically Disabled', London: David Fulton.

Cornwall, J. (1996) *Choice, Opportunity and Learning: Educating Children and Young People who are Disabled*, London: David Fulton.

Cornwall, J. (1997) *Access to Learning*, London: David Fulton.

DfEE (1998) *Excellence for All*, London: HMSO.

Driedger, D. (1989) *The Last Civil Rights Movement*, London: Hurst.

Fenton, M. and Hughes, P. (1989) *From Passivity to Empowerment: Living Skills Curriculum for People with Disabilities*, London: RADAR.

Forest, M. and Pearpoint, J. (1991) *Two Roads: Exclusion or Inclusion*, Centre for Integrated Education and Democracy, Toronto: McGill University.

Maslow, A. (1962) *Towards a Psychology of Being*, New York: Van Nostrand.

Moore, J. and Morrison, N. (1989) *Someone Else's Problem*, Sussex: Falmer Press.

QAA (1999) *Promoting Higher Quality* Section 3: Students with disabilities, London: DfES.

Webber, A. (1991) *In-Service Practical Approaches, Attitudes and Equipment for Staff Working Alongside Students with Disabilities*, UK: Folens.

Other factors that affect learning: epilepsy, HIV/AIDS, puberty and mental health issues

Sue Soan

Introduction

It is the aim of this chapter to introduce a few areas of need that educators frequently think about and occasionally meet in their everyday practice, but which they have little, if any, knowledge. It will discuss the difficulties and how they can affect the learner educationally, paying particular attention to the current national agendas.

Educators have a crucial role to play in including learners with many varied additional needs in a mainstream classroom. The educational achievement, social and personal happiness of the individual learner, the other pupils and the adults in the classroom will all depend on how the educators handle situations. If great thought, joint planning and sharing of information are encouraged and the educators act and think carefully about all the possible envisaged situations that might occur, then the successful inclusion of individuals with severe or often socially difficult needs can be supported. The educators also need to be able to communicate well to all those involved, fostering tolerance and understanding.

Learners with medical conditions

In any given year there are some 100,000 children and young people who require education outside school because of illness or injury. In addition there are a significant number of children and young people who experience clinically defined mental health problems. The situations of these children and young people will vary widely but they all run the risk of a reduction in self-confidence and educational achievement.

(DfES, 2001b)

There are many learners with many needs who quite rightly should be placed under this heading, but for the purposes of this chapter AIDS/HIV and epilepsy are going to be the two issues discussed, but transferable ideas and information will be included that may be useful for other medical conditions that might be met within educational settings.

Epilepsy

Epilepsy is a neurological disorder that affects 1 in 200 of the population.

> Epilepsy is an established tendency to recurrent seizures, which occur as a result of biochemical changes in the brain. It affects children of all ages, backgrounds and levels of ability. It is not an illness or disease, but is indicative of a physical disorder.
>
> (McCarthy and Davies, 1996)

If a child only has one seizure this would not necessarily indicate epilepsy. Epilepsy means that the child has recurring seizures. The symptoms and duration vary greatly depending on the type of epilepsy, but also it affects children in different ways. Epilepsy is abnormal brain functioning and this produces fits, attacks or seizures. Children may have muscle spasms, convulsions, involuntary movements and changes in perception and consciousness. These seizures are usually over in a few seconds or minutes, the same processes that caused the seizures having triggered other mechanisms in the brain stopping them.

The Tonic–Clonic Seizures, previously known as 'grand mal' epilepsy, are the most disturbing for all involved and indeed can be quite frightening not only for the child experiencing the seizure, but also for other pupils and adults. In this situation the child may make a noise and then fall quite suddenly, followed by convulsive jerks. Saliva around the mouth may then start appearing and sometimes bladder or bowel control might be lost. Within a few minutes the child will regain consciousness, but is quite likely to feel dazed and confused for a few hours, very tired with the possibility of a headache developing.

If this is not the first time a child experiences a seizure it is not considered a medical emergency. However, a child may have caused harm to himself when he fell or may have been unconscious for quite a long time. If this is the case, it is always better to seek medical attention.

The other types of epilepsy are not so easily identified, but as one in three of the children with epilepsy fall behind academically, it is essential that educators are aware of signs that MAY indicate a neurological disorder. Table 15.1 illustrates the type of epilepsy and some of the symptoms.

Case study 1

Brian was a Year 2 pupil causing concern to his educators, as he seemed not to be making the expected progress. Other concerns highlighted included a high level of tiredness and lack of concentration. Meetings with Brian's parents did not throw any light on the difficulties that were manifesting themselves, although the parents said that Brian always slept very well and for long periods. They were concerned though that he did not concentrate and that he would frequently appear not to listen to them or have any memory of activities he had carried out only minutes earlier. It was decided that the SENCO would observe Brian to see if any clues could be obtained. Within a couple of days following discussions with the class adults it was felt that Brian had absence seizures (petit mal). During a games lesson Brian was practising catching and throwing a ball with a partner. The SENCO observed that for a few seconds Brian just stopped moving his arms in an attempt to catch the ball and stared into space. Then without any recollection of his 'blank' period he would continue in the activity from where he had 'left off.' This type of incident also happened during lessons, but the blank sessions were so short that it was unlikely a class teacher or teaching assistant would notice the seizures, other than thinking they were due to a lack of concentration or effort. After discussing the concerns with Brian's parents he was taken to the doctor and given medication to help prevent these seizures.

Table 15.1 Indicators of epilepsy (other than tonic–clonic seizures)

Names of seizures	Symptoms
absence seizures	Sometimes known as 'petit mal'. Learners may stare into space or day-dream. Some may only flutter their eyelids. Learner will be totally unaware of these seizures.
complex partial seizures	Only part of the brain is affected. The seizures occur as small involuntary movements, such as dazed walking, lip smacking or plucking at clothes.
simple partial seizures	A learner may experience a disturbance of feelings or a smell, taste or perception. A learner may also experience a tingling in a limb.
sub-clinical seizures	These cannot be seen, but such seizures may be identified when an educator notices a sudden drop in performance or in oral or written work for no obvious reason.

Source: Adapted from information presented in McCarthy and Davies (2002).

Discussion

As has been mentioned, learners with epilepsy experience seizures in many different ways. Can you think of a learner who may possibly be experiencing a form of epilepsy?

Treatment of epilepsy

Medication can be prescribed that enables learners to lead normal lives, building up a resistance to seizures. However, there are a number of factors educators need to monitor and be aware of. Learners on medication for epilepsy should not appear drowsy, over-active or inattentive in school or have seizures. If such behaviour is noted, then the parents and doctors need to be informed immediately, as the medication may well need adjusting. This can be a problem that is not easily corrected and parents may well make very different decisions that educators need to be aware of so that they can support the learner as well as possible.

Case study 2

Debbie suffered from tonic–clonic seizures and was constantly on high levels of medication as the doctors were unable to stabilise the seizures. This had tremendous side effects on her self-confidence, self-esteem, levels of energy and academic progress. However, after discussing it with Debbie's parents, it was felt inappropriate to lower the levels of medication as Debbie was still suffering two or three large seizures a day, causing great concern for her actual physical well-being. In response to this information her educators wrote a new individual programme for Debbie focusing on her very individual needs, recognising she would frequently be very tired and lack the ability to focus for long periods of time.

Case study 3

Sharon, another Year 6 learner, also experienced tonic–clonic seizures, but these were occurring very infrequently. Sharon felt that the medication was preventing her from learning as much as she could and was causing her to be very tired all of the time. Sharon's parents discussed the situation with the doctors and with Sharon and decided to stop the medication. The school monitored the situation very carefully, keeping daily records of her behaviour, health and learning progress and for the final eight months of the academic year Sharon did indeed make exceptional academic progress. Sharon also did not experience any further seizures and quickly gained in confidence and self worth. These were two very different situations that demanded very different educational responses and an openness of educators to meeting learners' individual needs.

If a learner in your classroom is diagnosed as having a form of epilepsy, list the actions you would consider necessary to enable him/her to be beneficially included into the school and the class with regard to:

- other pupils;
- parents;
- other adults in the classroom;
- unstructured social opportunities;
- school activities.

Note any particular clues that may indicate if the learner is about to have a seizure such as a change in behaviour or in body temperature. This can be very helpful, because the removal of a jumper may prevent or lessen a seizure and other warnings may mean that the learner can be moved to a safer environment prior to a fit or seizure. An adult can learn to notice these changes and quickly support the learner without too much fuss.

Learners may be very embarrassed if they know that their peers have witnessed a fit, especially if they lose bladder control or salivate. The educators need to handle this extremely sensitively, educating the other pupils so that teasing or an unwillingness to socialise with the learner with epilepsy does not occur. It must be remembered that if adults treat the learner with epilepsy with respect at all times and with the same high learning expectations as everyone else, then this will encourage the other learners to do the same.

Epilepsy is only one of many medical difficulties that learners can experience when attending an educational setting, but one that can be used as a pattern for other similar problems.

HIV/AIDS

HIV and AIDS infections are an increasing problem all over the world with 47 million adults and children having been infected since the beginning of the epidemic in the 1980s; 18.8 million have already died. Although the highest prevalence of cases are still to be found in some of the least developed countries, it is quite possible that educators in the United Kingdom may find they have a learner with HIV or AIDS in their class, or indeed a colleague.

When considering what the issues are for people working in educational settings, the first to come to mind is not, I suspect, academic success for those infected. Indeed, the first concern for the school community is the physical safety of all adults and children and the risks that are involved in including a learner with this infection. However, many of these learners are in the classroom without the knowledge of the educators or perhaps even the parents. Also as Naude and Pretorius (2003: 138) say: 'Ethical considerations are also an important factor to consider within schools; even if a teacher knows that a pupil has HIV/AIDS, this information may not be made public.' Hence it is necessary, it could be argued, to organise health and safety issues for all the community, as if there is an adult or child in the school with this infection. If this is achieved, then the physical risks to others is limited and identifying individuals to a wider public becomes unnecessary, when considering this aspect of care. Wearing clinical gloves whenever dealing with bodily fluids is always good health and safety practice, and protects the carer at that time from risk of cross-infection. A simple practice, not always easy to fulfil in practice when adult support is short, but one which immediately protects all involved in such incidents.

Learners with HIV/AIDS undoubtedly also have many difficulties that include psychological, neglect and social interaction problems, but it is the educational impact of this infection that is to be considered in greater detail. This is fast becoming an important issue as effective anti-retroviral drugs mean that many more children with this infection are surviving through to adulthood (Safriel *et al.*, 2000).

One of the major areas of the body that the HIV/AIDS infection affects is the central nervous system and this is important as it is clearly obvious that certain areas of the brain can affect academic performance. Related HIV/AIDS illnesses, such as meningitis, HIV encephalopathy and non-Hodgkin's lymphomas also affect educational progress. This might mean learners have speech, motor, memory, vision and thought difficulties (Naude and Pretorius, 2002). If the individual learner's areas of weakness are known, educational programmes of support can be instigated and focus on the learner's strengths. Research suggests (Naude and Pretorius, 2003) that expressive and non-verbal skills are affected more than receptive language in learners with HIV/AIDS. Naude and Pretorius (ibid.) suspect that despite impairments, infected learners still are able to communicate effectively, to ask sensible and appropriate questions and also to develop and express their own ideas. However, pronunciation, written language expression and the ability to make decisions might well be affected. Due to other central nervous system difficulties that can affect this group of learners, focused attention and memory can be impaired. It is therefore thought beneficial to use *peripheral learning* strategies to help the learners. When teaching spelling and mathematics, therefore, an educator might use rhythm or songs to help learning to take place. Many educators already recognise that if they use activities that aid peripheral learning, memory and processing are also helped. Activities that include drama, puppetry, role-playing, singing, movement games and art therefore all support learners with HIV/AIDS. Again, in many instances including this active learning is considered good practice for all learners. Other factors this research indicates for consideration when planning curriculum content and delivery include those shown in Table 15.2.

Close collaboration with doctors, carers, parents and other social and health representatives is therefore essential if effective educational programmes are to be

Table 15.2 Educational strategies for learner with HIV/AIDS (adapted from Naude and Pretorius, 2003)

To be encouraged	To be limited
Silent reading	Reading aloud
Use matrix grid paper to help visual–spatial problems	Avoid spatial and gestaltic strategies
Linguistic approaches should be emphasised, e.g. phonic-dependent methods	Strategies dependent on visual memory and visual scanning, e.g. flash cards, look and say
For mathematics emphasise language-based instruction	Paper and pencil exercises
Use of ICT programmes	The need to memorise mathematical rules and algorithms
Cursive writing	
Colour coding to help give mathematical instructions	

made for learners with this type of difficulty. Finally, it must be said that: 'The critical need is for a holistic and individual approach to the education of children with medical conditions while, at the same time, remembering the importance of including them with their peers socially and educationally' (Closs, 2000: 3).

Discussion

How well do you think your educational setting would cope with learners with HIV/AIDS? Would the educational or social and medical issues predominate discussions and the successful inclusion of learners with these problems?

Learners unable to attend school due to medical needs

Many children cannot attend school due to their medical needs; some will be in hospital for a long time and others will need a variety of educational provision to meet their needs. However, it must be remembered that a medical diagnosis or a disability does not necessarily imply that the learner has special educational needs (DfES, 2001a: 88, 7:64). *Access to Education* (DfES and DoH 2001: 8) nevertheless states that LEAs should ensure that learners with medical needs are not at home without education for more than 15 days. Learners with long-term, recurring periods of absence, should also have access to education from day one and if this is at home they should receive a minimum of five hours each week. This statutory guidance also says that the education should include a broad and balanced curriculum and that it should be of similar quality to that available in a school.

There are a variety of provisions available for learners with these needs. They include:

- hospital schools
- hospital teaching service
- home teaching
- integrated hospital/home education service
- pupil referral units (PRUs)
- psychiatric units and hospitals.

It is important for educators that they can meet with and be involved in the planning of provision for any learner who is returning to or leaving for a period of time from a mainstream environment. Without this close liaison between professionals, learners can find themselves isolated, at risk of bullying and teasing, unable to cope with the curriculum, resulting in under-achievement and with their medical needs misunderstood by staff and peers alike (DfES, 2001a, 2001b). *Every Child Matters* (HMSO, 2003: 91, 6.33), a government Green Paper, also rigorously supports this joint working approach: 'The Government is committed to working with children's workers to deliver world class services. To that end, the Children's Workforce Unit will examine how to develop collaborative approaches with frontline staff to identify and overcome barriers they face.'

Educators also need to be aware that learners returning to school from a long illness may well get tired very easily, be anxious about meeting friends again or catching up on missed work. They may well be emotional or display behaviour difficulties and some of course may still be on medication such as steroids that can make them more emotional than normal. Individual reintegration pro-grammes, written collaboratively, should enable all such areas of concern to be discussed and planned for proactively.

When learners miss school intermittently for a term or two, due to illnesses such as glandular fever, it is essential that this is planned for and that the learner receives appropriate homework that is regularly sent home and regularly marked. Contact with parents and other agencies is also vital so that everyone involved is aware of changes and that educational needs are met.

Case study 4

Beth had been absent intermittently for nearly two terms with glandular fever, during which time her mother had regularly sent in medical certificates and requests for homework. Her mother only received one phone call from the guidance teacher and one package of homework, and felt that there should have been more contact and, 'They could have made a wee bit more effort.'

Source: Norris and Closs (1999: 31)

Discussion Who would be the guidance teacher in your educational setting? Have you experienced a similar situation, perhaps when work has not been carefully thought about and regularly sent home? Can you think why this was the case and what changes could be made so that other learners with medical needs requiring absence from school can be handled more effectively?

Other medical needs may include helping learners cope with allergies. Asthma and hay fever will be the most familiar to educators, but more complex needs may be met. The following case study shows how a school adapted their practice and the environment so that a learner could be included without social or educational repercussions.

Case study 5

Pippa was extremely allergic to peanuts, so much so that a medical pen filled with medication had to be close at hand at all times. Also if this was required, staff needed to be able to confidently inject the medication via the rectum to Pippa. Understandably this caused much concern and fears that the school would not be able to keep Pippa safe. However, the staff did not wish to exclude her from her local school and set about making changes to the school environment. The following are areas that were changed enabling Pippa's safe and successful inclusion:

- The school nurse arranged training regarding the medication to TAs who were trained First Aiders and willing to carry out the treatment if ever necessary.
- The school put photographs and allergy alert warnings of Pippa up in the office, the class register and the dining hall so that ALL adults would have a visual reminder of Pippa's medical needs.
- All staff were informed of Pippa's particular allergy and reaction to any contact with peanuts.
- All pupils were asked NOT to bring peanut sandwiches for their lunches due to a peer's risk.
- The SENCO arranged a timetable of cover that meant that the class teacher, a trained teaching assistant or lunch time supervisor wore a light, over the shoulder handbag with the medication in it at all times (and there was always a second or third possible person in case of sickness etc.).
- A First Aider regularly checked the medication making sure it was in date and she was responsible for contacting Pippa's Mum, if this needed to be changed.
- Regular meetings were held with parents to keep up to date with Pippa's needs.

The plans put in place to ensure Pippa's safety meant that her education was not disrupted in any way. Expectations from educators were high and social interaction with her peers did not have to be adapted as it was the adults who had altered routines enabling her to play and mix normally.

Puberty

Due to our improved health and diet many more children are experiencing puberty at a much earlier age. This can cause great disruption to the education of these learners if great care and consideration does not take place. Girls who physically enter puberty at primary school, perhaps in Year 4 or Year 5 can experience many difficulties that can separate them from their peers. They can be teased about their physical appearance and about the need to use the female teachers' toilets at certain times of the month. This can lead to an unwillingness to attend school on PE days and to feelings of exclusion from her immediate peer group. Emotionally these girls can also experience massive mood swings, causing arguments and tantrums at school, with both peers and adults. Educational attainment as a consequence is affected, and even behavioural problems can prevail. It is therefore essential that a member of staff is identified as a 'friend' who can support these learners and that facilities are provided, to lessen the need for identifying their particular needs. A good relationship needs to be established with a class adult so that if feeling unable to cope physically or emotionally, a girl can seek assistance, hence avoiding unnecessary reprimands or confrontations.

Boys also can be affected by early or late puberty, many adults expecting far more from physically mature young men than from those less advanced. Frequently they are felt to be more emotionally mature and also able to cope with higher academic pressures. Socially they can also stand out, sometimes literally, towering over their peers, causing them embarrassment and self-consciousness. Educators need to make efforts to observe how learners experiencing early puberty in particular are coping generally and from day to day. Again, with joint collaboration and sharing of information professionals and parents can prevent detrimental emotional and educational responses from occurring.

Educating school-age parents

Pregnant pupils should be able to be supported in school and indeed the government states that 'Pregnancy is not a reason for exclusion from school' (DfES, 2001c). It is the government's aim to reduce teenage pregnancy by 50 per cent in 2010 from 90,000 in 1998, but it still recognises the need for a strategy to encourage these young parents to continue in education, hopefully avoiding the risk of social exclusion and promoting better opportunities for future employment for the parents. The *Guidance on the Education of School Age Parents* (DfES, 2001c) clearly identifies the provisions available for pregnant or young parents, but still states that the mainstream school should oversee the education, frequently even setting and marking work. Many issues are mentioned within this document that educators within a school need to be in a position to handle effectively through policy and allocated roles.

The *Guidance* (DfES, 2001c: 14.7) says:

- There is no evidence that keeping a pregnant girl or school age mother in school will encourage others to become pregnant.
- Effective personal, social and health education (PSHE) can alert teenagers to the risks and realities of early parenthood and can be used to encourage understanding of young parents' situation amongst the other pupils, taking care not to reinforce negative stereotypes.

Discuss these statements. How does your educational setting support pregnant teenagers or young parents?

Child and adolescent mental health services (CAMHS)

In 1994 a Department of Education circular, *Pupils with Problems* said: 'schools ... play a vital part in promoting the spiritual, cultural, mental and physical development of young people ... the emotional development of children must continue to be a concern of mainstream education'. Teachers can identify learners with SEBD, but there is, understandably confusion about the boundaries between 'normal' SEBD and mental illness. Figure 15.1 illustrates the relationship between SEBD, mental health problems and mental health disorders. However,

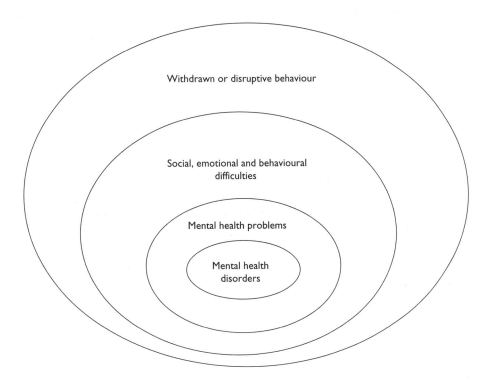

Figure 15.1   The relationship between SEBD and mental health disorders
Source: Weare (2000)

the Special Educational Needs Code of Practice (2001a: 140, 10.27) says: 'Many children with mental health problems, but by no means all, may also be recognised as children with emotional and behavioural difficulties.' It also informs the educator that there are a range of specialists to help with these issues and that a referral to CAMHS may well benefit many learners for the assessment and treatment of mental health problems.

So what are mental health problems and mental health disorders?

According to Atkinson and Hornby's model, there will be a proportion of learners with SEBD who will be severe enough to be diagnosed with a mental health problem and a small number of these will have a mental health disorder. Atkinson and Hornby (2002) write:

> A mental health problem is defined as 'a disturbance of function in one area of relationships, mood, behaviour or development of sufficient severity to require professional intervention' (Wallace et al., cited in the Department of Health, 1995: 10). A mental health disorder is defined as 'a severe problem (commonly persistent), or the co-occurrence of a number of problems, usually in the presence of several risk factors'.

> (ibid., 1995: 10)

Mental health disorders include:

- conduct disorder;
- attention deficit hyperactivity disorder (ADHD);
- eating disorders;
- anxiety disorders;
- substance abuse;
- depression;
- suicidal behaviour and deliberate self-harm;
- obsessive-compulsive disorder;
- schizophrenia.

(Atkinson and Hornby, 2002)

How can educators identify learners at risk of mental health problems?

It is not possible to identify those learners who will develop mental health problems. However, there are some risk factors which might indicate that a learner may develop mental health problems and these are cumulative: 'If children are exposed to one risk factor, the likelihood of developing a mental health problem is between 1 and 2 per cent, but with four or more risk factors this increases to 20 per cent' (Atkinson and Hornby, 2002: 7). The Mental Health Foundation (1999) listed the following as risk factors: physical illness, learning disability, difficult temperament, parental conflict, inconsistent parenting, homelessness and socio-economic disadvantage. Understandably, therefore, these factors can affect learning and achievement, because as Greenhalgh (1994: 2) wrote: 'The realm of feelings, of our subjective experiences, can indeed both facilitate and inhibit growth, development and learning.'

It is therefore vital that if an educator has concerns about the mental welfare of a learner that further assistance is sought. A decline in academic abilities, of deteriorating relationships with peers or an experience of loss, all may alert an educator to a problem. As Long (1999: 6) says: 'Our aim in school is to offer appropriate and informed support to the pupil – not to act as a therapist.'

Key issues

It is anticipated that you will now:

- be able to feel more confident about supporting learners with medical conditions in mainstream settings;
- be able to identify some of the factors that schools need to consider when including learners with infections such as HIV/AIDS;
- be able to understand some of the educational difficulties that can be associated with HIV/AIDS;
- be able to work more closely with other professionals to develop individual programmes of support for learners, such as those in early puberty, or teenage mothers, enabling effective education to take place;
- be aware of other types of provision that may be able to support learners with a specific need;
- be willing to consider mental health problems as real issues for learners and to seek appropriate support and care.

Professional Standards for Higher Level Teaching Assistants (HLTA)

If you can demonstrate your understanding and professional use of the key issues illustrated within this chapter, it is hoped that you will be able to fulfil the following HLTA Standards:

1.2	1.4	1.5	2.5	3.3.7

The individual statements are not highlighted throughout this chapter as it is felt a holistic understanding of these particular issues is required, before a HLTA can demonstrate these Standards are being met.

Useful documents

DfES (2001a) *Special Educational Needs Code of Practice*, Annesley: DfES.

DfES (2001b) *Inclusive Schooling: Children with Special Educational Needs*, Annesley: DfES.

DfES (2001c) *Guidance on the Education of School Age Parents*, London: HMSO, available on: http://dfes.gov.uk/schoolageparents (downloaded: 22.12.2003).

DfES and DoH (2001) *Access to Education: For Children and Young People with Medical Needs*, Annesley: DfES.

DfES, *Reintegrating Teenage Parents Back into Education: Exclusions and Alternative Provision*, London: DfES, http://www.dfes.gov.uk/exclusions/related_policies/teenage_pregancy.cfm (downloaded: 22.12.2003).

HMSO (2003) *Every Child Matters*, Norwich: The Stationery Office.

Useful contacts

Action for Sick Children
Tel: 0181 542 4848

Association for Children with Life-Threatening or Terminal Conditions and their Families (ACT)
Tel: 0117 930 4707 or 0117 922 1556.

NAESC/PRESENT (The National Association for the Education of Sick Children)
Advice line: 01159818282
Email: naesc@ednsick.demon.co.uk

SCENT: Sick Children's Educational Network for Teachers
Email: majordomo@ngfl.gov.uk (facilitated through BECTA)

References

Atkinson, M. and Hornby, G. (2002) *Mental Health Handbook for Schools*, London: Routledge Falmer.

Closs, A. (2000) (ed.) *The Education of Children with Medical Conditions*, London: David Fulton.

Cornwall, J. and Robertson, C. (1999) *Individual Education Plans: Physical Disabilities and Medical Conditions*, London: David Fulton.

DfE (1994) *Pupils with Problems*, London: HMSO.

DfES and DoH (2001) *Access to Education: For Children and Young People with Medical Needs*, Annesley: DfES.

Fox, M. (2003) *Including Children 3–11 with Physical Disabilities*, London: David Fulton.

Greenhalgh, P. (1994) *Emotional Growth and Learning*, London: Routledge.

Long, R. (1999) *Understanding and Supporting Depressed Children and Young People*, Tamworth: NASEN.

McCarthy, D. and Davies, J. (1996) *The SEN Resource Manual for Schools*, Ilford: Specialist Matters.

Mental Health Foundation (1999) *The Big Picture: Promoting Children and Young People's Mental Health*, London: Mental Health Foundation.

Naude, D. and Pretorius, E. (2002) 'Addressing educational needs of children with HIV/AIDS', *Journal of Research in Special Educational Needs*, vol. 2, no. 3, available on: http://www.nasen.org.uk.

Naude, D. and Pretorius, E. (2003) 'Proposing an instructional framework for children with HIV/AIDS', *British Journal of Special Education*, vol. 30, no. 3, pp. 138–43.

Norris, C. and Closs, A. (1999) 'Child and parent relationships with teachers in schools responsible for the education of children with serious medical conditions', *British Journal of Special Education*, vol. 26, no. 1, pp. 23–8.

Poursanidou, K., Garner, P., Watson, A. and Stephenson, R. (2003) 'Difficulties and support at school for children following renal transplantation: a case study', *Support for Learning*, vol. 18, no. 4, pp. 170–6.

Safriel, Y.I., Haller, J.O., Lefton, D.R. and Obedian, R. (2000) 'Imaging of the brain in the HIV-positive child', *Pediatric Radiology*, vol. 30, no. 11, pp. 725–32.

Weare, K. (2000) *Promoting Mental, Emotional and Social Health*, London: Routledge.

Index